A Collection of Memories, Discoveries,

BETWEEN

Observations, Hopes, Dreams, Realities

THE LINES

and Other Little Pieces of Life

Anna Gotlieb

Bristol, Rhein & Englander
Princeton, New Jersey

Copyright © 1992

Published by Bristol, Rhein & Englander
Princeton, New Jersey

Distributed in the U.S., Canada and overseas by
C.I.S. Publishers and Distributors
180 Park Avenue, Lakewood, New Jersey 08701
(908) 905-3000 Fax: (908) 367-6666

Distributed in Israel by
C.I.S. International (Israel)
Rechov Mishkalov 18
Har Nof, Jerusalem
Tel: 02-518-935

Distributed in the U.K. and Europe by
C.I.S. International (U.K.)
89 Craven Park Road
London N15 6AH, England
Tel: 81-809-3723

Book and cover design: Deenee Cohen
Typography: Nechamie Miller
Cover photography: Solaria Studios

ISBN 1-56062-115-X hard cover
Library of Congress Catalog Card Number
92-70691

PRINTED IN THE UNITED STATES OF AMERICA

TO MY PARENTS,

MY HUSBAND

AND MY CHILDREN

TABLE OF CONTENTS

BOOK ONE: ADJUSTMENTS

BOOK TWO: TRANSITIONS

BOOK THREE: IMPRESSIONS

BOOK FOUR: REFLECTIONS

BOOK FIVE: CONNECTIONS

BOOK SIX: REALIZATIONS

$\mathcal{A}$CKNOWLEDGMENTS

Thank you to my parents for warm boots in the winter and goldfish in the wading pool, for helping me with the fifth grade report on Mexico, for listening to everything I've ever written before it appeared in print, for wiping tears, for fostering laughter, for allowing me to lean and encouraging me to stand tall, for all of the hours of conversation and all of the years of guidance, for the immaculate kitchen and the soft sheets and the kind words.

Thank you to my husband for taking on a wife and two children, for including me in his warm and wonderful family, for introducing Yiddishkeit into our home, for learning Torah with my son, for helping with the social studies homework, for drying dishes, for coaching baseball, for intelligence, patience and insight, for serving as the in-house editor of this book.

Thank you to my children for teaching me to be a parent.

Thank you to my sister, brother-in-law and their children for being friends, for seeing me through transitions.

Thank you to my in-laws and my brothers-in-law and sisters-in-law, nieces and nephews. Thanks to Brooklyn, Chicago, Paramus and Staten Island for homemade pickles, pistachio cake and separate dancing.

Thank you to Rabbi and Mrs. M. Roberts and family for the first pot of *cholent* and all that it represents.

Thank you to the Yeshivah of Rockland County and former principals Rabbi Harry Mayer and Mrs. Miriam Nussbaum for *Chanukah* programs and Model Seders. Thanks for the *Birchas Hamazon*, for allowing me to be a hot lunch mother and a class mother. Thanks for reaching out and taking me in.

Thank you to JEP and NCSY for classes and courses, for songs and stories, for encouragement and support.

Thank you to the family in Meah Shearim for an orange and pink plastic tablecloth and for inspiration.

Thank you to Tuvia Rotberg for suggesting that I contact C.I.S. Publishers.

Thank you to Rabbi Yaakov Yosef Reinman of C.I.S. Publishers for reading between the lines.

Thank you to Raizy Kaufman for answering endless questions, for constant enthusiasm, for thoughtful suggestions.

Thank you to Chumi Leshinsky for typing the entire manuscript.

Thank you to the Rockland *Journal News*, where many of the essays appeared originally as columns.

יהיו לרצון אמרי פי והגיון לבי לפניך, ה' צורי וגואלי.

May the expressions of my mouth and the thoughts of my heart find favor before You, Hashem, my Rock and my Redeemer.

INTRODUCTION

I talk to myself. Sometimes out loud. Sometimes in my head—often on paper. I do this to set things straight. To put my thoughts in perspective. I do it to try to keep the reins on fear or pain, to capture joy. I converse with myself as a means of confirmation. "So this is what I think," I say, and in the saying make it so. And I talk because I must. Because for as long as I can remember, the words have pushed their way from brain to mouth to pen or typewriter or computer.

In cardboard boxes in the attic are aging diaries reflecting me at nine and ten and twelve. In manila envelopes are written images of the teenager I once was. Somewhere under stacks of photo albums lie words I penned while waiting for my children to be born. Throughout my life, I've spoken to myself in every tone of voice—in anger and panic, in ecstasy and resignation. I've admonished myself, encouraged myself. I've listened to what I've had to say. And some of what I've said, I've saved.

I've saved it in case I'd want to know what life was like

when I was alone on a winter night after the children had gone to sleep. In case I'd want to recall the way in which the imitation Tiffany lamp made shadows on the kitchen table as I sat with pen in hand—while the past rushed furiously towards me, fighting to be captured on the sheaf of papers before me, and the future begged me to begin a different tale.

And so it is that I present the following—a collection of writings. A decade's worth of conversations with myself, many of which appeared originally as newspaper columns, some of which are printed here for the first time. The whole is a chronicle of everyday life—the skinned knee, a child's first day at school, laughter, a pot of soup, shopping, the backyard tree. And, a second chance at marriage, an introduction to *Yiddishkeit, kashrus,* day school, *Shabbos, Pesach, Sukkos, Purim, Torah,* discovery of the *neshamah* striving to emerge between the lines.

BOOK ONE • ADJUSTMENTS

$\mathcal{A}$DJUSTMENTS

INTRODUCTION

A period of adjustment. That's what they called it. Well-meaning friends, relatives and neighbors carefully labeled that space of time just after the divorce. "It will take a while," they patiently explained, "but just you wait and see. Before you know it, you'll feel completely comfortable in your new life." That concept, though, was difficult to swallow. Did I really want to feel comfortable with my "situation," as my status was euphemistically termed? Was adjustment something towards which I should ultimately strive? And if not, what was it that I hoped to achieve?

Peace of mind, I think. A reprieve from emotional turmoil. Back then I wanted simply to feel better. I wondered vaguely if I'd ever smile again. The concept of going it alone (with a two-year-old and a four-year-old) was frightening. Parenting, I'd only recently discovered, was an all encompassing job and suddenly I found myself facing motherhood without a spouse. The first night in the apartment was awkward. The place and I had not yet made friends. I heard my foot fall on the wooden floor and thought the sound was hollow. The tiny kitchen was odd after the spacious one I'd left behind. I was lost, confused in the rooms where I could hear the voices of other people filtering through thin walls. I remember offering simple explanations to my son and daughter, attempting to make them understand that Daddy would no longer live with us. I recall trying desperately to connect the abstract with the immediate. When I wanted to make dinner, the oven would not work. The pilot had not been lit. I knocked on a neighbor's door for help, feeling as I watched a stranger strike a match that I was rather inept and vulnerable. Eventually, though, I fed the children.

Next, I bathed them in the rose-colored bathtub and dressed them in their Dr. Dentons. And just then, as I combed their freshly-washed hair and put the damp towels in the hamper, just as I completed the familiar bedtime routine, I knew a sense of accomplishment. I—we had made it through the day. Night had fallen and my offspring had clean bodies and full bellies. The old life was over forever, and this new life had begun.

The future was an awesome responsibility weighing me down in my apartment at the top of the stairs. And yet, on that first night I understood that I would be all right. In celebration of this insight, I took the children for a walk. I followed behind as they padded through the long carpeted hallways of the building which we would call home for nearly five years. "People live behind each one of these doors," I remember telling them. "There are probably lots of boys and girls for you to meet. Living here is going to be so much fun." And the children, being optimists at heart and trusting in their mother's words, smiled happily at the confidence I seemed to feel.

Eventually, I began to believe myself. I learned to balance the checkbook. I landed a part-time job. I hired baby-sitters, made new friends. I spent countless hours on the telephone with old friends. I worried about my children's psyches. I worried about money. I thought about things— life, family, the universe and me. I thought about myself. And then there was that other thing. That spark. That secret pinpoint of light which sometimes burned in the distance or in my mind; I could never tell which. There was that gnawing sense of something greater than I, which saw me through the days and nights and years, and tugged at me and beckoned me to follow it—something which said that it would lead.

 ORKS OF ART

When I moved from a four-bedroom colonial to a two-bedroom, second floor apartment, I left my old life behind— including the husband and the furniture. I decided it would be best to carry as few memories with me as possible.

Friends warned me against the decision. They said I'd regret not taking my dresser, and didn't I really want the little old marble-topped table? But in my conviction to begin anew, I was sure I'd want pristine surroundings. I forgot about one thing, though. I was taking the kids.

The walls in the apartment were white. I thought that would signify a new start, sort of a clean slate. But in less than six months, the white walls were covered with lollipop-smudged fingerprints. I had, of course, left all the artwork behind. When the smudges began to take over, I had to cover the walls with something. Now the dining area and hallways are a gallery of scribbling and collages, the paintings of a five-year-old and a three-year-old.

Then there was the fiasco of the glass-topped, wicker end tables. I couldn't keep the children out of the living room when we had a joint playroom and a bedroom for each. How could I have expected them to stay put in the one small room they currently share with their blocks, books, games, puzzles and trucks?

I bought some interesting baskets and wind chimes to display on the wall, but they abut the front door where the donkey of pin-the-tail fame hangs. The bathroom was done in shades of pink and maroon with enlarged postcard art reproductions on the wall opposite the tub. Beneath that wall sit three dolls, two boats and six empty shampoo bottles.

I used to love plants, but I can't afford the large ones these days so I bought some little ones instead. I told the kids they could take care of them. Now the plants stand on the glass-topped tables next to the paper cups the children need for "watering," and the toy guitar they play to lull the greenery to sleep.

There's a portacrib in my bedroom for when my nephew comes to visit and two pairs of training pants hanging from the shower curtain, testimony to last night's "accident." I've got Pampers boxes interspersed with perfume in the cabinet under the sink and forty-three Golden Books hiding Hemingway, Faulkner and Edgar Allan Poe on the shelves. There are magic markers in my etagere and colored construction paper in the drawer where I intended to keep placemats or tablecloths or whatever else adults keep.

The only photographs on display show a little girl in pigtails and ribbons and a boy in a blue shirt.

Before a friend arrives, I do my best to vacuum the Cheerios from the rug and erase the pencil lines from the hardwood floor. But inevitably, I miss the crayons someone hid in the cookie jar or the kids' toothbrushes stuck between the cushions of the brown velvet chair.

In the peace and quiet of the evening when the children are asleep, I sometimes look around and redecorate in my mind. But the stick figure drawings taped to my walls are probably just as interesting as any work of modern art. And besides, I've got the originals.

AN INKLING OF SHABBOS

Friday nights get me down. There is something about the end of the week, years of memories of not having to get up for school or work on Saturday. It doesn't matter that I'm a mother now and have neither school nor a career in my life. It's still the weekend. Friday night. And I can remember the combined fragrance of chicken soup and cleaning fluid that filled the house of my childhood at four o'clock on dreary, wet, slushy winter afternoons. The damp clinging chill melted instantly as I walked through the front door. Home and peace. Oh, for those days!

Then there was the marriage and a lovely little cottage in the woods and waiting for my husband to come home on Friday night. The expectation of the weekend ahead. And I'd have supper waiting and the baby would be awake and eager for Daddy to arrive. Oh G-d, for Friday nights of a full, satisfied family feeling!

It is bleak out today, a midwinter, foggy day with snow

melting to rain. I need desperately to be where the warmth is, with a Saturday morning ahead and a Saturday night with "plans" and a Sunday with that sad, weekend-over feeling. Now I look forward to Mondays where routine fills my hours, the part-time job, shuttling the oldest child to nursery school and back, taking the baby to the sitter. Home at the end of the day, tired enough to be glad the evening is short. But Friday nights are different. They're meant to be long and lingering and forward looking. They're meant for staying at the dinner table and continuing to eat after the meal is done. Friday nights were created for the children to play happily with their toys while the parents relax over a cup of coffee. On Friday nights, you can get into pajamas early and read or talk and later have a snack. You can curl up in bed because there's still Saturday night left.

When I think of all the things I miss, it's Friday night I miss the most.

FOOD FOR THOUGHT

Peanut butter and jelly for lunch is bad enough, but macaroni spaceships for dinner is the end of the line. And I've reached it.

I can recall a time, not so long ago, when dinner meant chicken or steak or fish with a side dish and a vegetable. But that was when there were two adults in the house. Now that it's just the kids and me, it seems a waste of time to cook when they won't eat anything but spaceships.

There is still some variety to my meals. The little ones will tolerate elbow macaroni and cheese, hamburgers if the buns are made of white bread and there's lots of ketchup, or spaghetti if it's long, skinny, cooked with butter and "no sauce, Ma."

You remember those married days when your husband wouldn't be home for dinner. You'd sort of relax and whip up something fast, like omelets or hot dogs or even macaroni spaceships. Well, I find that now I truly look forward to dinner guests. It gives me a rare opportunity to settle for something appetizing.

It isn't that I haven't tried. I've made a London broil for four, hoping to lure the little guys by the sheer fragrance of the cooking meat. But they always say "yech." I wind up giving them oatmeal, and I eat an entire London broil myself.

Or the steaks packaged in pairs, one for me and one for the two of them to share. I've eaten two full steaks myself, cleaned up the kitchen and started over with tuna sandwiches for the children, because you can't let them go to bed hungry. In the past year, I've eaten more pancakes, salmon croquettes made in the shape of footballs, pastina and eggs than I care to remember.

According to my friends, however, there is a solution. If the solo adult craves lasagna and the children can't stand the stuff, you make one enormous lasagna, cut it into parent portions and freeze it. When you break out the pancakes for the kids, you can simultaneously defrost the lasagna. Then everyone's happy. While you're boiling the hot dogs, you can be broiling a steak. Of course, it means an extra pan, but hot dogs are unhealthy for growing grown-ups anyway.

Periodically, I long for a quiche or veal scallopini, but the kids will eat veal only if it's dipped in bread crumbs and eggs and only if it's fried in oil. There seems to be just one solution. Cook two meals, one for the kids and one for yourself. Consider yourself as important as the man for whom you used to cook. But then, the thought of sauteed mushrooms eaten while blowing on oatmeal to "cool it, Mom," detracts somewhat from the culinary experience.

Last night, I placed a tablecloth on the table, turned down the lights, lit candles and played classical music on the stereo. I served chicken with apricots, broccoli and parslied potatoes at six o'clock.

The kids wanted to know why I could not read to them instead of playing music. Whose birthday was it anyway? Couldn't they at least blow out the candles? Why did the potatoes taste funny, and what was that thing next to the chicken? They ate a little broccoli. I gave them a peanut butter and jelly sandwich before they went to bed.

 A GOOD SPORT

At the age of thirty-four, I'm learning to pitch a ball, dive off a diving board and ride a bike without training wheels. This in the name of parenthood.

When your three-year-old son hands you the huge bat and ball his Daddy gave him for his birthday and looks at you expectantly, what can you say? I haven't pitched a ball since junior high school. And even then, I was the kid nobody wanted on her team. But you can't say that to your child. Anyway, I've got custody, so I figure that includes athletics. It wasn't easy at first. I couldn't even show him how to hold the bat. But I did manage to find an older boy with a decent grip. He showed me, so I could show my son.

Now for the pitching. I knew about overhand and

underhand, and with some practice, I even managed to aim the ball pretty close to the bat. When the ball and bat actually connected, I was as thrilled as the three-year-old.

Now, diving was another matter entirely. My daughter wanted to learn to dive. My daughter wanted me to teach her to dive. I can't dive. Or, I couldn't dive until this summer. I watched her jump off the board (all twenty-eight pounds of her). It didn't look that difficult, so I did it. I got some water in my ears, but I didn't drown.

Then I saw her kind of bend over and fall in. "Is this how?" she asked. (I don't know, I thought.) "I think so," I said encouragingly. "Yeah, that looks right." And she went in, under and back up. "Your turn, Ma." So I walked to the edge of the board. The first five times I couldn't make myself fall in. I leaned over, but just before the plunge I held my nose and jumped. "Look Ma, if you bend your knees a little, it's easier," she explained, with the wisdom of a five-year-old. But remarkably, she was right. Anyhow, I can sort of dive now.

Then there was the bike. I have a bike, old, one-speed, rusty and unridden for years, but I pulled it out of storage and had the tires fixed. At the same time, I had the training wheels removed from my daughter's bike. So, here we are at thirty-four and five-and-a-half, wobbling around the parking lot of the apartment building. Sometimes when she's at a friend's house, I practice alone. I can even go on the street now if it's not too crowded.

If I were still married, chances are I'd leave the sports to the man of the house. But now that I'm on my own again, I am really pleased to discover that I'm not as much of a *klutz* as I thought. For instance, I can do a cartwheel. In the seventh and eighth grades, I was the only girl on the cheerleading squad who couldn't do a cartwheel. But when my little girl learned to do a cartwheel I figured it was time to learn, too. So I did. She taught me. I can do it on the grass, on the sand, in the living room. If I had known at twelve what I know now, I might have been a gymnast.

And that's not all. My three-year-old conned his Daddy into buying him a soccer ball last week. He's watched all the big boys playing. Last night, I actually went into the yard with the boy and the ball and tried to figure out how to bounce the thing off my head.

I can roller skate again and, if the kids have their way, I'll be learning to ice-skate this winter. I figure, if I keep going at this rate, by the time I'm forty I can coach a Little League game, and by forty-three I'll be ready for football. To be perfectly honest, I like the Band-aids on my knees.

GIRL'S DAY

Among the most difficult aspects of being a mother is that there's just one of me to divide between the two children. What with working and washing, cooking and cleaning, it's sometimes hard to determine which child needs more attention at any given moment.

On Friday, October 10, as I was kissing my daughter good night, I noticed that she looked older. So on the spur of the moment, motivated by the fleeting of time and the child's advancing age of almost five and a half years, I issued a whispered invitation. "There's no school on Monday, it's Columbus Day," I said. "How about if we make it Girl's Day? We'll find somebody to watch your little brother, and you and I can spend the whole day together."

She was ecstatic. She promised not to tell the little guy beforehand (so he wouldn't be jealous). And she made me promise not to invite any other girlfriends (mine or hers). "Just the two of us," we pledged.

After she fell asleep, I made three phone calls to line up a sitter, a substitute sitter and a substitute substitute sitter for my son. I wanted to be absolutely sure nothing would stand in the way of Girl's Day.

Throughout the weekend, my daughter periodically reminded me of our secret. Her excitement was contagious. And I think the anticipation was as important as the idea itself.

By ten a.m. on Monday, my son was already with the first-choice sitter and Girl's Day had begun. My daughter and I dressed very carefully. She helped select my outfit and I helped her choose hers. We fixed our hair, complimented each other and set out for a local gift shop to buy each other matching presents.

"May I help you?" asked the lady behind the counter.

And, in total seriousness, my little companion answered. "It's Girl's Day. We need two of the same things." For the next thirty minutes, we combed the shop. I rejected the matching twenty-seven dollar soft sculpture dolls (although I had to agree they were lovely). She rejected the six dollar gold bracelets with tiny jade circles (too simple). At last we settled on the perfect compromise, two rainbow pins. Bright, cheerful and three dollars each. We paid the lady, attached the pins to our sweaters and left our coats unzipped so everyone could see.

Next, we went to the restaurant. We decided to have breakfast for lunch; pancakes, eggs and two cups, one with coffee and a little milk, one with milk and a little coffee. We showed the waitress our rainbow pins.

After lunch was dancing school. She danced, I watched. Normally I drop her off and return for her in an hour, but on Girl's Day, I stayed.

My daughter and I had spent an entire day together talking and laughing and sharing our lives. She's growing up fast, but I'm determined to take the time to enjoy her.

HELPING HANDS

It began with a discussion of responsibility and ended with blueberry yogurt and cold fried fish for breakfast.

Several weeks ago, after a particularly harrowing day, I read one more bedtime story and commenced my lecture. "Children," I said, "I'm beat. All day long, I've done things for you. I cooked for you, washed you, dressed you, took you to school, played games with you. I've picked up your toys and read you your books and brought you one more drink of water and another glass of juice. And I'm really tired. From now on, I think we need cooperation. I may be the only grown-up person in this house, but I'm not the only person. I'd like some help from you."

The next morning, nobody jumped into my bed to announce the arrival of dawn. It was a strange feeling to lie there in my room listening to the scurrying and whispering of the kids. They were definitely up to something. With my eyes half-closed, I watched them run past my door on their way to the kitchen. In the five and a half years since I've become a mother, I believe this was the latest I've ever stayed in bed. They came to get me at eight forty-five.

"Wake up. We've got surprises for you. We did a lot of

work." And indeed they had. The five-year-old is an old hand at dressing. But between the two of them, they'd somehow managed to clothe the three-year-old. He was magnificent in his red pants and orange and brown striped shirt.

"We even got on my underwear and socks," he crowed. "Now close your eyes and we'll show you something else."

They took me by the hand and led me to their room. "Okay, you can look now." And there, amidst last night's pajamas and teddy bears, and the morning's washcloths and toothbrushes, were the two lumpiest, bumpiest, most beautifully made beds in the world.

For the *piece de resistance*, I was led to the kitchen where they had set the table with forks, spoons, Sesame Street plastic plates, paper cups and the meal itself—a heaping portion of last night's cold fried fish and their own addition, an entire container of blueberry yogurt. This was to be washed down with one full-to-the-brim paper cup of water.

They pulled out my chair, helped seat me, and then, with their eyes riveted to my mouth, they watched until I had devoured every last morsel. "It was the best breakfast I've ever had," I said. And I meant it.

Since the morning of the first breakfast, my children have continued to give me a hand in a variety of ways. With the slightest encouragement and a little praise, they can sweep a floor, dust a room, help fold laundry and clear the table. They can dress themselves and get into their pajamas. Their beds are still lumpy, but I don't remake them. I keep Cheerios on a shelf they can reach for the times they "cook."

Last night, after a particularly good day, I read one more bedtime story and commenced my lecture. "Children," I said, "I feel great. All day long we've done things together. We've cooked and washed and dressed and gone to school, played games, picked up the toys and read the books. I may be the only grown-up in this house, but I'm not the only person. I like your help, and I love you."

$\mathcal{M}$Y DOCTOR

In this era of impersonal group medical practices and impervious group medical receptionists, there still exists the doctor with a good bedside manner. It took some doing, but I found him by phone Monday night.

My son couldn't breathe. Literally. My daughter was hanging onto my leg, and the receptionist in the pediatrician's office said I'd have to speak to the "group" doctor on duty.

I mustered my strength. "No," I said. "I don't want to talk to the doctor on duty. I want to talk to the doctor I talked to this morning. I want to speak to the doctor I spoke to yesterday and last week. I want to talk to the doctor who knows my son's name."

And mine, I might have added. I want to speak with the doctor who knows me as the mother of this little boy. Who treats me with respect.

"But we have your file right here in the office, ma'am. The doctor on duty can give you advice."

I held firm. "No," I said. "I don't want to tell my story to someone new. I want you to call the doctor at home and ask him to call me back."

"I can't do that," said the receptionist.

"Oh yes, you can," said I. "I need to talk to *my doctor* right now."

There. I'd said it. "*My doctor.*" What an old-fashioned,

homey kind of phrase. It conjures images of a kindly man, trudging through ice-covered lanes, carrying his little black bag of cures. It brings to mind gentle tousling of a child's hair and a reassuring smile to dispel a mother's worries.

"Please call my doctor," I said again. "If he refuses to call me, that's his choice. Thank you and good-bye." I hung up.

Between my son's wheezing and my daughter's questions, and the churning of my stomach and my brain, I barely heard the phone ring.

"Hello?"

And wonder of wonders. It was *my doctor*. "Oh, thank you, thank you for calling," I said. "My son is wheezing now. It's nine o'clock (as if he didn't know) and I've got six different bottles of medicine in front of me and I don't know what, if anything, to give to this child. I'm scared."

"And it's difficult to make these decisions on your own," the good doctor added, reading my mind. "Don't be afraid. Here's what to do . . ." The physician spoke rationally and calmly for several minutes. He then suggested that I see him in the morning. By the time we hung up, I was confident that we'd make it till nine a.m., wheeze and all.

A sick child can be frightening, whether one is married or not. But when we're alone, sometimes the responsibility is overwhelming. Perhaps we would do well to tell our favorite "group" doctor that we're on our own. Somewhere in our child's file, the doctor could give permission for a receptionist to call him at home in case of emergency or extreme parental fear.

I couldn't see the doctor's reassuring smile and my son didn't have his hair tousled, but the physician's parting words helped get me through the night. "Don't worry," he had said. "Your little boy will be just fine."

Thanks, Doc. I needed that.

NEIGHBORLY ADVICE

"Sit here and don't move," I told the children. "I have to go back upstairs and get the suitcases."

I left the kids in the car in the apartment house parking lot, ran upstairs and returned three and a half minutes later with two huge suitcases and a blanket. I was carrying the teddy bear under my chin. I managed to get into the car without collapsing. The children were still there, and so was an irate elderly neighbor. "You young mothers are all alike," she scolded me. "How dare you leave these darling youngsters in the car alone? It's a good thing I came along."

"But it was only for three minutes," I started to protest.

"I don't care how long it is. There are crazies everywhere. Next time you have to leave them, knock on my door. I'll watch them." She glared at me, turned on her heel and marched back to the building.

As I finished loading the trunk, I replayed the scene in my mind, defending myself admirably. I could have said, "Look, there are two of them and one of me. I can't hold both their hands and get them safely to the car while balancing suitcases and teddy bears on my head, can I?" Or I could have said, "If I took the suitcases down first, I'd have had to leave the children alone in the apartment for three and a half minutes. Who knows what might have happened in that time? One of them could have turned on the gas, or stuck his finger in the socket, or broken his neck trying to climb on a chair to answer the phone if it started to ring."

Three, maybe four, times a day, I have to let them out of my sight momentarily so I can attend to some chore. I wonder if it is really necessary, for instance, to take them with me when I go outside to empty the garbage. And should they always accompany me to the laundry room, if it's time to do the wash? Somewhere along the line, I've had to make some serious decisions. For the laundry room detail I usually insist that they join me. They protest, and it is a harrowing experience to negotiate two stairways with two huge bags of laundry and two youngsters. But for the sake of safety, we do it together. When it comes to putting the laundry into the dryer, however, I have on occasion allowed them to stay in the apartment alone for a few minutes. (I take the phone off the hook so nobody breaks his neck while standing on a chair to answer it.)

For the most part, I think I'm a very protective parent. Still, there is only one of me. To a certain extent, though, my irate neighbor was right. Until she bawled me out for leaving the children unattended, I had not really asked for much help from the neighbors. But the interesting thing is, the neighbors don't mind helping. The wonderful couple across the hall has been known to "babysit" while I make an important phone call. The man downstairs has watched my children along with his, so his wife and I can start our separate dinners. I've called on friends in the building to take over for ten minutes while I run to the pharmacy for a bottle of baby aspirin. I've borrowed milk and eggs.

And when I'm going away with the children, I knock on a certain neighbor's door. "Can you watch the kids for a few minutes? I've got to put some suitcases in the car."

 A SUCCESS STORY

Some things are meant to be shared. Success is one of them. As a sometimes writer, one of my lifelong dreams has been to have a column of my own. That, I felt, would be a success worth celebrating.

A few months ago, I dropped one child off at dancing school and headed for the supermarket with the other. While my daughter shuffle-stepped the hour away, I purchased seventy dollars worth of toilet paper, toothpaste and other essentials. I had just finished loading four semi-ripped bags and one wailing child into the back seat when a very attractive woman tapped me on the shoulder.

I didn't recognize her at first. It seems she's met with some success of late. She looked ten pounds lighter, her new hairstyle was lovely, and she told me her career plans looked good. Alas, I was a mess. My dress was faded and three inches too long, and I was perspiring. It was one of those ninety-four degree, out-of-season, autumn days. I beat a hasty retreat, promising to call her soon.

I realized I'd better head home to unload the groceries before the milk spoiled and the frozen broccoli defrosted. It was four-fifteen and tap class ends at four-thirty. That gave me a quarter of an hour to get back to the apartment, unpack the perishables and return to pick up my little girl.

I heard the phone ringing before I turned the key in the lock. The three-year-old was screaming in the background. I dropped one of the two bags I was balancing (and discovered later that I'd once again broken four out of twelve eggs). "Hello?" I answered. *Success.* It was my very own small success calling. *They* had indeed agreed to allow me this column. "Thank you, thank you, thank you," I shrieked. And hanging up the phone I rushed to my son. "Did you hear that? Mommy's got a column."

He looked at the grocery bags. "For supper?"

"No, not for supper. A column for the newspaper."

I remembered to stick the milk in the refrigerator. It was

four-thirty. I was late for the dancer. Driving around the parking lot at breakneck speed, I missed my downstairs neighbor by an inch.

"What's the matter with you?" she yelled.

"I got the column!" I screamed through the car window.

"Oh," was all she could muster, still shaking her head as I floored the gas pedal.

"Where were you?" the dancer demanded. "You're late."

I grabbed her twenty-eight pound body in my arms and swung her around. "I did it, I did it. I've got a column."

She looked quizzically at me. "My new tap shoes hurt."

The first thing I noticed when we got home was one unpacked grocery bag and a puddle of strawberry ice cream forming at its base. We celebrated my joy with pizza for dinner. That at least was something to which the kids could relate. Then I called my parents, my sister and two old friends in South Jersey. Everyone was truly happy for me. But by eight p.m., with the children sleeping, I realized I'd spent my first three columns' pay on long distance calls. There was that moment of letdown. I no longer have a husband with whom to share my success. But then, if I had a husband I wouldn't be writing a column about bringing up my children on my own. So I phoned a few friends and invited them over. They may not have known exactly what we were celebrating, but I did, and that's what counts.

YOM KIPPUR THOUGHTS

Yom Kippur eve. What would I be doing if I had what I wanted? I would be getting dressed to go to services with my husband and my parents and my children. Candles would be dancing on the table, and we'd all listen to the beautiful ancient prayers together.

What am I doing? Listening to a French singer on the stereo, watching the children with runny noses play with puzzles and beads.

I would wear a white wool dress tonight, and I would be proud, with shining eyes. And the music would sink into my soul. And we would see old friends there. We would belong . . . but we don't belong. And I am scared. Their father was here today, sullen and gloomy. Each time he leaves I always want to cry for all that never was—that might have been. We might have had the holidays at least. The holidays when children hold their parents' hands and look into their eyes and ask them questions which their parents cannot answer. We might have had the festive meals when sons and daughter squirm and wriggle in their chairs. We might have been fasting on *Yom Kippur*. But we are not. I am not, and the children think tonight is just another night. There ought to have been a tablecloth and flowers in a vase. We should have been a family on our way to the synagogue, where our boy and girl would fall asleep to the sound of the *Kol Nidrei* melody. But the children are here with me, and *Yom Kippur* is somewhere else.

PURPLE SHOES

Last week, this family had two colds, one case of bronchitis, two vaporizers running all day, four boxes of Kleenex, two jars of Vicks VapoRub and three sleepless nights.

There is nothing like a sick mother caring for two sick kids to bring home some truths about parenthood. I know it's not supposed to happen this way, but I started the whole thing. I actually woke up one morning with a cold. But mothers are not supposed to be out of commission. So I went on with my work. I made breakfast, got the kids dressed, cleaned up the apartment and took two Bufferin and a glass of orange juice.

Truly, I tried to keep the germs from spreading. I flushed my crumpled tissues down the toilet lest the germs sneak out of the wastepaper basket. I sprayed Lysol everywhere I went. I kissed the children on the tops of their heads, and I even coughed with my mouth closed. Nothing helped.

I went to bed about nine p.m. the first night of my cold, and by midnight I knew I'd had my last three-hour span of sleep for a while. The six-year-old woke up first. (Why do kids always get sick in the middle of the night?) Her head was stuffy, her nose was runny, and her throat hurt. I took her into bed with me. We spent a restless night together. There is something not quite charming about curling up with a child who wads tissues under your pillow and insists on commiserating with you until the wee hours. As dawn approached, she finally dozed. An hour later, her little brother was awake and sneezing. Unfortunately for him, his colds always wind up as bronchitis.

The next couple of days are a blur of sticky medicine spilled on pajama tops, tea and honey stuck to tabletops and books, puzzles and crayons covering every inch of floor space. I spent the nights standing in the bathroom holding my son, while a hot shower spewed steam at us. Thus, after seventy-two hours of nursing duty, I felt quite the martyr. I had, after all, cured my daughter. And despite the lack of sleep, my cough had almost ceased and I could breathe out of one nostril most of the time. Even the four-year-old seemed to be getting better. It was cause for a celebration.

"Let's take a nap," I suggested to my son. "We'll lie down together and rest for a while."

I don't know if either of us actually slept, but after a few minutes, he poked me on the shoulder and announced he'd had a dream.

"What did you dream about, honey?" I yawned into his adorable little face. And after all my efforts at being a Super Mom during this time of stress, here is what he told me.

"Ma," he said. "You were smushed by a big machine. Flat out smushed. Then I saw this girl with a big yellow hat, blue eyes, a blue dress and purple shoes. I said, 'My Mommy was smushed, and I'm looking for a new Mommy.' And the girl said she'd be my Mommy, so I jumped up and down."

And with this, my little boy showed me how he jumped up and down and, I might add, clapped with glee. Then his little pixie face got very serious. "But, Mommy, I musta waked up because I looked around and you were still here."

So there you have it. I looked at myself lying there in my medicine-stained bathrobe and a pair of knee-socks, with my nose all red and my eyes all puffy, and I laughed like crazy. Why, I was half smushed already. Who wouldn't want a replacement Mommy? But purple shoes?

POPULARITY CONTEST

When two ten-year-old boys called for me after school, I knew I was in the running for most popular mother in the building.

Possibly it's because I've gone sledding with them. Maybe it's because they've played their favorite record album on my stereo ten times in a row. Or it could be the lure of my own four-year-old and six-year-old. But in all honesty, I believe the eight-year-olds, nine-year-olds and ten-year-olds that frequent my apartment have simply discovered that I'm home.

I've been told by other mothers and fathers that children begin to rebel against after-school sitters somewhere around the age of nine. And in an apartment building such as this, the anti-sitter rebellion may be stronger than that among nine-year-old house dwellers.

For one thing, there's a great deal of peer pressure in an apartment complex. In an era when so many parents work, and in a complex where so many working parents are also single parents, the kids have a lot in common. Of the ten or twelve youngsters living here, just a couple of kids will find a parent at home before five p.m. For the rest, fending for oneself is a matter of pride. Everyone over the age of seven has a key to his own apartment. I've watched them tumble off the school bus in a cluster to head for their individual homes. There, they drop off books, change their clothes and regroup in a matter of minutes. And notwithstanding fights, cliques and sometimes tears, these youngsters seem more capable than I thought possible.

I watched a ten-year-old carefully wrap a plastic bag around the cast supporting a nine-year-old friend's broken arm. "This will protect it, so it doesn't get wet when we play outside," the ten-year-old explained.

I heard an eleven-year-old admonish a chubby six-year-old for downing a sugary after-school snack. "An apple would be better," the older child suggested. "It's important to watch what you eat so you'll grow up big and strong."

Between dismissal and the time they get home from work, parents can be fairly confident that their offspring will be okay But that's a matter of only an hour or two. A no-school day is different. And that's where I came in.

On the year's first snow day, eight a.m. brought a flurry of activity in the corridors of the building. School was canceled, but work was not. Parents rushed up and down the hallways hiring resident teenagers to babysit for the youngest of the children. A few adults decided to stay home from the office. And one mother knocked on my door to ask if I would watch her nine-year-old. "He really doesn't need a sitter," she said. "Just check on him once in a while if you would. He's downstairs in our apartment."

Since I had not yet served breakfast to my own children, I decided to invite the nine-year-old to join us. I rang his bell. "Would you like some French toast?" I asked.

"French toast?" he answered. "Sure."

"French toast?" came an echo from the depths of the apartment. It was the nine-year-old's ten-year-old friend.

Anyway, between the invitation to breakfast and the return to our door, we somehow picked up four additional guests, all of whom were "too old" for sitters but not too old for French toast, omeletes, juice, milk and hot buttered bagels. I also discovered that they were not too old to draw pictures, play games, sing songs, listen to records and tell stories.

I had a terrific time with the children, and they seemed happy here. Why? Was it the breakfast? Or the novelty of spending time in a different apartment?

Nine-year-olds, as they were quick to tell me, "do not need sitters, not even on snow days, and definitely not after school." But somebody else's mother isn't a sitter. She is just sort of at home.

A WALK IN THE ORCHARD

When my six-year-old asks if I'd like to go for a walk, I know that I've been feeling glum. The suggestion to stroll is my son's way of taking me away from it all. Usually, he succeeds.

He has a favorite walking spot in an orchard near our apartment. He holds my hand, and we wander together among the apple trees for an hour or two. Sometimes, if my child thinks I'm in need of a longer change, we pack a picnic lunch. The orchard is one of those places where my son and I can be quiet together without feeling penned.

My need for "a little air" is usually brought on by an acute bout of disappointment—sometimes a string of disappointments. In work, social life, finances, there are always rough and rougher times. I guess the disappointments show. I wander around the apartment grim-faced and silent for a day or two. At particularly difficult times, I become a functional mother. I cook. I clean. I answer the children's questions. But I don't look interested. I rarely smile.

My son, a kindergartner, arrives home at midday. If my mood has been silent and sullen, I suppose he doesn't much look forward to an afternoon with me. Sometimes, he suggests a walk. He knows I will feel better. He is right.

I believe I must take credit for the initial stroll in the orchard. It might have been a bad day for me, or maybe not. Anyway, I remember pointing out the shape of the apple trees and the straight lines of earth between the rows. I showed my son some clouds and bunches of wildflowers along the side of the road. I told him then that the orchard makes me happy. It smells good there, and the air is clean. I also told him that peaceful, pretty places like orchards become peaceful, pretty pictures in my mind. So when I feel unhappy, I can think about the pictures to cheer up. And if thinking doesn't work, visiting usually does.

My son and I saw the orchard last spring. In summer, my daughter joined us, and we walked for miles in the hot air. In fall, we watched the leaves turn colors. We noticed apples rotting in colorful piles on the ground. In winter, we made footprints and wrote our names in the snow among the apple trees. And now it is spring again.

As I write this, it is afternoon and I am glum. I have had a few disappointments. It is drizzling outside. But my son has made a suggestion.

"A walk in the orchard?" he asks.

I am smiling now. I think we'll go. The orchard will be pretty in the rain.

 LICES OF LIFE

Just this afternoon, someone asked me where I get the ideas for my columns. "Oh, things sort of happen," I answered.

Take tonight, for instance. I made chicken for dinner. The children and I were having a semblance of table conversation when my daughter choked on her chicken. I totally forgot the Heimlich Maneuver and instead insisted that she down three glasses of water while gagging and crying. In my state of panic, I figured the water would wash down the chicken. Eventually, I remembered to call the doctor. I told him the child was breathing but seemed to have something stuck in her throat. He agreed to see us immediately.

Somehow, I was able to avoid an accident as I sped through red lights on my way to the doctor's office. By the time we arrived, my daughter was no longer in tears. The coughing had subsided. The chicken apparently had been swallowed. The doctor checked her throat, listened to her lungs and pronounced her cured. He gave her a yellow balloon. He gave her little brother a green balloon. And he gave me the bill.

We got back in the car. Relieved at having averted disaster, I suggested we do something a little out of the ordinary to top off the evening. "It's a beautiful night, isn't it, kids?" I asked. "I was going to do the grocery shopping in the morning, but since we're already in the car, how about if we shop now?" (Somebody once told me, if you speak with enthusiasm, even a chore will begin to sound like fun.)

"Wow," they said. "Let's shop."

I didn't have the grocery list with me, but I remembered the necessities, and we managed to fill the cart in twenty minutes. For eight p.m., the line at the checkout seemed unbelievably long, but since we'd come this far, there was no point in quitting. So I cracked open the box of doughnuts I'd not yet purchased.

"Have one," I told the children. "Isn't this fun? Doughnuts for dessert at eight o'clock in the supermarket."

"I can't eat mine," said my daughter. I wondered for a moment if the chicken had returned to her throat.

"Can't you swallow?" I asked her.

"I can swallow, but I have to go to the bathroom . . . badly. It's an emergency."

"Can't you hold it?"

"No."

I knew it was those three glasses of water I'd made her drink.

Have you ever used the bathroom in the stock room of a supermarket? There are crates and boxes and carts and pulleys and stock boys. The ladies' room is at the end of the obstacle course.

Eventually, we returned to the checkout line only to find that four people had gotten in front of our cart. About fifteen minutes later, we paid the bill. I hoisted the two heavy bags into my arms and walked outside, kids in tow. And what I saw was amazing. Forty-five minutes earlier the sky had been hued with pink and orange, a perfect summer sunset. As we exited the supermarket, we encountered a torrential downpour.

By the time we got to the car, kids, bags and mother were soaked through. But I did manage to get home and upstairs to the apartment without dropping a child or grocery bag. I cleared "dinner" off the table, washed the dishes still piled in the sink and unloaded the produce. I was just beginning to feel that things were under control when my daughter came into the kitchen.

"Mommy, it's still raining pretty hard outside, isn't it?"

"Yes," I said.

"Well, you know that bedspread you washed this morning and hung on the terrace to dry? It's getting very wet."

NAP DECISIONS

I am a creature of habit, a slave to routine. The idea of a *change* usually sends me running back to the nearest known mundane task. How did it happen then that I left two bags of dirty laundry, an unvacuumed carpet and several unwashed dishes to make a three-and-a-half-hour journey with two kids and a picnic lunch?

It was a sunny summer morning. I was about to attack the housekeeping chores when I noticed the expressions on my children's faces. They were bored.

"Well, kids, what should we do this afternoon?" I offered a choice of predictable, safe, uncomplicated alternatives. "Wanna go swimming at the lake?" (The lake is a man-made local body of water filled with tubes, rafts and children.)

"Naa," the kids answered.

"We could go to the library."

"Naa."

"I have one other suggestion," I tentatively suggested. "I have an aunt and uncle who own a house way, way down the shore near the ocean. They've invited us to visit them any time we want. They've got a couple of grandchildren about your age who'll be there . . ."

"Wow," my son jumped from his chair. "The ocean?"

"Neat-O." My daughter clapped her hands. "Come on. Let's go."

"Can we swim? And play with the kids? Can we bring our sleeping bags? Can we go? Oh please, oh please, oh please." The children were dancing around the apartment.

"Hold it," I ordered, stopping the cheerful commotion. "I said this was an invitation. I didn't say we could do it. It's a long, long ride to get there, and you don't even remember my aunt and uncle, and you've only met their grandchildren once, and it's already the middle of the morning, and I'd have to call and tell them we were coming. And anyway, it might rain."

"Mommy, you said it was a suggestion. Why did you tell us about it if we can't do it?" my daughter challenged.

I thought quickly. Should I be honest and tell my

children that spur of the moment decisions frighten me, that I feel safe with the boredom of routine. Having gotten them all excited about the prospect of a trip to the beach should I dash their enthusiasm with a firm No? I decided I should not. So I said, "Yes. Let's go."

And we went. We phoned my aunt and uncle to announce our impending departure. We packed a hastily made picnic lunch to eat in the car. We threw our bathing suits and pajamas into a suitcase. (And I did not bother to fold them.) I remembered the toothbrushes and the Caladryl lotion. We double-checked the apartment. It was not the epitome of neatness. In fact, it was sort of a mess. I suppressed the urge to straighten it up.

"Let's get going," I commanded. "I'm sure glad you kids agreed to do something different for a change. Do you realize there are people who can't make spur of the moment decisions? Aren't you glad we're not like that?"

A PENNY SAVED

How can I teach them the value of money? The allowance, of course. The allowance, I felt, would instill in my youngsters a feeling of independence, pride and a basic knowledge of mathematics. Eventually, it should help them understand why I can't buy every toy they see. And thus inspired, I launched my course on economics at a cost to me of a quarter per week per child.

One Friday afternoon, I gathered the family around the kitchen table to make an announcement. "Henceforth, I will give you an allowance at the end of every week."

"What's a week?" the four-year-old asked.

And the six-year-old quizzed, "What's an allowance?"

"A week is seven days," I answered. "And an allowance is the money I will give you for your very own. You can spend it right away or save it for a few weeks until you have enough to buy something special. Or you can use it to buy something for somebody else. Like me, for instance."

I handed each child two thin dimes and a nickel.

On their first shopping spree, the kids discovered that twenty-five cent toys are hard to find. It took the six-year-old twenty minutes to settle on a pen. She spent the next hour muttering about the high cost of living.

On the eve of the second allowance, I paid in pennies. They were thrilled—momentarily. "This looks like a lot, but it's the same amount as the two dimes and the nickel," I explained.

"Then one of these pennies is hardly anything, Ma."

"Right."

It was the four-year-old who remembered the piggy bank. "There are more pennies in the piggy," he said. "If we crack him open, we'll have lots of money to go with the allowance."

Simple addition. I was proud of him. I took out a hammer and broke Piggy. We spent ninety minutes counting pennies and arrived at a total of six dollars and fifty-two cents, a little more than three dollars for each child. Both kids went to sleep that night with delusions of grandeur.

The next morning, I explained the value of saving for a rainy day versus spending. My daughter decided to save. My son chose to spend. He stuffed his entire hoard of pennies into a baggie and shoved it into his pocket. We set out for the department store. He desperately wanted Superman pajamas.

"I'm not sure you have enough," I cautioned. "You might have to wait for a few more allowances."

"It'll be enough," he grinned. It was. Superman was on sale. He even found the correct size. He marched up to the cashier, plunked his find on the counter and spilled out his bag of pennies. And now, a thanks to the cashier. She must have been a parent. She patiently counted out three hundred and forty-nine pennies, bagged the purchase and handed my son his two cents change.

As for the anonymous customers behind us in line, I apologize for the wait. But look at it this way. How often will you see someone cashing in his life savings for a pair of pint-size pajamas?

HOMEWORK

My six-year-old daughter ran off the school bus, slammed through the apartment door, shed her shoes in the kitchen and plunked down on the living room rug. She rummaged through her book bag, pulled out the spiral notebook and turned to a page headed by the letter B. Then she spilled all her crayons on the floor and hastily scribbled a picture of a ball.

Still in a flurry, she closed the notebook, put it back in the book bag and stood up. "Done," she announced.

"Done?"

"Done. I'm done with my homework."

Somehow, by osmosis or through her friendship with "big kids," she's learned that it's a good idea to do your homework. "Right away, as soon as you get home from school. First, before you do anything else, you sit down and do your homework."

And this "Letter B" homework was mighty special, since it was her first assignment ever, in her first week of school in the first grade.

"Can I see what you did?" I asked tentatively.

"Okay." She unbuckled her book bag again and pulled out the notebook. There it was, a rather lopsided ball hastily colored in pale blue. She was proud of it, proud of being in the first grade and proud of having homework to do, just like the other big kids. But the assignment itself—was she proud of the ball?

"Ah, honey . . ." I began. Then I stopped—my first encounter with the question: to interfere or not to interfere? "Ah, honey, don't you think . . . ah well, couldn't you maybe have drawn the ball a little more neatly?"

"Ma," she answered condescendingly. "The teacher said to draw something blue. She didn't say it had to be neat."

"Oh," I answered and let it go at that.

But not really. Later that evening, I pondered the ball, the debut of homework. There'll be days, years of assignments, and I'll be the sole supervisor. Suppose I was still married. My spouse and I would be relaxing after dinner. I'd turn to him and casually say, "Well, our little girl had her very first homework assignment today."

"How'd she do?" he'd ask.

"I don't know. She loved having homework, but she was more interested in getting it done than in getting it done to the best of her ability."

"Well, did you ask her to do it over?"

"Not exactly. Should I have?"

Anyway, in my hypothetical conversation with an imaginary mate, we'd continue discussing our thoughts on how, when and to what extent parents should interfere in homework. And I imagined we'd reach some mutual conclusion.

But there is no husband here. There will be no mutual conclusion in this home. For the most part, I'm on my own. I want my child to enjoy learning. I want to help her, but not too much. I must learn when to step back and when to step in. Suddenly, I'm awed and a little frightened by this process called education.

 DAY'S WORK

My daughter has a stuffed nose, my son has spots on his tongue, my car died in line for the drive-in window at the bank and the cat got stuck between the storm door and the screen. It hasn't been one of my better days.

When the alarm rang this morning I could hear the coughing from the children's room. They sounded awful. I went to check. "Looks like you two won't be going to school today."

"Hurray . . . why?"

"Because you're sick. You sound terrible. Here let me look at your throats . . . stick out your tongues and say ahh."

"Ahh," said my daughter, spewing coughs in my face. The tonsils looked okay to me.

"Now you, little guy," I ordered my son. "Open your mouth and say ahh."

My daughter looked first. "Oh, yuck, he's got spots on his tongue."

"Where?" I said. "Let me see!"

He did, indeed, have spots on his tongue.

So we went to the doctor.

"It's not the spots that concern me. They'll disappear," the doctor said. "It's the ear infection."

"Ear infection?"

"Here's a prescription."

So we went to the pharmacy. I got the medicine for my son's ear infection. We drove home. I gave the children lunch and listened to my daughter cough. Cough! I'd forgotten to buy the cough medicine.

We got back into the car to head for the pharmacy, when I remembered I had no cash. "We'll just have to make one quick stop at the bank," I told the kids. I got in line for the drive-in window. (I didn't want my sick children to have to get out of the car and walk to the bank.) But the car stalled and absolutely refused to start again.

"I will remain calm," I told myself and the kids. "I will gain control of this situation."

First, I put the flashers on so that the people behind us in line would know something was amiss. Then I hauled the ailing youngsters from the warmth of the car out into the cold, where we stood on the walk-up line next to the drive-in line. Then we went back to the car which still wouldn't start. So we walked to the gas station across the street, where we found a mechanic willing to accompany us back to the car. He announced that the car had a cough, an ear infection and spots on its tongue. He pushed it to the station, where he said it must remain hospitalized overnight.

I called a friend who picked us up, took us to the pharmacy for the cough medicine and drove us home. Ahh, home at last. I turned up the heat. The children were chilly from our invigorating outdoor adventure. I gave them medicine and tea.

Okay, so today wasn't so terrific, I tell myself. In fact,

today was terrible. But it could've been worse. At least I rescued the cat.

$\mathcal{A}$ WISP OF MEMORY

We did something good last night. Something important, I think. We filled an empty space.

The children were already in bed when the idea came to me. I had been sitting on the brown living room chair, scanning the paper, daydreaming, feeling bored, lonely, isolated, when the thought settled in and took hold. It was Friday night. *Shabbos*. Other Jewish people were out there feeling part of a community, and I was yawning.

I knew the children were almost asleep, snuggled in their beds, surrounded by stuffed animals. But they would rally, I was sure. They would sense my determination and enthusiasm and they would understand.

Without hesitation, I marched into their room and whispered loudly to them. "Wake up. Hurry," I said in a cheerful voice. "We're going someplace special."

They rubbed their eyes and stared at me as I turned on lights and opened their closet door. "Pick out your nicest clothes. Find something beautiful to wear. We're going to services. It's *Shabbos*."

Shabbos, at eight o'clock on a Friday night, in winter at the Reform temple across the street from our apartment. I felt conspicuous settling into a plush gray seat near the *bimah*.

"But I want you to see what is happening," I told the children. My daughter smiled brightly, eager for a new experience, elegant in her lace-collared dress. My son squirmed on my lap, sucking loudly on his bottle of apple juice. I cuddled him and waited anxiously for the familiar sound.

The sound. It was a long time in coming. First, there was a great deal of English: readings from a scripture translated to suit the American tongue. Then, there was the organist and choir, the effect of which seemed like a church. And the rustling of pages as the congregants found their places in the books which read from left to right, an innovations which struck me as not quite authentic. Next was a sermon with some arm flailing and pontification. Finally, came the sound—the sound of Hebrew spoken in unison by the fifty people filling the cavernous room. The cadence of the ancient language swirled in the air. And that was when the tears began to form, brimming over in my eyes as the Hebrew words danced around and around. I felt something at that instant, something I had felt before at times I could not name. I understood something, believed something, knew something in those fleeting moments as the sound surrounded me. There came a wisp of memory, the names: Moses, Abraham, Isaac, Jacob. A place, a link. And then the sound stopped. The tears dried. The service was over.

We ate cookies at the *oneg* in the many-windowed room to the right of the sanctuary. We bundled into coats and walked outside into the chill night. The heel of my left shoe fell off as my foot sank into a pile of hardened graying snow piled on the sidewalk. I laughed, hobbling home.

When, at last, the children were once again pajama-clad and wrapped securely in their beds, I kissed them each on their foreheads.

"Good night," I said. "Good *Shabbos*."

"Good *Shabbos*," each one answered back.

THE ANNIVERSARY

My daughter was busy printing "important events" on her calendar. Along with Thanksgiving and her cousin's birthday, she made a note of Grandma's and Grandpa's anniversary. Then she turned to me. "And when is your anniversary, Ma?"

A momentary pang hit me in the gut. "I don't have an anniversary anymore. Remember? I'm divorced."

"Oh," she answered. "That's right." She went on to Washington's Birthday and the Fourth of July.

It has been years since I felt any pain on my anniversary. In fact, last year, the month passed without my even remembering what had once occurred on the 17th. But when my daughter inquired, I had this fleeting feeling of having lost something important.

Since the divorce, I've lived without my own washing machine and dryer, my own back yard and, obviously, my anniversary. Comparatively speaking, I miss the washer and dryer more than I do the day of celebration marking my wedding. Still, the day did occur.

I became nostalgic and whipped out some old wedding pictures. Me—in a white gown with a veil and in-laws beaming. Me—with a bouquet of flowers and the face of a young girl. Me—with a long satin train and a head full of dreams. Me—before children. I had to smile.

Me before children is probably more significant than me before marriage, before divorce, before anything else. No matter what has occurred since 1969 (the year of the wedding), the advent of the offspring has challenged me every step of the way.

"How was I born, Mommy?"

"How do fish talk?"

"How do airplanes stay up, Ma?"

"If G-d made everything, does that mean He made all the buildings and the streets and the sky, too?"

"Why did somebody kill that man Sadat?"

"Who was that guy on my necklace with the silver dollar? You know, Kennedy or somebody?"

"What is frostbite?"

"What's the mumps?"

"What is a handicapped person?"

"What does retarded mean?"

"Does everybody die?"

"What are artificial sweeteners?"

"What are additives?"

"Why is sugar bad for you?"

"Can I have some of your coffee?"

"Can people really die from cigarettes?"

"Why do people have wars?"

"Why did you get a divorce?"

"Are there people on other planets?"

"Can I wear my baseball hat to sleep?"

I put away the wedding pictures. So I don't have an anniversary anymore. I do have two children though, and had I never been married to that particular man, I'd not have had these particular youngsters. Therefore, I am grateful.

Happy anniversary to me.

TIME TO REAP

"I'm late . . . I'm late . . ." Feeling not unlike Alice's white rabbit, I floored the gas pedal of my aging car. It was two-thirty in the afternoon. My daughter gets home from school at two-forty. I was late and a mite panicky.

For the past twelve months, I've been preparing my child for the possibility of my not being home when she gets off the bus. But until today, I'd always been there on time. And if for some reason I knew I'd not make it on the dot, I'd always have a friend, a sitter, someone waiting for her when she walked through the door. But this afternoon, the time had slipped by and I'd not realized I'd be *late* until it was too late.

As I swerved into the apartment house parking lot, I realized one of two things could happen. I could find my daughter in a state of hysteria, paralyzed in the center of the living room, certain that I'd deserted her forever. Or maybe, just maybe, she'd remember what I'd begun teaching her a year ago. It was conceivable (although I had my doubts) that the six-year-old had indeed gone to a particular neighbor's apartment when she discovered my absence.

As I turned the key in the lock, I braced myself for the hysteria. But instead, I found my child, a sheet of paper in hand, just about to exit the apartment.

"Oh, hi, Mommy," she said. "I was just going to tape this note to the door for you, so you wouldn't worry if I wasn't here when you got home."

I read the note. It said, *"Dear Mommy, I'm gowin* (that's going) *nxtedor* (that's next door). *Love . . ."*

Ecstasy! I hugged her a hundred times and twirled her around. How marvelous, how terrific, how mature, grown-up and thoughtful of my daughter. She'd remembered everything I'd taught her. She'd seen that I wasn't home and was prepared to go to the neighbor's apartment. But more than that, even better, was the fact that she'd left me a note so I wouldn't worry. She'd understood everything—that it's not a good idea to stay all alone in the apartment and that I would be concerned about her.

I was patting myself on the back for being such a good mother/mentor when there was a gentle knock on the door. "Hi," said the towheaded seven-year-old from downstairs. "Do you mind if I stay here for a while? My sitter wasn't at my apartment when I got home from school. I waited for her, but she's pretty late, so I think I should stay with you. Oh, I should call my Mommy at work to tell her."

Okay, so my daughter isn't the only thoughtful, intelligent, knowledgeable child in the building. And I'm not the only adult who has prepared her child for a change in plans. But I'm proud nonetheless. Next time I'm a few minutes late, I won't be quite so hysterical.

 N EQUAL RIGHTS

"Gimme my baseball cap," my son demanded. "I gotta wear it to cover my hair. My hair is ugly. I look ugly."

"You do not," I said. "You look . . ." (I was going to say adorable, but five-year-old boys hate being adorable) ". . . very handsome."

"Do not," he scowled, pulling the red cap farther over his eyes. His hair, about two inches too long, was jutting out every which way from beneath the brim. "I think my hair looks disgusting." He turned away from the mirror in anger. I promised him a trip to the barber shop after nursery school. For a few hours, at least, we averted a crisis. You see, during the past month, my son has discovered vanity.

"This shirt is not cool," he announced one morning.

"This shirt is a stupid shirt. I need a cool shirt. I need an army shirt."

"What?"

"An army shirt, like the cool kids wear."

He also needed a pair of miniature construction boots and a football sweatshirt. He refuses to wear any but the most faded and torn pair of pants in the drawer. He has put the kibosh on overalls with elastic waists and polo shirts with trucks or bears printed across the chest. He has even become picky about his slippers.

For all my efforts at instilling a sense of individuality, my son is hooked on fads. And, what's worse, he doesn't like his coiffure.

I thought the haircut would help. It didn't. The very evening of the cut, I was doing the dinner dishes when my son marched into the kitchen wearing the baseball cap again. "My hair doesn't look like it did in the barber shop. It looks disgusting."

I was at odds. If I told him he looked handsome, I'd be reinforcing the importance of handsome, right? If I giggled, he'd be crushed. If I said I love him no matter how he looks, he'd be furious. If I told him he's adorable, he'd go into a rage. I thought quickly (and not particularly intelligently). "You know what?" I said. "I think you are very strong." (I was trying to change the subject.) "In fact, I think you are so big and strong that you can carry out the garbage for me." (I was standing next to the garbage can in the kitchen at the time this inspiration occurred to me.)

"Yeah?" he brightened.

"Is he stronger than I am?" His seven-year-old sister had apparently been listening. "Why can't I take out the garbage?"

Now, here was a real dilemma. If I told my son that he

and my daughter are of equal strength, then I wouldn't be bolstering the boy's self-image. I made another snap (and incorrect) decision. "Well," I told my daughter, "I think maybe your brother is just a tiny bit stronger than you are."

As soon as I'd said it, of course, I knew it was a mistake.

"Stronger than I am? That's not fair." She was reasonably calm for about thirty seconds. "You don't even know. You just said that because everybody thinks boys are stronger than girls, and that's not right. Not at all. Girls are just as good as boys and just as strong and I can take out the garbage, too . . ." And so on (with tears and foot stomping).

Older, stronger, cooler, better, bigger, smarter—all those awful words I'd been working so hard to avoid. Now, I see, I have a heavy task before me. I must teach my children that neither strength nor beauty nor gender matter. It's what's inside a person that counts.

I left two angry youngsters standing in the kitchen as I lugged the garbage bag outside. When I got back to the apartment, I washed my hands and caught sight of myself in the bathroom mirror.

"Oh, yech," I remarked unthinkingly. I called to my son, "Hey, slugger, c'mere. May I borrow your baseball cap?"

QUEEN ESTHER WILL WEAR PINK

"Queen Esther will wear pink."

"Pink," she repeated. "With beads and sparkles and a beautiful crown. Oh, and fancy shoes." Here, she paused for emphasis. "And lipstick."

"And rings and bracelets and necklaces?" I asked.

"Yes," she answered, turning 'round and 'round, her scrawny pigtails flying. "Necklaces with diamonds and stuff. And I'll wear socks with lots of lace and ribbons in my hair. Big ribbons, Mommy. The pretty kind, 'cause queens are pretty, right? And maybe earrings with pearls and things and some polish on my nails. Okay?" she asked me with a smile.

"Okay," I agreed, exuding confidence. "I'll make the costume tomorrow."

A rather weighty promise, don't you think? I admonished myself some minutes later. Considering that you do not own a sewing machine and wouldn't know what to do with it if you did own one.

"But I can sew the costume by hand," I answered back. "Can't I?"

I wasn't sure.

"Of course, you can," I told myself.

And I was right.

Like so many other things I've come to learn of late, costume-making is not much different from diapering the baby or getting a job. One does what one has to do.

And I had to make a costume for the *Purim* party my daughter would attend. I had to find a swatch of pink taffeta and a bunch of beads, a little glitter, pompoms, some velvet rickrack and a bow. And then, I had to sit down at the table to cut, to snip, to stitch and sew, to create this glorious dress for a little girl who was determined to emulate the Queen.

And then I thought of the Queen, and the magnitude of her trials, the courage and conviction with which she faced her foe. I realized that, in part, because of Esther's determination, my daughter now holds the right to celebrate her faith. And as I thought, I worked, until at last the task was done.

Queen Esther will wear pink.

EBELLION

"It's very late. Put on your nightgown and get into bed."

"No-o-o."

"I said, put on your nightgown now."

"Which nightgown?"

"The blue one."

"Oh no. Not that one. Do I havta? I don't wanna."

"So put on the pink one."

"But you said I havta put on the blue one."

"I did not say you have to put on the blue one. Just put on a nightgown right this minute. Do you hear me?"

"Well, which one do I havta put on?"

"Oh, forget the nightgown. Here, put on a pair of pajamas. *And hurry up!*"

I grabbed the yellow pajamas from her top drawer and flung them at my seven-year-old daughter. She flashed a vicious look my way.

"I don't want to wear pajamas, but you're gonna make me, aren't you?"

I straightened my shoulders, turned and walked out of the room, closing the door behind me. In the kitchen, I faced the sink. Speaking directly to the faucet I said (aloud), "The kid is driving me nuts. I say blue, she says pink. I say now, she says later. All of a sudden, she's fighting me every step of the way. What's happening?" The faucet responded with four consecutive drips. I must get that fixed. It's downright irritating.

Lately, everything has been irritating. The nightgown is only one example. Yesterday morning, she said she was cold. Well, not exactly cold. She said, "I'm freezing. May I have a sweatshirt?"

"Sure, honey," I answered. (Maybe I didn't really say

honey.) I removed her red and blue sweatshirt from the closet. "Here, sweetheart. Here's your sweatshirt."

"Not that sweatshirt! That's not my sweatshirt! That's *his* sweatshirt!" (*He* is her little brother. And *he* and *she* are about the same size. And a sweatshirt is a sweatshirt. Right?)

But I acquiesced. "Okay. I'll get a different sweatshirt." I went to her dresser and removed the white sweatshirt with the red satin heart. This was definitely *her* sweatshirt. I pulled it over her head and helped her get her arms through.

"Now look what you did," she accused. "You messed up my hair. This is a sweatshirt. I didn't want a sweatshirt. I said I wanted a sweater."

(Remain calm, I told myself. Do not let this get to you.) "I thought you said sweatshirt. I'm sure you said sweatshirt, *honey.*" (This time the "honey" was definitely tinged with sarcasm.)

"Well, I can't help it if I get the words mixed up. I want the green sweater that buttons down the front."

"*Coming right up, dear.*" (My voice was shrill.)

Once she'd donned the sweater, I was able to return to the kitchen sink to discuss my dilemma with the faucet.

"What am I going to do?" I asked. Eventually, I decided to check the old psychology book. There must be something written about sweaters, nightgowns and defiance. Actually, the chapter I found had to do with unkempt hair and untied shoelaces, but the essence was the same. My daughter, said the book, is declaring her independence. She is finding my nagging and bossiness bothersome.

Well, how about that! According to the experts, she's right on target. She's trying to gain a sense of "dignity." Dignity? (That's what the book said.)

Feeling relieved, I walked up to my daughter and gave her a hug. "You know, we've been arguing an awful lot lately, haven't we?" I said.

"Yeah."

"Well, I just looked something up in a book about kids and it said this is just what's supposed to happen. You're supposed to want your independence now."

"What's independence?" She smiled sweetly.

"Freedom."

And then, without warning, something inside her said, "*Rebel!*" Suddenly, I was *wrong again*. She wrenched out of my arms and burst into tears.

"It's not right," she shouted. "Not right at all. I do not want my whatever-it-is!"

FISH TALE

It took three five-year-olds just thirty seconds to teach me the meaning of stuffed to the gills. Truthfully speaking, I never asked for a working definition of the phrase. But as with so many of life's minor trials, I've become an authority on gill stuffing by firsthand experience.

It was an overcast, No-you-can't-go-outside-it's-going-to-rain-any-second-now day. The afternoon loomed ahead. (Isn't it wonderful how half-day kindergarten gives the little ones hours and *hours* to have fun at home with Mom?) Anyway, my son definitely could not go outdoors. And he did not want to color, paint, work with clay or listen to records. So we invited two friends to the house to play. The friends, a pair of identical twins, did not want to color, paint, work with clay or listen to records. They, and my son, preferred instead to race the trucks across the kitchen floor, park the miniature cars behind the couch and sprinkle potato chips in the plastic gas station. They found the cowboy hats and rode imaginary horses through the bedrooms. They instructed their cattle to graze on the living room rug. They caught wild tigers and lions bare-handed as the animals roared in the jungle just inches from the laundry basket which doubled as a tree. And they flew imaginary airplanes into bookshelves that they said were really clouds.

Finally, I decided they'd had enough healthy, creative exercise. I suggested they think of a quiet activity.

"May we feed the fish?" asked one of the twins. (I don't know which one and he never confessed.)

I thought it was a fine idea. And thus did I allow the boys to approach, unsupervised, the ten gallon tank which held all of our current household pets.

It wasn't until hours later, when the twins' mother came to pick them up, that I entered the children's room and thought of the fish. Perhaps it was the discoloration of the water which caught my eye, or that it appeared to be snowing in the tank.

In any case, it seems the twins (and my son, too, although he claims he didn't help but simply "watched") had managed to offer goldfish and company a year's supply of Fancy Flake Food in one serving.

The man in the pet shop (I called him at the suggestion of the twins' mother) said I'd best do something right away or the poor little goldfish would be quite lifeless by morning. So bucket by bucket, I emptied the tank, scrubbed the walls, wiped the floor, refilled the tank and performed telepathic therapy on the African frogs who appeared to be hiccupping. Finally, when all was done, I stood back to study the fish. And that's when it occurred to me that the creatures were, indeed, stuffed to the gills.

RUISED EGO

I was reduced to tears by a five-year-old. It started the night before last. He refused to go to sleep. He said he wasn't tired, but he'd try to fall asleep if I'd sit on the edge of his bed. So I did. But he didn't fall asleep. Then he said he was thirsty. He would fall asleep if he had a drink. "Can you bring me a drink?" So I did. But he didn't fall asleep. Next, he said he was hungry. He would definitely fall asleep if his belly was full. Could I please, please get him something because he was "starving"? So I did. But he did not fall asleep. Finally, I left his room, bellowing a stern, *"Good night."*

Five minutes later, I heard quiet sobs. "Mommy, Mo-o-o-mmy."

He sounded so utterly pathetic, I had to see what was wrong. "What is wrong?" I asked from the doorway.

"I'm lonely."

"Your sister is in her bed right next to you. How can you be lonely?"

"Because she's not awake," he answered logically. "Can't you sit here with me?"

"No," I said. "You are a big boy, and I can't sit with you. Why don't you just hug Barney?" (That's his teddy bear). "He'll keep you company."

"No, he won't," pouted the little debater from his bed. "He can't keep me company, because he's not real."

At this point, some people would say I allowed myself to be manipulated. Others would accuse me of surrendering. I prefer to think of it as a rational compromise. The clock read 11 p.m. It was too late for further negotiations. So I curled up on the edge of my son's bed. He remained awake. I fell asleep. Eventually, the boy dozed off, and I woke up long enough to find my own room. But nothing had been resolved. Morning came too quickly. Everything was wrong.

The five-year-old said his shirt was wrong, his breakfast was wrong, the storybook was wrong. It was raining. (How dare it rain when the sun was supposed to shine?) Where did I put his socks? Why couldn't we have cookies and soda? With each accusation, his voice grew more hostile and shrill. I could feel the hair bristling on the back of my neck. Finally (although I knew he hadn't had enough sleep and was simply overtired), finally (although I knew he was really disappointed about the weather and taking it out on me), finally, I did what I hardly ever (honestly) do. I gave him a swat on his well-padded bottom.

He was outraged. "*You broke my bones,*" he hollered in horror. "You are a bad mommy. You broke my bones." He stormed off to his room in a huff, his hand rubbing the injured "bones," his eyes on fire with humiliation.

We never did resolve yesterday's battle, and the rain never stopped. Whenever possible, he reminded me of his "broken bones." But I remained unmoved. I didn't feel like being nice to him. At last, night came. I tucked my son into bed and kissed his defiant little face. He dropped into a snoring slumber. I stood there watching him for a long time with tears falling down my cheeks. Sometimes being a parent is mighty trying.

THE OMELET

This one's mother cooks gourmet meals. That one's mother is into arts and crafts. Somebody else learned to do macrame 'cause guess who taught her how? Lately, I've learned of mommies who weave, crochet, knit, perl, comparison shop, bargain hunt, coupon clip and who are manicured and pedicured as well.

All this parental comparison might have made me insecure. But I put things in perspective. Like cooking, for instance. It's quite obvious that cooking is not my favorite pastime. Yet, everybody's got to eat. So last Sunday morning, I took out the frying pan, the eggs, the mixing bowl and the cheese.

"What's that gonna be?" my daughter asked.

"An omelet," I answered.

"Yech, I don't like how you make 'em."

And then, ta da, an inspiration! "How about if you make the breakfast?" I wasn't being defensive, argumentative or even parental. I simply realized my daughter might be a better chef than I am. At least where omelets are concerned. After all, she's a better rug hooker.

"Can you teach me how to hook a rug?" she asked me last winter.

"Who me? No way," I had to answer. "I've never seen a hook rug face to face. And truthfully, I don't think I care if I never do. But if you want to learn, we can buy the kit and hook, and you can give it a shot. Maybe you'll like it."

It has taken a while, but I'm finally beginning to recognize my children as people separate from their mother, little human beings with talents and interests of their own. At times, it's discouraging, frustrating, even disappointing to find that the kids don't even like what I love (or vice versa). But that's what makes them special, I guess. After all, at the age of seven, my daughter has already learned to cook an omelet, ride a bike and read. What more could you possibly want? Whoever said nobody's perfect?

SPARE THE ROD

"Can't he walk?" *they* would ask.

"Of course he can walk," I would answer, clutching my two-year-old son more tightly to my hip. "He just needs to be held right now."

"Suit yourself," *they* would say. "But it looks like you're spoiling that kid."

Spoiling that kid. I hate the sound of those words. I hate the authoritative way *they* were always telling me to put my child down or leave him alone or stop being such a nervous mother. "You'll make the kid neurotic," *they* would tell me.

But *they* didn't understand. I was new at parenting without a spouse. I was insecure. I believed I had failed at marriage. I was convinced that I had received an F in the pass/fail grading system of matrimony. My greatest fear was failing at motherhood.

To hide this fear, I held my son.

My little boy was a whiny, cranky, cantankerous, moody (melancholy?) impossible two-year-old. He was, I suppose, very normal. But I am a single parent. My son is a child of divorce. I saw each of his whines, cranks and moods as a reflection of some terrible inner turmoil. While other parents were enjoying their youngsters' first attempts at artwork, I was busy scrutinizing crayoned drawings for signs of emotional instability.

I was frightened. I was threatened. And I didn't want anyone to know. Lest the world find out that my son could be a pain in the neck, I kept him attached to my hip. I hugged him tightly so no one would hear him whimper. I figured if no one heard, they wouldn't suspect any problems. If they didn't suspect problems, they couldn't blame me for wrecking my child's life by getting divorced.

But of course, *they* didn't have to blame me for anything. I was quite capable of blaming myself.

Fortunately, most of this is in the past. I am not nearly as insecure as I used to be. I am not nearly as defensive. I am happier, more confident. I never carry my five-year-old son. (He hardly lets me hold his hand in public these days. He says hand-holding is for babies.) I think I am a better person, a more secure parent.

Still, I flinch at the slightest suggestion that I might be spoiling my child.

LC

I fell off my bike. The handlebars rammed into my armpit. My knee dragged along the pavement. I lay there on the grass, bleeding and bruised. My pride was hurt. I wanted to cry. At that moment, I realized I hadn't been hugging my daughter enough.

For the past few years, when my little girl has gotten hurt, I haven't gone running instantly with Band-aids and sympathy. Instead, I've encouraged her to swallow the tears and act like a . . . what? I guess I haven't wanted my daughter to be tagged a simpering female. But maybe she should be allowed to simper after all.

When I fell off my bike, I hurt all over. My daughter came running. "Oh, Mommy! Are you okay?" She helped me upstairs. "Put ice on it, Ma. There . . ."

She took my hand. "Do you feel better?" When she was satisfied that I would survive, she admonished me, "Mommy, you know you shouldn't wear sandals when you ride your bike." She went to my closet and took out the running shoes. "Here," she said. "Put these on. It's not safe to ride in sandals. Show me again where you got hurt."

The more solicitous she became, the more guilty I felt. (For some time now, I had been letting her wash her own skinned knees.) My unspoken motto has been: minimize the injury. Maybe my motto is faulty. At thirty-six, I was not above needing a hug when my armpit hit the handlebar. I was perfectly willing to accept an ice pack for my bruise and a seven-year-old hand to hold mine. I have sometimes accused my daughter of crying wolf. ("You scream the same for a stubbed toe as you do when you fall out of a tree. You should only yell for something important.") But now, I see, where injuries are concerned, what's not important?

So from this writing on, I intend to listen when my daughter yells, to hug her when it hurts and to kiss the boo-boos even when they're mostly in her mind.

ON A SMALL SCREEN

It was odd, to say the least. *Rosh Hashanah* on TV. Well, not exactly. It was actually closed-circuit television. The rabbi conducted services from behind the podium, in a large, crowded sanctuary. The rest of us watched him from a different room on a screen activated by the grace of technical wizardry.

My ex-husband grimaced. "This is ridiculous," he said straining to find a seat. "It's impossible."

I couldn't have agreed more. But I suppose, in part, I was to blame. The children's father had been planning to visit anyway when I'd reminded him that he would arrive on *Rosh Hashanah*.

"So shouldn't we take the kids to services?" I'd asked. And he'd said yes.

I guess he could have said he'd take the children to a synagogue by himself. Or I might have told him that that's what I had planned to do, that he could visit on a different day. But neither he nor I had thought it through enough to plan. And we were left instead to grapple with our private awkward situation in the public television room. The experience was hardly uplifting—on any level. We two adults did not belong together anymore. We'd agreed to this joint *Rosh Hashanah* event in an attempt to show unity in the area of religion. By default, we'd wound up with a mockery of things spiritual.

"It wasn't like this when I was growing up," he said to me, as we maneuvered our way through the crowd and back outdoors. I nodded, feeling sad. It hadn't been like that for me either. I'd walked to *shul* on *Rosh Hashanah*. My parents and my sister and I had traversed the mile of sidewalk from our house to the house of worship annually throughout my youth. I'd sat through years of holiday songs and speeches, straining to make sense of what was said and sung. I'd comprehended little, yet I'd always known that there was much to know. The rabbi had been enormous in my eyes, looming high in his white *tallis*. How small a rabbi looks when he's shrunken to fit a television screen.

We climbed the stairs to the apartment in silence. The children were cranky, aware of the tension we tried to hide. I served a semblance of *Rosh Hashanah* lunch to the semblance of our family. We made small talk and avoided accusations. But the effort of pretense was exhausting. I was relieved when at last the children's father left. I heard him slam the car door and drive away into the night. *Rosh Hashanah*, I thought—a new year had commenced.

 OUTHS OF BABES

"Mommy, do you wish I was still a baby?"

I looked at my five-(and-a-half) year-old son walking next to me. He wore his uniform: jeans, baseball jacket and sneakers. His hair was rumpled, his gait was determined. He looked like a kid, not a baby.

"No, of course not. Not at all. I loved you when you were little, but it's terrific that you're so grown up. Now we have conversations, and you dress yourself and you help me. Of course, I don't wish you were a baby."

I'm not sure he believed me, though. You see, he started kindergarten this year. And for the first few weeks of school, I well . . . I guess I did baby him. I mean, nursery school was one thing. But real kindergarten, a real yellow school bus, milk money, now that's another thing. Something crumpled up inside me when I saw him wave good-bye the first day. And I simply couldn't wait (shh . . . don't tell anyone) for my baby to come home. I think he must have sensed it. I sort of scooped him up and twirled him around and hugged him. I don't know, maybe I even said something gushy like, "How was kindergarten, my big baby boy?" I didn't think he was listening, and he misinterpreted my meaning. I don't wish he was an infant. I just miss the baby in him.

For about a week, the big baby boy seemed to love the attention. Once, he even asked if he could go back to school and come home again. "That's my favorite part," he said. He didn't elaborate, but I knew what he meant. All summer, he had had to share the spotlight with his sister. But with the start of school, the little guy had center stage to himself all afternoon. And he was thrilled. But maybe I was just a little overwhelming, doting on him, showering him with praise and talking baby talk with him. (Isn't that an awful thing to admit?) We'd have lunch together, and I'd take him to the grocery store. And there (horror of horrors) I'd say *yes* when he asked if he could have a toy. We took long walks together. I read stories to him. I played with him the way I hadn't played in quite a while.

Yet suddenly today, both my son and I seemed to realize the baby days are over. He asked for gum and a box of crayons and was indignant when I said no to both. (Enough is enough, I reasoned.) "You'll get cavities, and we're wasting money. The answer is no. You're old enough to understand."

And he couldn't have soda with his lunch. And I didn't read him the same book six times. He accused me of losing his favorite truck. I accused him of being a pain in the neck. Finally, with the wisdom which only a five-year-old can possess, my child looked me straight in the eye and said, "Ma, can I invite a kid over to play? I feel like having a kid here."

Such is life.

ALL IN GOOD TIME

"Come on. Let's go. Put on your jackets. We're ready. Everybody out the door. Come on, I said. Kids! Kids! Do you

hear me? Let's go! Now!"

"Just a minute, Ma. I've gotta do one thing."

"I'm warning you. We're going to be late. Everybody's waiting for us. *Move it. Now!*"

But the five-year-old had to dump the stones out of the dump truck before we left, or else there might be an avalanche in his absence.

And the seven-year-old had to return to her room for another pair of barrettes in case the two in her hair should rust during the next quarter-hour.

Then the five-year-old simply had to find the other half of the silly putty case. "Cause without it the stuff might stick to the inside of my pocket, and you wouldn't want that to happen. Right, Ma?"

And the seven-year-old had to go to the bathroom, again. "How would you like it, Ma, if I said you couldn't go when you *really* had to go? You wouldn't like it. Would you?"

And the five-year-old had to recomb his hair, change his belt and say good-bye to the fish.

So, I shrugged my shoulders and threw up my hands. It seems, no matter where we're going, no matter how early we started, the children inevitably have *just one more thing* to do before we leave.

And that's on a weekend with time to spare. It's the school mornings that really get to me.

"Okay. Here's your lunch box and your milk money. Here's your knapsack. Here's your jacket. Tie your shoelaces. Where's your homework? Fix your braids. Zip your zipper. Everyone ready?" (You'd think there were six of them instead of two) "Okay. Great. *Let's go. Out the door. Now!*"

"Ma . . . wait, Ma. Not yet. I forgot something. Just one minute. I'll just take one minute . . . I gotta get my book on

Indians. I promised the teacher I'd bring it to school today."

"Wait, Ma. Just a second. Just one quick second. I gotta get my bracelet with my name on it. I told the girls I'd wear it today. I promised. I gotta get it."

"Hold on, I havta find my pail. I'm takin' it with me to the park. And I need the shovel or won't be able to dig."

But I know I'm not alone. I hear it in the checkout line at the supermarket. "Wait a minute, Mommy. Just one minute. I gotta get some gum before we go."

And in the stationery store. "Give me five minutes, will ya, Ma? I can't just pick out any notebook. I gotta look around a minute."

And in the department store. "Will you please give me a chance to try on some things, Mom? I've got to have time. You want me to like what I buy, don't you?"

It's the children to their parents. "Wait a minute, Ma." And the children to one another. "Hang on a second. Hold it. Gimme a break." Even the children to the school bus driver. "Please don't go yet. I forgot something. I gotta run back to the house and get it."

Just one more time. Just one more chance. Just one more try. Just five more minutes, and I'll get up. Just one more song, and I'll turn off the music. Just another half-hour and I'll go to sleep. I'll take the bath later. Take out the garbage later. Do my homework in a little while. In a minute. In a second. *Later, Ma.*

How did this happen? How come my children are never ready when I call? I pondered the thought this morning as I finally, *finally* ushered them out the door. We got to the bottom of the steps. "Oops," I said. "You kids go on ahead. I'll be there in a minute. I forgot something. It'll only take a second. I'll be right there. Just a moment. Just an instant. How come I never seem to get out of here on time?"

GETTING LOST

We were in the supermarket *between the bananas and potatoes.*

"Ma, can I have money for the toy machine?"

"Not now."

Between the canned peas and the creamed corn.

"Later."

Among the American, Swiss, Parmesan and cheddar.

"Mommy! Mommy! Ma-a-a-a . . ."

"Oh, for crying out loud! *What do you want?*"

"A toy from the machine in the front."

My cart was almost full. I checked the list—nearly done, except for the tomatoes I'd forgotten between the potatoes and the bananas, and the tuna which had slipped from my mind after the macaroni and the pastina.

I rummaged through the change compartment of my purse. "Here. This is a quarter, a two and five. It's for *one* toy. Do you hear me? One toy where it says a two and five. I'll meet you at the checkout counter in two minutes."

The five-year-old grabbed the quarter and zipped away in his kid-powered sneakers. I returned to the yogurt and sour cream and whole versus skim milk.

One hundred and thirty seconds later, I rolled my cart to the checkout counter and scanned the toy machines for my son's blonde head. No head in sight. I called his name quietly. No answer. I parked my cart behind the man with six loaves of bread and twelve cans of cat food.

It was early. Just past nine-thirty in the morning. The store was practically empty. I had full view of the machines, but my child was gone. I panicked. Not externally. Not so everyone would know. It was just kind of inside instant hysteria. Someone had obviously walked through the supermarket door and eyed my beautiful blonde-haired son gleefully sticking his quarter in the machine. And, with silent expertise, this person had grabbed my child by the arm and carried him off somewhere; he was driving my child away right this minute. I would have to call the police. What would I tell my mother? Oh G-d. My beautiful little boy. I was *frantic*. I was frozen.

The voice came from behind my left leg.

"Ma . . . Mommy. See what I got from the machine? Look, I got a *glob* from the machine."

And you know the rest. *"Were were you?"*

"There."

"Where?"

"Right there." Looking at the batteries for sale or the slippers or the mittens or the soda bottles. Looking at the world, silly Mommy, smiling at everything. "You said I could go. You let me. Why do you look so mad, Mommy? Are you angry?"

"No . . . Uh uh. It's just that I almost got lost. That's all." I kissed him on the head. "Hold my hand a minute, will you, Tiger?"

AUGHING MOM

My daughter was standing on her bed, struggling to get the nightgown over her head. Her arms and pigtails were stuck inside. She called for help. I came to the rescue. The sight of her skinny, seven-year-old limbs jabbing at arm and head holes in pink flannel struck me funny. The more we tried to release her, the more entangled she got. The nightgown was twisted. The struggle was silly. Finally, her head popped through. We both collapsed into giggles.

She gave me a hug. "I like a mother who laughs," she said.

"You do?" I made a funny face and poked her in the stomach. "*You do-o-o?*" (She giggled again.) "Well, so do I."

I do like a mother who laughs. In fact, I like to be the mother who laughs. But parenting is not often a laughing matter. (Or perhaps I just take myself too seriously.)

Sometimes, at the end of the day when the house is quiet, the dishes are done, work is finished, the laundry folded, the toys put away and it's time to relax, sometimes, I stand over the children's beds and watch them. Every so often, I feel like waking them so they'll see me looking peaceful and calm. Sometimes, at those moments, I even feel like laughing. (And then, because it's really too late to wake them, I feel like crying because by morning the hurried, harried part of life will begin again, and the kids will have missed the laughing mother part.)

For despite my serious bent, I do have a silly side. It just doesn't surface as often as it used to or as often as it should. So many times during the past few years, I've shared somber thoughts with my children. With all good intentions, I've included my offspring in family discussions and decisions. Unlike the "old-fashioned" adults (who thought youngsters were "too young" to understand), I've let my kids know about the problems of life. I've told them about bills, the high cost of living, the broken vacuum cleaner, the leaky faucet. I tell them when I don't feel well, when the column I'm writing is coming out wrong. I let them know when I'm tired and when I'm miserable. I say when, and often why, things are the way they are. Maybe I say too much. In my attempt to share the serious side of life, have I forgotten to show them the frivolous part?

I must remember to laugh more frequently, because my daughter says she likes a "laughing mother . . . and you don't laugh enough . . . Mom."

THE INVENTORY

Within the walls of this apartment there are just three things to which I am sentimentally attached. Two of these are my children, the third is my typewriter. And even the typewriter is dispensable.

I wonder if I have always been this unfeeling about material possessions, or is it just since I've been living alone with my children? At one time in my life, I was half-owner of a house, two couches, two sets of dishes, twelve matching drinking glasses, an ornate framed mirror, a couple of end tables, a bedspread and a husband, among other items.

I can recall feeling mildly pleased with the symmetry of my dishes and glassware when I set the table. But the "things" themselves never really meant much to me. Yet, when we decided to part company, I chose to take nothing with me—not because the things were meaningless, but quite the opposite—they were meaningful. They had memories. It wasn't the mirror that counted, but the memory of where it had hung, in whose house, and by whom it had been purchased. It wasn't the couch, but who had sat on the couch, and when and where, and the conversations we'd had there.

So when we decided to divorce, I chose to leave with nothing save the two children, the typewriter, random pieces of furniture, a few necessities. That was nearly five years ago.

Today, I took inventory of my possessions. I wanted to see how much I've accumulated since my debut as solo parent. And I find that I've collected six wicker baskets, eighteen books, nine record albums, a stereo and a huge hoard of seashells. Not much, is it? So what does that mean? Should I be proud of my anti-material possessions stand? Or should I be wary?

At first analysis, I decided to be proud. But now, I think I'll be truthful. I believe I have chosen to reject possessions because they represent to me a kind of permanence or commitment which I still find difficult to face. Somehow, even after all this time, I cannot think of this apartment as home. If I were to purchase a painting (assuming I could afford it) for a wall in this, my home, I would be admitting that this really is my home. And although it is comfortable, cozy and friendly here, I still like to think I'll be leaving soon.

But when?

That, you see, is the fuzzy part. That's the part I've been avoiding for more than four years. "Soon," I say. "I'll leave when I have the money, the luck, the good fortune, the time." That's the part I can't really think about.

But by keeping myself free of "things," I guess I'm staying prepared for the moment's notice. If I'm prepared, I'll be able to pick up and go—just like that—when the time is right.

But where on earth do I think I'm going?

BOOK TWO • TRANSITIONS

TRANSITIONS

INTRODUCTION

Bashert. It's a word I've come to understand. But never did it cross my mind back then, nearly a decade ago, when my mother called at the end of a hectic day. "Do you remember him?" she'd wanted to know. "Were you aware that he is no longer married? You know the one I mean. And he's such a nice young man. He asked us all about you and we thought . . . Well, we decided, if you wouldn't mind, maybe your father and I would give him your phone number . . . that is . . . with your permission of course . . ."

I granted permission.

And then he came to visit. I liked him immediately—despite the fact that I thought he was *religious*. Actually, I liked him because of it. I admired his attitude and his having grown up with a lifestyle I'd only heard about. From the start, we spent hours discussing things—philosophy, education, parenting, Judaism, his great-grandfather, my children. We laughed often. Sometimes we argued. And then, there were the awkward days of introduction to parents, aunts, uncles, cousins, friends. There were endless attempts at verbalizing separate histories—two failed marriages to unravel and explain. There were questions, sometimes answers. Ultimately, there was the decision to marry, and the agreement to live together happily ever after in a kosher home.

"A kosher home?" I must have asked one hundred times. "You mean a really kosher home?"

Yes, he'd said. And I'd said "Well, why not, I guess it's only fair." Considering that he'd agreed to take on my two children, I decided that two sets of dishes didn't seem too much to ask.

But he hadn't told me about the separate *Pesach* dishes and all the different sets of pots and pans, and the mountains of silverware for meat and milk and for *Pesach* meat and milk. Still, it wasn't nearly as difficult as I'd imagined it would be.

We persevered. I stopped being defensive about the "Orthodox thing" and even began to study a little now and then. He stopped deferring to me and became adept at parenting. And the children did what children tend to do. They adapted to the new adult in their lives, to a new house, a new school and the Orthodox thing which blossomed as we nurtured it, because it was—*bashert*.

 HE GREAT-GRANDFATHER

"The great-grandfather." That's how he began the story which consumed more than two hours in the telling and left me feeling curious and vaguely pious—as though by the simple hearing of the tale I had absorbed the essence of the man.

"They say he was a mystic, born in Budapest to parents who had emigrated to Jerusalem in the 1800s. Slight and humble in demeanor, the great-grandfather had piercing blue eyes, which failed in later years. But he knew the Talmud by heart, and when he was no longer able to see, he continued studying in his mind through every waking hour. The grandchildren revered and respected him. He allowed them to climb on his knee. He played with them and sang to them. He smiled at them with gentle sweetness and seemed to have unlimited patience. He fasted every Monday and Thursday. Noted spiritual leaders of the day sought his advice. Neighbors asked for his opinions. He responded to all with equal sincerity and grace. Material possessions were of no consequence to him. He wore clean but threadbare garments and a fur hat on *Shabbos*. Family legend says his pocket watch stopped at the moment of his death. In life, the slight figure appeared to be fragile, yet no one would have called him weak. He was, in fact, a man of strength and infinite faith. He believed in G-d and set a continuing example for others to follow."

As the great-grandson spoke, I could envision this great-grandfather "in his two-room house with a small wooden table and stone floors." I could see the narrow face framed by *peyos* and a flowing beard. I could hear the voice of this soul who had so impressed the great-grandson seated opposite me and speaking in hushed tones, lest the memory of the beloved be somehow tarnished by the human voice. "His elderly daughter still lives in the same two rooms."

"As they were then, when you were a boy visiting your great-grandfather?"

"The same," he answered. "The place and the people are

exactly as they were ten years ago and two hundred years ago. Perhaps as they were two thousand years ago."

My voice dropped to a near whisper, adapting to the intensity of the message I was being offered.

"And if your grandfather had remained there, if your grandfather had not left Jerusalem to come to America, then his son, your father, and perhaps his son's son, meaning you, would be there now, wearing long *peyos* and a fur hat on *Shabbos* and knowing little of the outside world."

"Or a great deal more about the outside world than I do now."

I tried to comprehend. He seemed to be implying the existence of a different plane of life—some hazy order beyond the obvious. I grasped at the elusive fragment of his words, there and again catching portents of some intangible spirituality alive within the world—aware, as I listened, mesmerized by the story, of the great-grandfather's influence on the young man. And then the great-grandson was silent. He rose from the couch and said the hour was late. It was time for him to be going home.

And I lay awake half the night thinking about the great-grandfather, the great-grandson and the Wisdom which had brought them to my door.

STICKERS

Why did I let the kids put stickers on the dressers?

I asked that question today as I tried to scrape four years of glue from the walnut veneer of the bureaus in their room. Why did I allow the kids to decorate their furniture with uneven rows of cartoon characters? Whatever made me grant permission for this mess?

And why didn't I notice until yesterday?

Yesterday, I was sitting on one of the children's beds, glancing around the room. Their walls are filled with posters and pictures, banners and paintings. There are toys in every corner, dolls and stuffed animals on the pillows and trucks and cars in laundry baskets on the floor. There is a ten-gallon fish tank next to the window and an easel next to the door. The entire place is a confusion of children's interests. But there is a kind of order about the disorganization, a method to the madness, which doesn't bother me. Except for the stickers. Yesterday, the stickers were annoying.

"They look messy," I told the kids. "They look silly and sort of babyish. Don't you think so?"

Surprisingly, they agreed. (Not to the messiness, I suppose, but to the possibility of being babyish.)

And that was enough. They said they would help remove the stickers. It took us three hours, a large container of Comet, a gallon of boiling water and a sharp knife. And even now, after all the work, vestiges of stickers remain.

So why, I ask, did I let them start this in the first place? How could I have allowed them to deface their property when I must have known I'd be sorry later? What made me do it? Was it laziness? Guilt? Apathy? Boredom? Was it a touch of daring perhaps?

Some of the stickers were gifts from me to them. "I'm going out tonight, but here is a present for you. Listen to the sitter. Bye."

And some were, "Give me a break, will you, kids? I need ten minutes alone. Take these stickers into your room and put them someplace." (Anyplace out of my sight.)

A few were, "What's the difference? A couple of stickers on the dressers can't hurt. It beats having to play another game of Candyland." Or, "I don't care where you put them. Just keep them off the mirrors and the windows."

In any case, for whatever reason, by this morning's count, dozens of glue-backed characters had made their homes on the drawer fronts of my children's bureaus. And I had allowed it to happen.

But now I wanted it stopped. Reversed, really. I wanted the number stickers and letter stickers, the initial stickers and cartoons, all the silly, funny, collectible, ridiculous items cleared away.

But why? I ask again.

Why do I care? As long as the stickers were already there, why did I want them removed?

Because it is time to neaten things up a bit. It is time to tidy our lives, smooth out the rough spots and restore a little order. It is time to clean the slate, start fresh, begin anew. It is time to get ready. Now.

 IS SISTER

I'm a little scared. No, not scared. I'm nervous. He is so Jewish—so much more Jewish than I thought.

Last night, he took me to meet his sister. On the way to Brooklyn, he explained that his sister's husband wears a *yarmulka* all the time.

"All the time?" I asked. "You mean like a rabbi."

"Like a rabbi," he told me. "But he's not a rabbi."

I felt a knot form in my stomach. The same knot I think

I used to feel when, as a little girl, some adult would ask me a question about a Jewish holiday and I would not know the answer.

I was tense as we parked the car and walked the three blocks to the apartment building, unsure of myself as we mounted two flights of stairs. And then he said, "I used to wear a *yarmulka* all the time, too," and he pulled a small round skullcap from his pocket and attached it to his hair with a bobby pin.

A lump rose in my throat. "Wait," I made him stop in the narrow hallway. "Wait." The odors of other people's dinners sneaked through closed doors. I was beginning to panic. "How religious is your sister?"

"Not very," he told me. "She's modern." And he rang the bell.

Modern? What an odd word to have used. Modern in relation to what? I wondered then, and now, as I sit here contemplating last night's visit.

"Culture shock," I'd said aloud as we'd driven back home across the bridge. "Your sister was very nice . . . attractive, outgoing, modern, I guess. But her life is so different from mine."

"Different how?" he'd pressed, as though he hadn't noticed. But then again, maybe it was not obvious to him. Maybe he's used to all those Jewish books—dozens of them, big, thick, tall, leather-covered books with Hebrew writing on the bindings.

"I've never seen so many Jewish books before."

"*Shas*," I think he said.

And there was Hebrew music playing on the stereo, some new tape his sister said she'd wanted him to hear. And there were the paintings on the walls—a woman lighting *Shabbos* candles, a scene from Jerusalem and a bunch of others which I didn't understand.

So now I'm nervous because he feels comfortable with the *yarmulkas* and the Jewish books and the Jewish music and the Jewish art. I am nervous because I am a stranger to those things.

I am nervous because I do not understand.

I do not know exactly what it means to be a Jew.

I am nervous because I don't know how to act Jewish.

I don't know how to read Hebrew.

I don't know the words to the music or the prayers.

I am nervous because I do not understand.

I am nervous because I think I want to understand.

I do want to understand what it is to be a Jew.

 H Y ?

"Because I said so." Through clenched teeth, I hiss the words—the phrase I pledged I'd never utter.

When I was a young and idealistic mother (before my daughter learned to talk), I promised I would always answer her honestly when she asked, "Why?"

"Why is the grass green?"

"Why do onions smell?"

"Why do I have to go to sleep now?"

I vowed I would never be like those other mothers who scowl at their kids and grab them by the armpit when the children whine, "Why?"

"Why do I have to get out of the pool? What's so bad about thunder and lightning? Why can't I stand up in the front seat of the car?"

I would ask myself how the mother of a curious child could glare at her own youngster with such venom in her eyes when the child had only asked her, "Why?"

A parent, I believed, should be thrilled that her progeny asks questions. Frequently, after encountering a particularly mean mother, I would toss my head haughtily, hug my infant daughter and whisper promises in her ear. "When you grow up, I'll always be reasonable with you," I would say. "I will tell you the truth to the best of my ability. I will wait for you to finish your question before I answer you. I will never make you think your questions are silly. I will be proud that you asked."

But I was naive. I didn't know about eight. I did not understand that eight (and the accompanying questions) would put knots in my stomach and make me say things I thought I'd never say. At eight, my daughter wears purple sneakers and pink sweat socks and leaves them both in the middle of the living room floor. At eight, she asks me why she can't have ice cream before dinner, why she can't stay up till eleven p.m., why she isn't allowed to put her purple sneakers on the seat of the couch ("You useta let me"), why I can't interrupt my telephone conversation to fill her in on what I've been discussing with a friend, why she isn't old enough to babysit for her brother.

And those are the easy whys. It's the nonsensical questions which cultivate my rage.

"Please get out of the tub," I will say.

And she'll say, "Why?"

"Please come in for dinner."

"Why?"

"Put your dirty clothes in the laundry bag."

"Why?"

"Get in the car . . . out of the car . . . put on your pajamas, take off your pajamas, pick up your toys, turn off the light, wash your hands, brush your teeth, do your homework, take your vitamins."

"Why?"

Why? she will ask. Why? Why? Why? Until, ultimately, I will stare at eight with fire in my eyes, and through a newly developed, thin-lipped scowl, I will spit the words, "Because I said so, that's why!"

DANCING

"Will there be dancing?" I had asked.

And he had answered, "Sure."

Good, I remember thinking, pigeonholing the impending *bar-mitzvah* reception as typical of all the other such receptions I'd attended in my life. In the thirty seconds following his response to my question about dancing, I immediately pictured all of the guests in sequins and lace, charging across the floor to the Alley Cat. I saw everybody's Great-Uncle Somebody teasing children. I heard the adolescent girls giggling in the ladies' room. There was nothing to be nervous about after all, I told myself. A *bar-mitzvah* party is a *bar-mitzvah* party, and Jewish people are all basically the same.

Still, I had the jitters. This post-*Shabbos, glatt kosher* affair was the first family function from his side to which I had been invited. Although we've been seeing one another for several months, I am still unsure of my standing in the eyes of his relatives. I am, after all, the divorced mother of two young children, and non-observant to boot. It is not that I am irreligious, non-religious or anti-religious. I am, quite simply, uneducated in the orthodox sense of the word. Thus, I was rather relieved to hear there would be dancing. Not that I would know a tango from a rumba or a fox trot. But the thought of a raucous band with a crass, tuxedoed MC was, at the very least, familiar.

"Well, I'm ready," I recall saying, as we exited the car and walked the two blocks to the site of the event. I straightened my skirt. I checked my lipstick. I swallowed hard and prepared to meet the clan.

I could hear the music even before we entered the room. It was, as I'd expected—loud. And while it was neither the cha-cha nor the bunny hop, it was, I think, a recognizable *chassidic* tune. Something repetitive enough for me to assume that the aunts and uncles were in there doing the traditional *bar-mitzvah hora*.

And so, I remained calm. I said hello to his mother, who greeted me with a smile and a kiss on the cheek. I said hello to his sisters and brothers-in-law and to four or five female cousins from Brooklyn who were talking in the lobby. Greetings, salutations, comments about the weather, and then, finally, we were ready to join the festivities.

I followed the crowd through the double doors to the brightly lit room with its circle of yellow-skirted tables. Fine china, chandeliers, centerpieces of yellow and orange flowers—typical, traditional, predictable. I eyed the celebration slowly, deliberately—sensing the difference before I actually named it—before I saw it. Feeling it before I understood it. Knowing before I knew.

The beat of the drums throbbed in my ears and my chest. The people swirled before my eyes. 'Round and 'round they spun in circles within circles within circles. Surefooted and joyous. Stepping in time to the age-old melody. Some singing along with the band. Dancing, dancing. Beards and black hats and black coats and black shoes. Dancing in high-necked, long-sleeved dresses. Dancing with their feet and their arms and their hands and their eyes. Dancing the way their ancestors had danced. Dancing late into the night. The men on one side of the room, the women on the other.

Dancing, dancing. Separate dancing.

 HOVEL BROTHERS

I think it was the sight of his uncle with the thin gray beard and the *peyos* twirled behind his ears which made me face the fact—ours was a mixed marriage. Not in the traditional sense, of course. I mean, we are both Jewish and our parents are Jewish and their parents before them. But that's where the similarities seem to end.

We were seated around the dinner table for something which sounded like "shovel brothers." This ritual, I'd been informed, ordinarily takes place nightly during the first week after marriage. "But since yours is a second marriage, it's not exactly the same," I was told, which left me to ponder the implications of those blessings.

Yet, the custom sounded kind of nice, and we were being treated with affection. An abundance of food had been bountifully set out upon a table encircled by a combination of relatives, his and mine. Enjoy yourself, I told myself, and I smiled as I studied the guests.

The contrast was striking. Some of the folks from his family were wearing black hats. And some of the folks from my family had come to America five generations back. But it's not the differences which count, I thought. It's the similarities. It's the ancestors before our separate sets of families which connect us all. The garb is external. I tried not to stare at the cousins wearing *sheitels*. And I tried not to notice when the uncle with the beard began removing books from shelves and poring over passages with fingers pressed to eyebrows. I tried to appear nonchalant as other uncles gathered 'round until our two distinct families were separated by those immersed in books and those immersed in dinner.

At last, the bearded uncle cleared his throat and made a somewhat muffled announcement regarding the passages in the books which, it seems (according to the translation offered to me by my husband), indicated that the host and hostess had unwittingly waited a day or two past the appropriate period of time for shovel brothers when both parties have been wed before. And therefore, we would have to be content with another cup of coffee and the unofficial good wishes of those present at the party.

And while I know I would not have understood the words had they been said, and although the anticipated recitation of the blessings made me somewhat nervous, and despite the fact that it is difficult to miss what one has never known, still I must admit that I am kind of disappointed. I think I would have liked the *sheva brachos* after all.

GOOD WISHES

"Looks like married life agrees with you . . . hope you and your husband will have many happy years together."

My well-wisher owns the corner gas station. He has seen me through some trying times. He knew me when my car wouldn't start and I had neither jumper cables nor a husband to remedy the situation. He knew me when snow tires were more than I could afford. But he convinced me to buy them anyway for the safety of my children. During the past five years, he has offered friendly advice on proper car maintenance and appropriate child maintenance. During my weekly wait at the gas pump, the owner of this station has managed to impart his personal brand of knowledge and good humor in capsulized form. And now, he has taken the time to tell me he's happy that I've gotten married. I'm touched. I think it's nice of him to let me know.

And he's not the only one. The lady in the bakery has been doling out complimentary cookies to my kids for years. And with each cookie, she has commented on the state of my life. "Your son has a bad cough," she has said. "Try nose drops." Or, "You look tired. I think you should rest." And lately, "You've gotten married, have you? Well, I'm glad."

The bakery lady is, in fact, such a cheerful, smiling person that sometimes I stop just to make conversation with her. I like her, and I like the way she makes me feel.

Then there are the two women in the stationery store who know my children's names and ages. They've been selling me bubble gum and birthday cards since my eight-year-old was four. When at last I brought my wedding film to them to be developed, they insisted I put it under my new married name. They seemed to think it was important. So did I.

Then there is the proprietor of the clothing store, the pharmacist, the checker in the supermarket, the fruit market man, a favorite waitress in the delicatessen. There are all the men and women in the local shopping area whose friendship I enjoy, and whose good wishes mean so much to me.

And then there are the others. The readers. The anonymous ones and the ones who sign their names. The faceless folks who through the years have written to say, "I know what you mean and how you feel." Or, "How dare you feel that way?" These followers of my published words have written to commiserate, compliment, criticize. And now, they are writing again.

From New City, a woman wished our family "a long and happy life together." On gold flowered paper, she penned, "Your kids are lucky."

From Spring Valley, a seventy-two-year-old divorcee wrote that I had "proven beyond a shadow of a doubt that divorce need not and cannot be fatal."

From New City, an entire office staff sent their message on plain lined paper. "We wish you happiness," they said. "But we feel cheated. It's as if for years you shared a number of poignant, touching scenes with us, and then, all of a sudden, you tell us, 'By the way, I've gotten married.'"

From Spring Valley came the advice, "Be confident, relax and enjoy. You deserve it."

And from Monsey, single spaced on typewriter paper, two women wrote to say, "We were overwhelmed by a sense of childish rivalry. After all, we had been in this thing together for a long, long time . . . We're still going to be lugging groceries up the stairs by ourselves, and now you've got help. *Unfair.* Why couldn't our immediate response have been delight and rapture for you, our fellow struggler?" The women answer their own question. "Because we're basically insecure, and we're afraid that you will change and won't care about us anymore." Ultimately, the two agree to "think of it this way. We haven't lost a friend. We've gained a friend-in-law." And they say, "Congratulations, Anna."

And I say thank you for your good wishes. I appreciate your sincerity and honesty. I am glad you took the time to tell me how you feel. Although I am married, a part of me will forever remain a single parent—because single parenting is something one simply does not forget.

THE DAY SCHOOL

"Please give it a try," he had said. "I think it's important."

I was not sold—either on the importance or the trying. Day schools, private religious day schools in particular, were outside my realm of experience. I am a public school graduate. But I was newly married, anxious to please.

And somewhere within the reaches of my conscience, I could recognize a certain truth in what my spouse was telling me.

He and I, each married for the second time, have had to rely heavily on trust and maturity this time around. Although he has no children of his own, he has taken on my son and daughter with the warmth and caring of a dedicated parent.

So I said I would look at the day school. I said I would consider it because I appreciate my husband, because I believed he had my children's best interests at heart. I said I would look at the day school because I sensed, beneath our surface conversation about Judaism and faith, a depth of understanding which I envied.

My husband has a strong background in religion. He

attended *yeshivos* from kindergarten through college. He read, studied, argued, rejected, accepted. My husband was reared in an Orthodox home where being Jewish meant, simply, to be.

I, on the other hand, while labeling myself a proud Jew, am perhaps more honestly an assimilated American Jew. I hesitated at the thought of a day school for the liberated identity I thought my children would lose.

I wanted my son and daughter to mix with other youngsters, to know there are black people, yellow people, tan people. I want my son and daughter to feel strong and secure in a world of many races and faiths.

And my husband said, "They will. They will, because they will be strong and secure in the knowledge of who they are. They will be proud, and their pride will allow them to accept other people's individuality."

"But what about the indoctrination?" I asked. "Will the day school teach my children that Jews who eat McDonald's hamburgers are bad? That Jewish people who drive on *Shabbos* are not Jews?"

In my attempt to protect my offspring, because of my fear of the unknown, I wavered. "Too much," I said. "Perhaps a day school will be too much."

I cried. At one a.m. on a weekday night, three days before the start of school, I agonized at the change in direction my life might take. I cried until my daughter tiptoed out of her bedroom to comfort me.

"Mommy," she said. "Are you worried about the school, Mommy? Don't worry so much. Maybe the day school is an opportunity we shouldn't pass up."

She was right, of course.

The day school. It has added songs and prayers and a sense of security to my life. It has given my son and daughter an understanding of who they are. They tell me stories about their ancestors, my ancestors—brave, powerful, real men and women.

The day school has taught my children to accept differences among people, to see the good in others. They climb on the bus each morning, smiling. They come home singing, laughing, spilling their tales of math, social studies, science, literature, the prophets, the holidays.

They love no one more or less for his level of Jewish observance. They are growing quickly in their range of understanding. And they are teaching me.

They continue to play softball and baseball, to take music lessons, to play with children of all ages and races. They have lost nothing by attending the day school. They have gained everything.

And so have I.

US STOP

The school bus driver smiled at me as I kissed my children good-bye at the corner. "Nice of you to wait with your kids in the morning. Really nice," the driver said. "Every day you wait here." He shook his head from side to side and grinned as he maneuvered the bus away from the curb.

I watched until the bus turned the corner. I could see the backs of my children's heads through the window. I waved once and headed to our house.

This isn't the first time someone has been surprised that I wait at the bus stop with the children. But at least the driver seemed to approve. Other people have called me overprotective.

"They're old enough to wait by themselves."

"What do you want to stand out in the cold for?"

"Don't they mind having their mother wait at the bus stop with them?"

Maybe they do mind having me there. I suppose I could ask them. But not just yet. Anyway, I am not waiting at the bus stop for them. I'm waiting there for me. And I'm not ready to stop.

I like the idea of knowing the children are safely headed for school each day. I am aware that being safely aboard does not assure safety en route. But somehow, it makes me feel good to see them seated and on their way.

Still, the children's well-being is only one of the reasons I wait at the bus stop. The other reason is selfish. I enjoy it. I like standing there like the mailman in rain and sleet and snow and hail. I like walking to the bus with my children and watching them watch the seasons change. I am happy with the way they look in the morning. Their hair is combed. Their eyes are bright. I feel good seeing them puff frosty air out of their mouths on cold days. I've seen them stop to pet neighborhood cats and dogs. I've even heard them talk to birds. They are energetic and wide awake at that hour. It is good to see.

After the rush for breakfast and bathroom and "Where's my bookbag?" and "Did you pack my snack?" and "Do my braids, Ma!" and "Who's got my other glove?"—after that initial hectic time, it is good to walk outside at seven forty-five a.m.

I do not have to be at an office by nine. I have time for my children before school.

One day, they will probably ask me to stop waiting with

them. They will want to stand alone. But until that time, I plan on watching my son and daughter grow up at the bus stop in the morning.

Mother Knows Best

I don't know how to make a Q in script. I do not know why they need a radar station in Greenland. I don't even know who *they* are. I cannot recall what latitude we're in. Or if, indeed, we are in a latitude. Maybe we are between latitudes. But then that would make us point something latitude, and once we start with points, I have to leave the room.

I have forgotten my times tables except for eight times eight. That is sixty-four. And I do not remember the definition of a rancher. Actually, I don't think I ever learned that one. I have lost all ability to spell, especially words with silent letters or the hard C sound. America does sound like Amerika, doesn't it? I cannot list all seven continents, and I have no idea why temperature measures heat instead of cold. But my daughter thinks I should know. She expects me to remember.

And I do remember. I remember sitting at the formica-topped kitchen table in the big yellow kitchen where I grew up. My mother would be doing the dishes, and I would be slouching in a chair with each of my legs wrapped around a metal kitchen chair leg. I can picture myself twisting my hair on the pencil in my eight-year-old hand, drawing doodles on the loose-leaf paper, opening and closing the three-ringed binder just to hear the clicking sound.

"Mommy," I would say, "what is the capital of Washington? Will you help me with the spelling words? How do you make a capital P in script?"

I can recall hours of kitchen table studying. My mother was always nearby, drying the dishes, cleaning the countertops, wiping her hands on her apron (mothers wore aprons in those days). I can see the white porcelain sink that we owned before the advent of the dishwasher. And while I studied, my mother would give me a snack—chocolate cookies with white cream inside, or fig bars, or toast and jam.

In all the years of homework, it never occurred to me that my mother would have something more important to do with her time. I assumed she wanted to be there, listening to my questions, reassuring me, telling me the science quiz wouldn't be so bad, that I would do just fine. Throughout all those years, I never doubted that my mother knew all the answers and the questions, too. After all, she was an adult and my mother at that.

So I suppose I shouldn't be surprised when my daughter asks me when and why and where, and then falls asleep, feeling confident because her mommy has helped her study for the test.

PARENTING

I don't think I could do it. Get up in the middle of the night when somebody else's son coughs. Spend an hour helping somebody else's daughter with homework. I doubt if I would want to buy sweatshirts (just for the fun of it) for another person's kids. Or kiss them good-night. Or pick them up from school on rainy days. Or wash their hands and faces.

I don't think I'd relish regular softball games with another adult's offspring, and I'm sure I would not have it in me to admire an endless succession of barrettes and hair bands.

I don't mind all the effort involved on behalf of my own children, because they are mine. The demands of parenting, including softball games and remembering to compliment the choice of barrettes, come with the title. Being involved with one's progeny is a given, a fact.

From the moment of their birth (before their birth, actually), I accepted my fate as mother. I expected it. I tie shoelaces and take the youngsters roller-skating, because they are mine and I love them.

But would I, could I, do it for someone else's children? And if I couldn't, how can he? My husband. How can he feel the way he feels about someone else's children, even if they are mine? Even if they are the most wonderful boy and girl in the world?

I suppose it is impossible for me to be perfectly honest about myself. I could say, "Care about me, care about my children." And if the situation was reversed and the children were his, not mine, I would care about them, too, automatically. I could say I would be as good, caring and devoted a parent as he is. But I don't believe it's true. I don't believe I have it in me.

Maybe step-parenting is something innate, like eye color or the sound of one's voice. Maybe there are men and women born with a natural ability to mother or father. And given the opportunity, they succeed with ease, not because it is easy, but because . . . what? Because they see a job that needs doing and they do it? Because they have an extra sense, a larger capacity to give and love?

It would be nice for me to say, if he had the children, I would be his children's mother. I would love to be his children's mother. It would be nice for me to say, but I think it would be a lie.

I appreciate my husband. I appreciate him for challenging my mind, for making me laugh until tears run down my cheeks, for being studious and silly and for caring about me. I respect him for many things. But perhaps, I respect him most for his ability to take on this family without making the son and daughter (or their mother) feel as though they are a burden, an obligation, a strain.

For all my experience at first-hand parenting, I find that, at times, I look to this new father for advice, approval and understanding. He is a good person.

And I wonder about myself.

FIRST CLASS

Maybe it is easier to learn from a stranger than from a husband, less threatening, less familiar. Maybe it's because this particular stranger was a teacher, trained to work specifically with people like me, newcomers to the fold. From the start, she seemed able to anticipate my questions as though she'd heard them all before. Or maybe it had less to do with he and she and I, and more to do with time itself. Perhaps I was ready to listen when, finally, I joined her class. Had I already made that leap of faith both he and she had said were part and parcel of the course? In any case, her answers worked where his had not. His answers were too long.

"And complicated," I would complain with a whine. "I cannot understand a thing you're telling me." My husband would try again, with infinite patience, quoting famous rabbis, ancient texts, the names of which I'd never heard. "Sources," he would call them. And I'd drum my fingers on the tabletop or shake my head from side to side.

"What is the Oral Torah?" I would want to know. "Tell me, in a nutshell, what it's all about." What's the *Mishnah*? Who is Rashi and what's so special about him? What do you mean, marshmallows aren't kosher? What's the difference between the Satmar Rebbe and the Lubavitcher Rebbe? What is everyone learning when they're "learning"? What's *Tishah b'Av*? And what's a *tish*? Where exactly is the Red Sea? And what's *Taanis Esther*? Who was Abarbanel? What really happened in the holocaust and why? What are *tefillin* made of? Where is free will in all this religious stuff? Who wrote the rules of the *Pesach seder*? Where's the law which tells about not mixing milk and meat? What's a red heifer? And who is Morris Ein?

"Simple questions," I would say. "Why can't you give me simple answers?"

He would shrug his shoulders, straighten his back and attempt to respond once more. I suppose I should have been flattered by the scholarly replies he gave to my surface inquiries. He assumed I carried with me the names and places and dates upon which he'd been reared from birth. His answers were too long and deep for me. And so I'd feel the need to argue, to vent my frustrations, to strike out against the hours and days and years of history which seemed to be the foundation of religious observance. I was angered by the futility I saw in trying to catch up, overwhelmed by the millions of facts I knew I would never master, never comprehend. And yet, I longed to find a niche.

"To be on the inside" is how the teacher phrased it, summing up precisely how I felt. "To be on the first rung or the second or the one hundredth climbing up, to be part of the process. Is that it?" she asked, knowing that it was, pointing to the metaphorical ladder she'd drawn on the blackboard. "Your very presence here is evidence of your commitment. You've taken the first step, and now the doors will open. You will see."

 RYING SHOES

My friend's three-year-old daughter left her red shoes out in the rain. The mother discovered the shoes soaked through and muddy the next morning. She placed them near the front door to dry.

When the three-year-old saw them sitting there, she was greatly concerned. "Mommy," she said, lifting the shoes gingerly, "my shoes are crying."

My friend was charmed by her child's choice of words and repeated the story to me.

That evening, while my own youngsters were preparing for baths, the tub water reminded me of the wet shoes, so I relayed the tale. "And you know what the little girl said?" I smiled. "She said her shoes were crying. Isn't that funny?"

Neither of my children laughed.

"Why?" asked my son.

"Because they were wet," I explained, assuming he

wanted the scientific explanation for the sad shoes.

"No," my daughter interrupted. "Why were they crying?"

I was surprised. How could she ask?

At six and eight, both my son and daughter are old enough to know that shoes can't cry. I was confused. Their serious response to the shoe story stayed on my mind for several days until, finally, I recognized the problem. I see things as an adult. But my offspring are still children. They may know the difference between fact and fiction, but they are still young enough to accept the reality of pretend.

The issue was not really whether or not my children believe in crying shoes. The issue was that my children believe in children. They placed their faith in the three-year-old. They understand what it is like to be at one with your shoes, your pillow, your toothbrush, your lunch-box. My son and daughter have conversed with trees and clouds. They have created whole worlds around the trials and tribulations of popsicle sticks upon which faces have (or have not) been drawn. My son has shed tears over a torn teddy bear. My daughter has blown the nose of a stuffed parrot. As recently as yesterday, I heard my children say good-night to a candle, a goldfish and one another with equal solemnity.

Although they allow for the difference between reality and pretend, they continue to fight for the right of make-believe to exist. Instinctively they applaud imagination. They cherish it and guard it in one another and themselves.

At some stage, they may lose this ability to commune with inanimate objects. But until that time, they and the other children of the world apparently understand that a pair of crying shoes is no laughing matter. And for that I envy them.

LOST CAUSE?

I found myself thinking of juvenile delinquency and drugs, alcoholism and robbery, fear and hostility and hopelessness as I sat waiting patiently in my car behind the yellow school bus.

It was midday in December, shortly before winter vacation. I watched the youngsters disembark—a collection of small children, kindergartners probably, judging from their size and the time of day. The little ones, mittened and scarved against the elements, grabbed waiting hands as mothers or grandmothers or baby-sitters came to greet them at the bus stop. I saw the smiles and the hugs and the hurried crossing of the street, as guardians of the little lives protected their charges from the chill winter air and the traffic. Compact bookbags and brightly colored lunch boxes were handed from youngsters to adults in a practiced ritual.

The children, taken in at a glance, massed together in my casual appraisal, looked cared-for and protected, save for one little boy, sandy-haired and thin, hatless in the wind, clutching a large construction paper creation in one hand. He descended with difficulty from the bus, holding tightly to his prize—some handmade holiday decoration intended for home, the place where he was headed.

I followed him with my eyes to the ramshackle structure on the right side of the road, a house of sorts among a group of similar houses with plastic-covered windows and broken bits of metal strewn across the yard. A house whose look of desolation seemed even more pronounced against the gray sky and winter-brown grass. Faded paint of a nondescript color barely covered rotting wood, a sagging staircase looked dangerously unstable in the light of day. But the boy ran on, smiling—with his paper gift in hand. I watched him running, running on five-year-old legs to his home—where no one stood guard at the door. And I hoped, as I sat in the warmth of my car, that within this place of poverty someone waited for the child.

I wished, as the last of the youngsters tumbled from the steps of the school bus, that some person would take the hatless boy's paper decoration and hang it proudly on the wall in the house with faded paint.

But the chance of that seemed unlikely to me. I've seen the place before, wondered about its inhabitants in summer as in winter, admonished myself for staring at a way of life so shabby amidst the surrounding middle-classness of the community. The box springs and useless cars and lifeless tires piled beside the shack looked bizarre in summer, even more so in winter with no green to soften the sight. But in warmer weather there were always people—scrawny, shirtless boys playing with bottles or sticks or dogs, chasing one another among the trees.

In December, the one small boy running home seemed a much sadder sight. A tiny human being destined for trouble and pain.

 EA FOR TWO

My little girl wants my undivided attention. She is in there now, lying on the living room couch, drawing pictures, sipping juice, pulling the blanket around her shoulders. She has the chicken pox. She wants my undivided attention, but she can't have it—because her brother is home, sick with the flu.

He finished the pox two weeks ago. While she boarded the school bus alone each morning, he snuggled in the corner of the couch with the juice and the crayons all to himself. For a full week, he basked in the spotlight while she brought him messages from his friends and inquired daily how he was feeling; was it itchy, was he very uncomfortable, did he need anything?

During the time her brother was suffering with the chicken pox, my daughter was a kind, sympathetic, attentive, solicitous sibling. She was also waiting her turn. Sooner or later, she knew she'd be a victim, and she looked forward to it eagerly for fourteen days.

On the Thursday morning of her first pock, there was, indeed, a celebration. The mark appeared on her stomach after she was already dressed for school. She didn't even try to hide her glee. "Hooray," she said. "I got 'em and I get to stay home from school, and he" (she grinned at her little brother) "has to go."

So off he went, grumbling at the injustice of it all.

"But you already had a week at home."

"So what. You'll probably get to stay home longer." He did manage to make it through one full day. He boarded the bus solo, sat through classes and returned home with messages from his sister's friends.

"I did it today," he announced in the evening. "But I can't go to school tomorrow."

"Why not?" I asked.

And he answered, "Because I'm sick."

He did look a bit peaked. (Could envy of his sister's getting all the attention cause his complexion to pale?) I felt his forehead. He was warm. Actually, he was hot. The thermometer registered one hundred and three degrees.

To his sister's chagrin, her brother was really sick. He stayed home on Friday, but he was relegated to the brown living room chair. The couch is reserved for children with chicken pox. The next day, he seemed a little better. By Sunday, the fever had disappeared. He remained home from school on Monday as an extra precaution "to build resistance. But tomorrow you're going back," I said.

And almost before the words were out of my mouth, my son developed a cough. It isn't a dry, hacking, phony cough. It is not even an I-don't-want-to-go-to-school, whimpery, pretend cough. Somehow, he has managed to contract a good old-fashioned, throaty, there-is-no-way-the-teacher-will-let-him-stay-in-class cough.

So there he sits on the brown chair with his blanket, juice, crayons and tissues, coughing his bronchial cough and sharing center stage with his sister.

She, in the meantime, is recuperating rapidly from the chicken pox. "And it's not fair, Mommy," she says. "It's just not fair."

I suppose it is not. But it could be worse.

TAKING A STAND

She came home from school in tears.

"Sara and Rachael had a fight," she said. "And Rachael said if I'm friends with Sara she won't be friends with me. And Sara said if I'm friends with Rachael she won't like me anymore. And Tamar said I should side with Rachael. And Deborah said I should side with Sara. And Esther said that Sara said that Rachael is wrong." And so on.

Except for intermittent sobs, it sounded like a rewrite of "Who's on First?"

I asked my daughter to repeat the story. "Who did what to whom?" I said. "And why?"

She wasn't sure. She knew one thing only. She was being asked to take a stand. And in doing so, she was sure she would lose "the other half of the friends."

I offered a suggestion. "Why not tell them you want to be friends with both?"

My daughter looked at me—stricken. "Wahhh." The tears streaked her face. (Obviously my idea was ridiculous.) "I can't do that. I have to be friends with one or the other. If I tell them I like them both, they'll both hate me because they're mad at each other, and then I'll have no friends at all . . . waahhh."

A part of me hurt for my daughter, caught in the dilemma of cliques, spats and best friends. The other part of me felt like smiling for the bittersweet memories of my own third grade days. I recall well the feeling of having to decide between two friends when they had had a falling-out. And, I remember the major disappointment when, after having made a choice, I found that the girls had made up with each other and left me out. If memory serves me, these great love-hate relationships between little girls at ages eight, nine and ten are precursors to the teenage years. So I grinned inside at what was to come and put on a serious face for my daughter.

"There is really nothing I can do for you. However," I lectured, "if I were you, I'd stay out of the fight entirely, even if it means playing by yourself for a few days until things simmer down." The answer was definitely unsatisfactory, but it was the best I could do.

My daughter slept fitfully that night, fretting over the

confrontation. She whimpered about having to board the school bus in the morning. "Who should I sit next to?" she asked. "If I sit next to Rachel, Sara will be mad. If I sit next to Sara . . ."

So I told her to sit next to her brother. That seemed to satisfy her temporarily. Apparently, though, it did not satisfy her little brother.

With all my maternal wisdom, I had chosen to remain out of the fight. I hadn't offered to call the girls' mothers. I wanted my child to handle things on her own.

My son had a different plan. And he carried it out alone.

When the children arrived home at the end of the school day, both were smiling.

"You look happy," I commented to my daughter. "Did the girls make up?"

"Yup," she said. "Somebody must have told the teacher about the fight. The teacher called each of us out of the classroom separately and fixed up everything. Now we're all friends again." She beamed. "I wonder who told the teacher?"

And very quietly, from across the room came the matter-of-fact and unexpected answer.

"Me," said my son. "I saw your teacher and I told."

"But why?" we asked.

And he responded. "Because I couldn't stand thinking about my sister walking around the house with no friends."

SNEAKERS

New sneakers. An American tradition. A suburban celebration. A rite of spring.

"A madhouse. This place is a madhouse." I wiped the perspiration from my upper lip and scowled at my six-year-old, as he tripped over a pile of boxes strewn across the shoe store floor.

"I want these." My eight-year-old grabbed a pair of iridescent running shoes and held them aloft for me to see. "Do you like them?"

"Like them? How could anyone like anything in this crowd?" And I thought I'd been so smart. "Let's beat the rush," I'd said to the children. "It's the first beautiful day of the season, but it's still a little early for sneaks. Let's go get them now."

I guess everyone had the same idea. The discount sneaker store owner was handing out numbers as patrons entered. I nodded in commiseration to other disheveled mothers, and I unzipped my jacket. It was sweltering in the shop, but a tail end nip of March-like weather had forced us all to wear our winter garb. So there we sat, stood or squatted, parents and progeny in wool and down, participating in an annual event.

I listened to the sounds of spring. "How about these, Mommy?" My daughter brought me a pair of green tennis shoes adorned with pink, yellow and blue stripes. "Which do you like better, the sparkly ones or these? I love them both."

Isn't it wonderful how we humans have come to love sneakers? I smiled thoughtfully as I watched the sneakered saleswoman hand two pairs of miniature sneakers to a young mother whose baby sat squirming on her lap. The young mother, also wearing sneakers, chose the navy over the red. The little canvas shoes fit in the palm of her hand.

An elderly grandparent with a furrowed brow squeezed one sneaker in her right hand, another in her left, testing each as though it were an unripe fruit. "You never really know till you get home," she confided, "but I can tell you from experience, its the toe that counts." And she pinched the material to prove her point.

I heard a teenager order track shoes. "Do you run?" asked the salesperson. It seems there are shoes that look like running shoes for "imitation" running. And then there are real running shoes. Only the salespeople know the difference.

"Can you feel the difference?" I heard the man ask my son. "Walk across the room and show your mother."

My six-year-old didn't walk, he stomped his way towards me, frowning. His lip quivered. "I hate these," he said, staring down at the sneaks. "And the man called me Junior."

I suppressed a smile. My child's little feet looked enormous. I hugged him quickly, because he doesn't like to be hugged in public anymore. "If you hate this pair, we won't get them. Pick out another pair and show the man. Oh, and he knows your name isn't Junior. He's just being friendly."

He ought to be friendly, I thought. It's his shoe store, and it's packed. The man must be rich.

With thoughts of money and friendship crossing my mind, I approached my daughter. She had reached an impasse. "I want both," she said of the iridescent and the green. "I can't decide."

I turned away. Sometimes if I leave her alone, my daughter can make a choice. Otherwise, she can make a scene.

Thus we passed the better part of an hour. But as in other emotionally charged events, when at last we emerged from the discount sneaker shop, we were slightly changed people. We carried with us two pairs of sneaks (one for my son and one for my daughter), a mild headache for me, and a renewed spirit for the season of spring.

KNITTING

I bought her a skein of lavender wool and two knitting needles. I think I made the proper choice. For several years, she's been asking me to teach her how to knit. "I can't," I've said. "I never learned to knit, and I don't want to learn. I have no interest. Some people knit, and some people don't. I don't."

And there the issue has stood, a moot point by the time she was seven. Maybe I was a bit overzealous in my lack of interest. "I just don't care for that sort of thing. It takes a lot of patience. There are other" (more important?) "things I'd rather do."

I guess I was trying to take a stand. Knitting, I suggested subliminally, is something contemporary women simply do not do. But I never quite worded it that way. And she never quite understood the implication anyway. She likes ruffles, lace, ribbons and black velvet pumps. She probably can't relate to my liberated opinions regarding knitting.

Besides, it is her birthday.

So I acquiesced. Without telling her, I purchased the needles and the lavender yarn and arranged for my mother-in-law to give her lessons.

Then I hid the gift in the corner of my room. And while it sat there unobtrusively buried in its Yarn Barn baggie, I got to thinking.

What was I like at nine?

Not unlike my daughter, I decided. The year before I turned ten, when my interest in dolls was beginning to wane, I developed a sudden burning desire to sew. The summer of my ninth birthday, I wanted more than anything else to make a shirt to wear over my bathing suit.

It makes me grin today, looking at those knitting needles

intended for my daughter, to remember how ardently I wanted to create the perfect shirt. It was to be red and white striped with a bow in the front, and everyone would be jealous. At night, before falling asleep, I would plan the way I'd lay out the pieces and bind the back and front together. I can recall imaginary conversations I had with people who would notice the beautiful shirt and ask where I'd bought it.

"I didn't," I would answer them. "I made it myself." And they would be amazed.

But it never happened that way. I never told people I had made the shirt. I never sewed the back and front together. In fact, I never asked my mother to buy the material. It was, I suppose, a passing fancy, a daydream. Still, I wonder sometimes what might have been if I had tried to sew.

So I've decided to give my daughter a chance. Perhaps in the long run she will be a contemporary woman who knows how to knit. And will that really be so bad?

FIRE

Fire gutted the entire place—ate away the structure and everything inside. The people were saved, but the flames demolished the objects in the house—their house—a house that was part of my childhood.

I knew the rooms in their house nearly as well as I knew the rooms in mine. I can describe the wallpaper in their kitchen, the color of their living room carpet, the way the beds in the girls' room abutted the windows. Their house stood solidly next to our house with only a row of over-grown hedges between. At the far end of the hedges, toward the backyards, we sneakered children wore through a dusty path, a secret passageway from their house to ours.

Our house was huge, with a stone foundation, a wrap-around pillared porch and wooden stairs leading to the glass-enclosed vestibule. In the yard was an oak tree and the swing set. For half my childhood, our house was green. Later, we painted it tan and brown. I lived there with my parents and sister.

Next door was their house—painted white with black trim. Always. Inside lived Mr. and Mrs. (we called them Aunt and Uncle) and the three girls (one my sister's age, one my age and one two years older). Later, the baby boy was born.

In the foyer of their house hung the portrait of the girls at ages three, six and eight. Their hair was brown, they wore pastel party dresses and carried nosegays.

In the living room, the grand piano filled the space near the bay window. At the back of their house, a den was added with paneled walls and a fireplace. Upstairs were the bedrooms and bathrooms—the secret corners, the places where we hid and giggled, fought, told stories, the corners where we grew up.

Except for the sporadic squabbles ("Don't you dare come into my yard again, you're not allowed!" said with hands on hips and tongues stuck out), we spent days on end in one another's kitchens and lives. We knew each other's aunts, uncles, cousins, grandparents. Our mothers and fathers were young adults together. We were babies together. We went to kindergarten, junior high school, high school together. I rang their doorbell to call for my friend on the way to school. We visited one another in college. We attended one another's weddings. We kept in touch long after we left our childhood homes to begin lives of our own.

Eight years ago, when my parents sold our house to buy a more suitable, modern home, I felt a vague betrayal of my youth. I knew no other place would ever be the same. I was, I suppose, comforted somewhat by the knowledge that "Aunt" and "Uncle" still lived next door to the old house and I could visit when I liked.

And during the past eight years, I have on occasion driven to the old town, parked in front of the old house and gingerly walked past "ours" and "theirs." All their children are gone now, of course, some with children of their own. Their baby boy is six feet tall and a doctor. But "Aunt" and "Uncle" have remained the same, glad to see me, giving me snacks and hugs, allowing me to be perpetually seven-and-a-half, allowing me to wander through the rooms, to flirt with a piece of my past. They have helped me to arrest time for the time it takes to drink a cup of coffee.

Their house has been a good friend, a fine place with all the memories contained between the walls. But the walls were destroyed by the fire.

And the house is gone.

THE MUSIC BOX

He held the small round plexiglas music box in his hand. The delicate sound was clear and sweet as my son spoke.

"I miss Daddy," he said. "I hardly see him." He cast his eyes downward and played with the cover of the music box, watching the tiny workings through the glass.

The lump rose in my throat. Maybe it wasn't such a good idea after all . . . the music box. It had been an afterthought, a spur of the moment extra birthday gift for my seven-year-old son. My husband (my son's stepfather) and I were treating him to a Knicks' basketball game for his birthday. It had been the child's decision. He had chosen the game over a party. He had said he wanted it more than anything else, more than a cake, hats, blowers and a bunch of kids. "Okay?"

"Okay," we'd agreed.

But it had seemed so grown up. He is only seven, I'd reminded myself as I purchased the red and blue crepe paper to decorate the house. (Even though there would be no real "party," I felt he needed decorations.)

And while he'd already told me he didn't want a cake, I couldn't help buying candles for the cupcakes, so he could make a wish.

But the music box was truly extra. It was as much a gift for me as it was for him. I knew the basketball game would be fine, but I had to give him something else, something special.

I found the gift immediately. It cost eight dollars and it plays, "My Way." It is small enough for him to hold in the palm of his hand, and the saleswoman told me he could put a picture in the clear glass cover. (I thought he might choose a picture of one of the basketball stars.)

But he didn't. He didn't even consider it.

When I handed him the music box, I was unsure—tentative. "This is for the soft part inside you," I told him. "Everyone has a gentle, sweet place, and this is for yours—and you can put a picture on the top."

He opened the package slowly, and slowly wound the key, and then he sat there staring at the music box quietly, listening carefully to the sound. I watched him walk to his dresser. Still holding the music box, he unearthed a small photo album and removed the wallet-size picture of himself taken in the hospital on the day he was born. He asked me to trim the edges of the picture to fit the music box. Then, he returned to the edge of his bed where I left him holding his gift. I walked out of the room feeling proud of the tender soul inside my son.

Ten minutes later, he came to me with a serious mouth and an observation about his father. "I miss him," he said. "I hardly see him . . ." And the sound of the music tinkled slowly in the little boy's hand.

Then I remembered (just as my son must have remembered) the sound of another music box, a small hand-held wooden music box his father and I had played for him when he was an infant. That music box and his father both left our lives when the child was twelve months old.

Between his first and his seventh birthday have come other toys, bigger ones, louder ones, bicycles, drums, matchbox cars. And between them, too, have come changes: an apartment, a new house, school, friends and, recently, a loving stepfather. Between one year and seven, much has happened to the child and the father. The old music box was thrown away.

But the memory stayed intact.

COMPANY

"We're having company for dinner tonight," I said.

"A-g-a-i-n . . . ?" they whined in unison with that long drawn out sound which implies that Mommy is intentionally making life difficult once more. "Why again? We're always having company for dinner."

I had to check their faces to judge the mood. A truly injured whine is different from an I'm-going-to-give-you-a-hard-time-but-I'll-come-around-Mom whine.

I figured this to be the latter.

"They're very nice people. You remember them, don't you? They have three little children. We went to their house once, and they gave you candy and potato chips and chocolate ice cream." (And stomach aches.)

"Oh, them . . . Are they bringing the kids?"

I had to check my offspring's faces again. "Are they bringing the kids?" could mean, "Yeah. We liked their kids. It's okay that they're coming." Or it could mean, "No way, Mom. Those kids are terrible. They're gonna take our toys and mess up our room and ruin our games. You better do something quick, Mom."

Actually, their expressions showed neither acceptance nor annoyance. My children's eyes registered disinterest. The company kids are younger, just past baby stage, neither interesting enough to encourage enthusiasm, nor threatening enough to be a problem. They are just kid company, their parents, adult company. Both types of which have been joining us often for dinner lately.

In the past few months, we have entertained every sister and brother-in-law on both sides of the family, both sets of in-laws and a pair of ex-in-laws who will remain forever my children's devoted grandparents, assorted aunts, uncles, cousins and friends. We've had overnight guests, breakfast guests. We've served everything from soup to nuts—literally—and here it is Thursday evening and we're having company—again.

"But why, Ma?"

I've often wondered about that myself. During my first

marriage, when the children were little, entertaining made me nervous. I recall planning meals weeks in advance and agonizing over the appropriate quantities for the number of guests. I remember feeling harried, holding a ten-month-old on my hip while trying to mash potatoes with a dented fork. I was insecure, inexperienced.

During the time of life when I was without a spouse, the thought of planning anything—dinner parties, vacations, a trip to the dentist—caused me great difficulty. I lived a flexible, albeit neurotic life as a solo mother. Existence happened one day at a time. There was no room for organized entertaining. I suppose I didn't want to know what I'd be doing on any given Thursday night, particularly a week in advance. I preferred imagining that perhaps I'd be offered the Nobel Prize for Literature on that Thursday, or I'd win the lottery or meet the man of my dreams. I could not tolerate the thought of knowing I'd be serving lasagna to two adults and their three kids.

But things are different now. I am married again. And older. My children are more mature. I know how much chicken to serve a family of six (and how much extra to make in case four more show up). I'm not afraid to plan in advance. I enjoy the routine and certainty of my life. (If the neighbors are coming for lunch next Sunday then I'm sure I'll still be living in this house and married to my husband next Sunday.) There is a kind of reassurance to my plans.

But it is more than that. It's a pride I feel, a need to show off to the grandparents, aunts, uncles, cousins and friends. It is my personal desire to tell the world that I feel good— good enough to share my bread, lasagna, coffee and cake. I want people from my past to see my present. I want them to know that I'm okay.

Okay?

TAKING FLIGHT

How fortunate for him to be able to stay home from work to help with the babies.

The thought crossed my mind at six-thirty a.m. on a recent morning. I was standing beneath the tree in our back yard, watching the comings and goings of two small brown birds who had, a day or two earlier, become parents of two, three or four smaller brown birds.

In the heat of the early morning, or because I had not yet had breakfast, I truly forgot that I was watching birds and found myself pondering the merits of paternity leave. It crossed my mind that this father was, for some period of time, not going into the office. His boss had either found a temporary replacement for him or would simply do without him for whatever time it would take to get the little ones off the ground (or out of the nest).

I laughed at myself standing there in the driveway. "Come here, kids," I called to my pajamaed children. "Come outside and see how that father and mother both feed the babies. Look at that. He's going to sit on that branch and guard the nest until she returns with a worm."

And then it was her turn.

And then his.

We watched on and off all day and the next and the next. I called my mother to tell her about the birds.

"Beautiful to see, isn't it?" she asked.

And I answered, "Yes."

The infant birds grew. Their O-shaped mouths remained open almost constantly with chirping and peeping for sustenance. The parents, diligent and dutiful, were ever-present with the food.

Aren't they exhausted? I wondered. At day's end, doesn't

the mother lie prostrate with one wing over her forehead whimpering to her mate, "Won't these kids ever go to sleep? Can't you do something for goodness' sake? I'm too tired to cook tonight. You'll just have to order in pizza for dinner."

At sunset, with the O-mouths still beeping, didn't the father look disgustedly at his frazzled spouse and long for a day in the office? Did he say, "Listen, honey, I really have to get back on the job tomorrow. The guys have been having a rough time without me. You can handle it here now, can't you?"

But I wonder if in their bird brains they thought at all. Or was this effort at parenting simply instinctive? Did some internal mechanism direct the parent birds to collect food and deliver it with delicacy into the mouths of their babes? Was this nature taking its course or were the birds contemplating their actions? If they knew what they were doing, I could foresee a split in the family. The babies were becoming a burden. One or the other of the adults was going to take off.

I decided to help. Corralling my children and their neighborhood friends, we tore strips of bread into bite-size pieces and covered the ground below the bird house.

And then, I stepped back to watch. But the blue jays and the squirrels discovered the bread and, what's worse, the home of the infant birds. Despite my good intentions, I had interfered where I was not needed. Now the bird parents had double the work. They had to keep guard for stray jays and feed their offspring simultaneously.

It was a difficult time for all of us. I eagerly awaited the day when the little ones could fly off on their own. I assumed they might fall from the nest a few times and I would have to be around to pick them up and put them back. I thought the mother and father might need me to lend a hand here and there. But such was not the case.

Towards the week's end, I was away from home for a few days. When I returned, the birds were gone—all of them—male, female and babies.

I was worried. I called my mother. (She knows about such things.) "Ma," I said, "the birds have left. I can't see them in their house anymore, and they're not chirping and the mother and father aren't flying back and forth with food. I'm concerned. What do you think happened to them, Ma?"

And my mother answered in her serious and wise way. "They grew up," she told me. "They did what all children do. When they are strong enough and old enough, they leave the nest. And that is the way it is supposed to be."

PLANS

I was organized. But my plan is deteriorating into chaos.

In the beginning of the summer, I said to the children, "Children, if you cooperate with me every morning, I will take you swimming every afternoon. Fair enough?"

"Fair enough."

So we devised a schedule. The older one would do the laundry, the younger one would be in charge of sidewalk and driveway sweeping. The two would make their beds and clean their room. I was assigned to floor washing, bathtub cleaning, dusting and vacuuming. My husband (who leaves for work at six forty-five a.m.) would retain his year-round job of grocery shopping. Theoretically, while the children were completing their chores, I could handle my end of the deal and write a column or story with time to spare.

I figured that by rising at six a.m. to jog, I could be back home before my husband was out of his morning shower (thereby assuring that the children would not be left unsupervised while I exercised). But I had forgotten how difficult it can be to crawl out of bed at sunrise.

However, I was determined. By my calculations, I should have been able to head for the pool, park or lake each day at noon with firmer muscles, neatly folded laundry, a well swept sidewalk and an article or two under my belt.

It is now eleven thirty-five a.m., and I have just sat down at the typewriter. I have cleaned the bathroom floor twice since seven a.m. I personally handled all the laundry today, and no one has swept the driveway, watered the lawn or offered to wash the dishes.

But there are extenuating circumstances. I did the laundry because the nine-year-old overslept. I allowed her to oversleep, because she went to bed after ten last night. I let her stay up till ten, because she said, "There's no school in summer, so why do I have to go to bed so early?" And this morning, I didn't have the heart to wake her.

Furthermore, she needed her rest for the nine-thirty a.m swimming lessons. I hadn't remembered the lessons when I worked out the summer schedule. I'd forgotten to include the lost hour between nine-thirty and ten-thirty while my offspring are learning the elementary backstroke and no one is cleaning the stove. But the backstroke is important. And when we return from the daily swimming lessons their lips are purple and their teeth click together. How could I refuse them warm baths, hot showers, a snack? But they track muddy feet across the bathroom floor, which is how I came to clean it twice thus far today.

Then there is lunch, which I had neglected to include in my master plan. And there are dishes to be washed and snacks to be packed for the afternoon at the pool. And I'd wanted the children to read this summer and write letters to their grandparents. I promised my daughter she could learn to bake (and then teach me). I keep running out of milk and juice. I lose my car keys. The children want to ride their bikes. Neighborhood youngsters ring the doorbell. Kids get splinters and skinned knees, and our African frog died.

These are minor matters, I suppose. But pet frogs must be buried, splinters removed, and one cannot let a ringing phone go unanswered or allow a child's thirst to remain unquenched. So it is after noon, and I am still sitting here at the typewriter. It doesn't matter though. Summer was probably never meant to be organized anyway.

SANDIE

Sandie is an optimist.

Her daughter has juvenile diabetes, and Sandie is an optimist. Her eleven-year-old child gives herself shots of insulin twice daily, measures her sugar level and monitors each morsel of food that enters her mouth, and still, Sandie manages to smile.

She more than manages. She spreads smiles. I have known this woman for thirty years. I knew her when she was her daughter's age. We rode the school bus together, went to college at the same time. I was the maid of honor at her wedding. I knew Sandie before she and her husband learned that their oldest daughter has juvenile diabetes. And I thought I knew Sandie now. But there is more to her than I had imagined.

At thirty-eight, she has the same wide smile, the same deep dimples and shining dark eyes that used to wink and twinkle when she was ten. She will still play volleyball, swim, sit in on a game of Monopoly with the gusto of a twelve-year-old. She is also a superb cook (the type who makes food appear effortlessly on the table). She is a good conversationalist and a fine friend. Sandie is fun.

"But how can you function?" I asked her during a recent phone conversation. "How can you get through each day knowing that your child is a diabetic? I suppose you just try and make the best of it," I commented—then realized that only a pessimist would make such a statement.

To Sandie, there is no best of it or worst of it. Juvenile diabetes is a fact of life, and Sandie deals with life head on. If she were to dwell on it, Sandie says she could worry about the future—about what might happen if her daughter's eyes fail and she loses her sight, if her kidneys stop functioning, if her heart stops beating. If she were to think about the negative possibilities associated with juvenile diabetes, Sandie's fears would be endless. "What good would it do?" she asks.

And I know she is right. But it is frightening. I am suddenly embarrassed by my good fortune. Yet Sandie tells me how lucky she is to be able to afford the pool in her yard so her daughter can exercise (juvenile diabetics need exercise). She tells me how happy she is that her husband could build the small gym in the basement so her daughter can climb. She tells me about the camp for juvenile diabetics, about the friendships her daughter has made. She tells me the things she is doing to help raise money for research.

"People really don't know about this condition," she says. "I guess they don't need to know unless they're directly affected. But we need money. With money, we will find a cure for juvenile diabetes. With money, we will discover a preventative. I am optimistic. I believe the answer is just around the corner."

So I hang up the phone and write out a check because I believe in Sandie.

 UI OUI

They said *merci* and *bon jour* and *bon soir*. They did not say yea and whatsnu and whadjasay. They sounded refined and cultured. I sounded tacky and coarse.

"Je ne parl (parlez? parle?) pas Francais," I eked out in broken French. And then, speaking slowly and loudly, I told the waitress in English that I wanted a Coke.

"Oui," she smiled at me. (Was she laughing behind those batting eyelashes?) "Coke?"

How was it that she could make a soft drink sound like champagne? How was it, I wondered, sitting there in the quaint little restaurant in Quebec, Canada, that all the waitresses, gas station attendants, tour guides and chamber-maids in this charming province sounded so highly educated? Was it simply the music of their language or is everyone north of the border just a bit more refined than I am?

When we'd first planned the trip to Canada, I had half hoped we would need our French. Between the two of us, my husband and I have a combined eight years of the language. Although we haven't had occasion to use it during the past seventeen years or so, I assumed it would be like riding a bicycle—once learned, never forgotten. But I couldn't recall the words for restroom or vegetables or left turn.

Maybe I never knew them in the first place. And I did not know how to say Mastercard and where is the laundromat in town?

If I never learned those practical things, what good was my high school French? And how is it that I can still say the sky is blue, but I don't know the phrase for how do I get to the other side of the river? Is it because the kids in the back of my ninth grade class were throwing paper airplanes while the teacher was trying to show me verb forms? Or is it because no one foresaw my need for conversational French?

So there I sat in the quaint little restaurant on the lovely cobbled streets of old Quebec City ordering Coke in tourist English and feeling mildly depressed.

Still, I suppose no one is perfect. *C'est la vie. N'est pas?*

SHOPPING SPREE

My mother took the children shopping for summer clothes. I went along to keep things under control. Experience has taught me that Grandmas get carried away.

"This time the kids just need a couple of T-shirts, Ma," I said.

"We'll see," my mother answered. "We'll see." And I caught her winking at the kids. The kids winked back. They know their Grandma all right.

And they know their mother. Their mother (that's me) wears T-shirts and simple skirts. I like this look. I strive for this effect. I hate shopping. I look like I hate shopping, and I want to look like I hate shopping.

But not Grandma. Grandma looks neat, sophisticated,

efficient and well-tailored. She looks as though there is something admirable about "getting dressed up." And the kids sense it.

"But they don't need fancy stuff," I told my mother. "All they need is shirts. Shirts make sense."

My mother raised her eyebrows. "When it comes to my grandchildren, I do not have to be sensible," she said. "When you are a grandparent you will understand." She grabbed each child by a hand and headed for the racks.

I slunk into a corner of the children's store to observe the shopping.

Grandmothers, I've noticed, are different from mothers. Grandmothers have patience. They don't care how many zippers get stuck, how many shirts have to be tucked in. They don't mind pinning up pants and tightening belts. Grandmas have good ideas about which tops match which bottoms and which skirts look prettier.

When I shop with the children, my motto is—fast. The quicker the better. If it fits and it's functional, buy it before anyone asks for anything else.

Not so with Grandmas. Grandmas take time. They are never frazzled. They really care about the way things fit. They are truly interested in the design on the front of the blouse or the ruffles on the dress. And in between try-ons, they take time to hug the kids. Grandmas give their undivided attention to the experience of shopping with the grandchildren.

From my position in the corner of the store, I could see the kids were loving it. There were no tears, no whines, no cries of "I wanna go home." Shopping with Grandma looked better than regular shopping. It looked like fun. It looked the way I think it's supposed to look—like a shopping spree.

OOK THREE • IMPRESSIONS

IMPRESSIONS

INTRODUCTION

We were a family. For the most part, we functioned as a tidy unit—sharing life's small pains and pleasures. Our little house was always filled with friends and neighbors. The children flourished in the stable atmosphere of their new two-parent home. The laws of *kashrus*, the day school experience, became second nature to us. And while I had not yet agreed to be *shomer Shabbos*, I was, I suppose, becoming so in measured steps. My husband imposed no strictures or rules. He guided gently, responded to questions and stepped aside as we moved forward towards observance.

Sometimes, we were reminded of our diverse pasts. The children's natural father visited, or they visited him. Our way of life demanded accommodation on this ex-husband's part. I worried that his disapproval of my chosen way of life would have a negative effect on the children. My fears, however, were unfounded.

When Little League practice interfered with *shul*, my

son opted for the local *shomer Shabbos* team. His new friends wore *tzitzis* under their T-shirts and *yarmulkes* under their baseball caps. My husband signed on as a coach, my boy learned to pitch, and I became a die-hard fan.

When my daughter's tap-dance recital was scheduled to begin before sundown on Saturday, she told the teacher that she would have to arrive a little late. "It's *Shabbos*," she explained. "I can't come on *Shabbos*."

Although our lives were in a state of flux, I discovered that the shift in direction was not drastic but rather smooth and pleasant. A friend advised me to concentrate on what I knew to be appropriate religiously. She said, "The rest will fall into place." I found that what I should not do on Saturday I could do on Sunday.

This was a time of peace for me, a comfortable segment after the turmoil of divorce, the demands of solo parenting and the excitement of second marriage. There came at last this period of calm between the children's toddler years and before the onset of the teens. I reveled in the tranquility—the sunrise in the eastern sky behind the oak trees, the mailbox on its crooked post beside the climbing roses. I loved the sounds of normalcy—the children squealing with delight in games of hide-and-seek, a neighbor calling "suppertime" from a kitchen window, a clean blanket of snow, the fireplace in the living room. I loved the little worries—the need to decide which flavor ice cream to choose, whether to water the lawn or take a walk, whether to make peanut butter and jelly or tuna for lunch, whether the children should wear their boots. I developed perspective. Life was glorious, like a picnic on a summer afternoon with high white clouds and chocolate cake. I drew comparisons with nature, with refreshing rain, sprouting tulips, clear blue skies. I felt fortunate. Serene. I was happy.

FEELING GUILTY

He makes me feel guilty. He's out there working in his yard at nine a.m. on weekends. With beads of perspiration running down his forehead, he's out there doing things in his yard that need to be done in my yard. But I'm not doing them. Nor is my husband. Nor are my children. We are inside in bathrobes and pajamas.

I always see him first from the kitchen window. In summer, he mows, clips and paints within my line of vision. I stand at the sink, filling the coffee pot, and watch him work. In autumn, he rakes, bags and fertilizes his lawn. In winter, he shovels. In spring, he plants and fixes.

In all four seasons, I look at him and wonder how he has the energy, the know-how, the desire to clean, sort and tidy on a constant basis. Sometimes, he makes me angry. How come he knows that driveways should be sealed? And if he knows, why don't I? And if by some quirk of fate I vaguely remember the necessity of sealing, how is it that he knows what to do and I don't? Why does he have the instinct to plant his garden at the right time, to fix the gas lamp before the flames set fire to the trees? Why can he adjust the wiring in his walls, sand the doors to his shed and paint his porch without getting spots on his shoes?

I can't. I never could. Or maybe I could, but I won't. I never do.

I see him out there with the birds, smiling as he completes each project in turn. It makes me jealous. Sometimes, it gives me false incentive. On Sundays, in particular, I make lists. I write: grout bathroom tiles, insulate attic, paint children's room, clean shed. I rewrite the list on the calendar page and put the calendar on the counter while I have a cup of coffee.

But one cup leads to another. I dawdle over breakfast. Breakfast becomes brunch. I read the newspaper, have a conversation, decide to visit a relative, take a ride, go for a walk, read a book, follow the football game. Somehow, I fill the morning with plans and the afternoon slips by. By day's end, I realize I have neither grouted nor painted (and if I'm honest with myself, I realize I had no intention of doing either anyway). Yet my neighbor has successfully completed all of his projects. I see him.

I know he is there in the evenings examining his work, checking out the freshly-sealed driveway, the newly-planted garden, the just-painted porch. On occasion, he has invited me to inspect his efforts. And I never lie. I tell him he has done a terrific job. I tell him I envy his energy and ability. I tell him it is a pleasure to look at his house through the windows of my house. (And I try not to think about the reverse.) I tell him how much I admire his stick-to-it-iveness. I compliment him heartily, and then I tell him the truth. I let him know how guilty he makes me feel.

N RETROSPECT

It's too quiet to write. The children are back in school, and I can hear the silence.

I know . . . I know there were times during July when the constant trail of kids in and out of the kitchen, the persistent banging of the screen doors, the never-ending cry for juice and snacks made it nearly impossible to write.

But I managed. I learned to put my thoughts on hold while I reset the sprinkler so the kids could cool off. I figured out a way to rephrase paragraphs in my head while wiping blood from scraped knees. I found time for iced tea and conversations with neighbors. I was able to examine the caterpillar the children found on the backyard bush. And I managed to retie the laces on sneakers at least ten times a day.

I know I complained about the chaos, the shouting, the balls which bounced against the kitchen window and which, one day, will shatter the glass. I realize I was tough on my offspring when I asked for eleven minutes of silence so I could reread what I'd started to write three hours earlier. I am sure I sounded ornery sometimes. But for the most part, I loved the noise. I loved the rosy cheeks, the tanned legs, the green grass and the kids. All of them. The ones from down the block and across the road and half a mile away. Maybe my columns were not quite as good from June through August. Perhaps they were disjointed, disconnected. I suppose they had the sounds of summer stuck between the lines.

But now it's gone—the warm, long afternoons, the bicycles screeching in the driveway, the ice cream truck and the kids.

The kids are all in school. And here I sit in the quiet of my room, looking out the window at the trees from whose limbs children stared back at me all summer long.

"Get down from there," I'd shout, my concentration broken. "Get out of that tree this minute. You're going to fall." And they'd tumble down, one, two, sometimes five of them rolling around on the grass like marbles or apples.

They would grin back at me through the screen of my first floor window. "What are you worried about? The tree's not high." And off they'd go to try handstands on the top rung of the monkey bars so I would have to interrupt my work again.

And I didn't really mind a bit.
And I wish it was summer again.
The silence now is much too loud. Too loud for me to work.

 HE SUKKAH

A cool breeze ruffled the roof of leaves and stalks. Paper birds swung on threads from their perch amidst the branches. The flimsy walls with crayoned designs billowed in the night air. And the candles flickered above the centerpiece of gourds, above the bowls of steaming food. The candles cast shadows on our faces as we sat around the table in our *sukkah*—my husband, my ex-husband, my son, my daughter and me. Together, preparing to share a meal.

My children's father and I have been divorced for five years now. My husband and I have been married for one. Yet the three of us—the former husband, the present husband and I—will remain forever in one another's lives by virtue of the seven-year-old-boy and the nine-year-old-girl.

My former husband, though Jewish, has said on occasion that religion can be a burden on society, a divisive rather than cohesive force. He would choose to ignore most rituals—in theory if not in fact.

My present husband considers Judaism a synonym for life.

But the children care little for subtleties or theory. They deal in truth. And the truth is, their father, their stepfather and their mother are Jewish. And they are Jewish.

And the children wanted to build a *sukkah*. They wanted

to decorate with crayon and paint, to cut pretty birds from colored paper. They wanted to light candles at sundown, to look through the *schach* at a starry sky, to proclaim their heritage. In their innocence (or was it wisdom?) they expected all of us—the father, the stepfather and me—to build the structure and to share a meal therein.

The construction began early on a day when the children's father was planning a visit. They had not told him of their intent to build the booth. They assumed he would be glad. They showed no signs of worry over whether or not their father would find such a display of heritage too flagrant in a world where assimilation was the norm. And they did not question the fact that their stepfather might feel uncomfortable with his wife's former mate dining beneath his roof of leaves and stalks.

They focused upon the walls and ceiling, the yellows, reds, blues. They concentrated efforts on the tablecloth, the pictures, the pine cones they hung to decorate the shelter.

And I did not know then, and I do not know now, if the children understood what they had wrought. But I can see us still sitting together at the table on the clear, chilly night with the candle flames dancing, the paper birds fluttering, stars, moon, the smell of autumn and the children's eyes glittering as they smiled at their father, their stepfather and me.

THE PIANO

I think my piano is smiling. Somebody cares again.
It's not that we'd forgotten about the piano standing

there in the far corner of the small room at the other end of the house. It's just that there hasn't been time. Or interest, I suppose.

It began when I was seven. I told my parents I wanted lessons. So they bought me a piano.

Not just like that, of course. I'm sure they discussed it with one another first. They probably gave me a little speech about the cost of pianos and the necessity of practice—the idea of commitment to a musical instrument. They probably said the study of piano is serious stuff. "Are you serious?"

And I probably said yes. Because before I turned eight, I owned a piano. And I had a piano teacher. Her name was Mrs. G. She had short fingernails (so they wouldn't tap on the piano keys), and her hair was wound in tight black curls. I liked her. She taught me to read the mysterious marks on the paper with the parallel lines. She taught me to listen for sound and beat and rhythm. She tried to teach me to practice. She probably said practice is necessary to the study of music. The study of piano is serious. She probably said, "Are you serious?"

And by the age of ten, I probably said I was not.

So I quit.

But the old piano stayed in the hallway of my parents' house. Through junior high school and high school, the piano stood there, solidly imposing in the hallway. It was always positioned in such a way that I had to brush against it as I walked past. And more than once, I'd feel a pang of guilt. Sometimes, I'd sit down and play a few melodies.

During my college years, the piano remained mute. Perhaps it was lonely in the hallway, with me not around to walk by it and pause for a song or two. Or maybe my parents were lonely with me not there? In any case, my father took pity on the old piano. While I was away at school, he hired a teacher for himself and began taking lessons. In earnest. He was serious. He understood the importance of practice. He learned to play. And he enjoyed music—enough so that he bought an organ and started taking both piano and organ lessons.

He'd alternate between the two, experimenting with tone and rhythm and melody. The music was his island in the midst of hectic life. He liked the sound and the serenity it gave to him.

And while my father played, I got married, had one child, then another. My husband and I bought a used piano. I sang silly songs with the kids. We let the children bang on the keys. Then my husband and I got divorced. We sold the piano. The children and I moved to a small apartment near my parents' home.

And one day, there was a knock on my door. Two moving men arrived with my good old piano, my childhood piano, my father's piano.

"A gift," said the men, "from your Dad."

"Concentrating on the organ lessons," my father told me when I asked. "No time to practice the piano. You play it for a while."

So I did just that. I unearthed old music. I taught myself songs. I played for the children and with the children. I played for the neighbors. I played loudly and long and rather poorly, but I spilled out my feelings on the ivory keys.

And then I met my husband-to-be. And there was less time or need for the piano. The children were happy. Life was good. After the wedding, we moved the piano to the far corner of the small room at the other end of our house. And there it has stood.

But yesterday my daughter told me she wants lessons.

(And I told the piano.)

BROKEN WINDOW

We said, "Do not play ball by that window." We said, "Move away or you'll break it one day." We said, "Play on the other side of the house. Play in the park. Play on the dead end street. Play anywhere but under the window." We said, "You are going to be sorry. You are going to break that window."

And he did.

Crash. Smash. Splatter into smithereens—thousands of them all over the rhododendron plant, the kitchen window sill, all over the ground, the grass, the driveway.

He came to the back door with eyes like marbles. The color had drained from his face. He stood there motionless with his buddy beside him.

"I broke the window," he whispered in a muffled monotone. He continued standing stock still.

"I heard," I said, trying to keep a serious face. He looked so funny with his ashen cheeks and his staring eyes. He looked like every memory of every window-breaking boy I've ever seen. And he hadn't even been able to run from the scene of the crime.

His sister and her friend arrived within moments to taunt in singsong, "Do you know what he did . . . oh, what he did. Did you see? Did you hear?"

And he still stood there—shocked. He had actually broken a window.

My husband says the shattered glass was probably less frightening to the boy than the knowledge that his mother and stepfather had accurately foretold the future.

His lower lip trembled slightly. He and his buddy marched off to the bedroom to await sentence.

My husband and I squelched our laughter.

He broke a window. He did it! He's big enough and strong enough and wild enough and happy enough to play ball with gusto. To play ball like a kid with nary a care. To play the way I never thought I'd see him play when he was little and I was alone and scared.

I guess there were times when my son and I were younger, that I wondered if he'd grow up rough enough. I wondered if—despite my doting care, my overprotective-ness—he'd be one of the guys. Would he ever roll around in the mud? Climb trees? Would he ever break a window?

And he did.

Like a rite of passage, a milestone, a major event, he crossed the line and smashed the glass.

So I celebrated a little inside myself as I stood with my husband before the accused to mete out the punishment—a day of leaf-raking in the back yard to defray the cost of the new pane of glass.

And I could have kicked up my heels as I left him sitting with his buddy on the edge of his bed, talking about the number of bags of leaves it would take to earn three dollars, talking about the size of the window, talking about how strong you gotta be to throw a ball that far, that high, that long. Humph! You gotta be good, pretty good. "Dontcha?"

MY MOTHER'S DRESS

It is a simple blue knit dress with thin silver threads woven into the material. Why do I find it so difficult to wear?

Because the dress belongs to my mother. The high necked, ankle-length, elegant dress belongs to a woman whose daughter I am. And if I am her daughter, her child, her little girl, how can I possibly be old enough to wear her clothes?

The blue knit dress is not new. In fact, it is one of those classic gowns the style of which remains in vogue forever. Maybe my mother purchased the dress ten years ago, maybe twenty. It doesn't matter. I know I've seen her wear it many times. It is lovely. It suits her. It is mature, sophisticated, regal, very adult.

"So why not wear it?" my mother offered. "It is perfect for the occasion, and it matches your eyes."

I tried to see it that way, tried to envision myself in my mother's blue dress. But I kept seeing her, a slim, tall figure, looking so like the woman I wanted to be.

Actually, my mother is not really very tall. We are the same height. But I feel so much smaller. I see her tall, in sparkling, high-heeled shoes which match the silver threads in her gown. I see the way she carried herself wearing the beautiful dress. And I remember me, her child at eighteen, at twelve, at five years old. I recall looking up at my mother, waiting for a kiss before she and my father would leave to go to a formal affair. Watching her dress before the babysitter would arrive to take care of me while she and my father would go out for the evening.

I remember the color of my mother's lipstick, the smell of her perfume, the way the bottles of cologne were set out on a glass tray on a vanity table in her room. I used to play with the lipsticks and colognes and powders. It was all so mysterious, the rustling of her skirt, my father's starched white shirt. Wherever they were going would be glorious, I knew.

"Okay, I'll try it on," I finally agree. "But I don't know if it will fit."

Reluctantly, I pull the gown over my head. I zip the zipper. I slip on high-heeled shoes. And then, I look in the mirror.

And I see a simple blue knit dress with thin silver threads being worn by me.

CLASS REUNION

I always thought I'd want to go. I'd want to see the old gang, tell the old stories, introduce my husband, meet their husbands and wives. I always figured I would want to see who got skinny or fat, who succeeded, who failed. I was certain it would be fun. But I have decided against it after all.

I am not going to the class reunion.

The realization that I've been out of high school for twenty years came six months ago, with a phone call from an old friend.

"Hello," she said. "How are you? What's new? What have you done with your life since last we met, and would you like to work on the class reunion committee?"

So I telescoped two decades into one paragraph and told her that I'd been to college, gotten married, had two children, been divorced and married again. That I've moved eight times, lived in four different states, had three full-time jobs, four part-time jobs. I've been sad, happy, lonely, calm, ecstatic, pensive, elated and dull. "And how about you?" I asked.

She said she had married a boy she'd known since high school days. They are the parents of three children, and they live in the same house where she grew up. "And will you work on the reunion committee?"

For a moment, I almost answered yes. For a brief few seconds, at the sound of her voice, with a flash of memories crashing through the phone lines, I reverted to high school days and nearly said I would. I envisioned cheerleaders in purple pleated skirts planning for the event. And I saw me (wanting to be a cheerleader but never making the squad) wanting, at the very least, to be part of the spirit. I saw the student council president perspiring in the overheated lunchroom with the plain round clock behind his head. I saw the literary magazine committee and the yearbook committee and class trip planning committee. At the sound of the voice on the other end of the phone, I remembered the full weight of too much homework on a night in the dead of winter, when I didn't want to have to take the biology exam in the morning or finish the algebra assignment after dinner or worry about who or if someone would ask me to the party. At the sound of the voice on the other end of the phone, it occurred to me that I did not want to attend any more committee meetings ever. So I told her no. "I cannot plan. And I will have to let you know about the reunion."

I realized I would have to let myself know first. I would have to decide if I care, if I am curious, interested. I would have to find out if the high school class of '64 means anything to me.

When the formal invitation arrived announcing the Saturday night gathering at the American Legion Hall and the picnic on Sunday, I could not answer. I could recall the circle pins and charm bracelets I wore. I could remember the records we played, the hairstyles we loved. I could summon back the years of plans and ice cream sodas and tests and lockers and blue gym uniforms, but I could not decide if I wanted to attend. I placed the invitation behind the tissue box on the kitchen counter. Later, I moved the invitation to the inside of my purse and then to the appropriate page in the daily planner calendar. But I did not respond. I waited.

I waited for something. I suppose I wanted a reason to say I could not go. The reason arrived in the form of an invitation to spend the weekend of the reunion at the shore with good family friends.

"And so you see, I won't be able to make it," I finally wrote. "We will be out of town on the evening of the get-together and the afternoon of the picnic. I am really very sorry. It would have been fun."

APPROPRIATE ATTIRE

It's not that I'm a stickler for style. In truth, where clothing is concerned, I have no taste. I wear what is comfortable, convenient, accessible. I wear what I like—a factor which may have contributed to my son's concept of acceptable attire.

"I'm ready," he announced, stomping loudly across the wooden floor. "How come nobody else is dressed?" His question was a statement of maturity, a show of self-sufficiency. He was letting me know that he'd selected his outfit for *shul* and donned the clothes all by himself. At 7:02 a.m. on a Saturday morning, he was smiling up at me from an additional inch of height gained by the brown cowboy boots he had chosen to complement his navy blue sweat pants which puckered at the knee.

"C'mon, hurry up," he commanded impatiently, "We're

gonna be late. Let's go already."

I swallowed my urge to laugh and stared somberly at the child. "You certainly are growing up," I mustered. "I don't think your sister has even gotten out of bed yet."

He accepted my words as a compliment and strutted cheerfully into the kitchen where the noise of his heels could be heard throughout the house. The pride of having beaten everyone at this business of "getting dressed" and the beauty of his cowboy boots were overwhelming. He marched across the floor like a soldier on parade.

How could I tell him to change his clothes?

In bathrobe and slippers, I stood before my closet, inspecting my own selection of garments, handling first one dress then another, distracted by the prospect of cowboy boots in *shul*. And those sweat pants were really out of the question. Still, I could not bear to dash his sense of accomplishment. I simply would not be the one to criticize his style.

Perhaps, I thought, I could turn the task around. Still formulating a plan, I called him to my room. "Hey, big boy," I greeted him, "since you're so good at getting dressed, how about helping me pick out my clothes?" He nodded, accepting the seriousness of the task.

"I was thinking of wearing this," I told him, removing an old, faded, somewhat wrinkled jeans skirt from the hanger.

"No," he said immediately. "Not that."

Then, I unearthed an ancient sweatshirt and held it up for him to see. "How about this?" I wanted to know.

"No," he said. "No good."

I frowned. "Why not? Don't you think this sweat shirt is appropriate for *shul*?" I glanced casually at his sweat pants as I posed the question.

"No," he answered. "Not appropriate." He likes it when

I use four-syllable words in conversation with him. "I'll show you what to wear," he said. With a little manipulative engineering on my part, he gave me a choice of two dresses, both tasteful and both acceptable for *shul*.

"So these are all right?" I feigned surprise. He said they were. "And what about shoes?" I asked, grabbing a pair of worn sneakers from the closet floor. He shook his head and handed me the black high-heeled shoes he's seen me wear with the dresses. "These, Ma," he told me, in no uncertain terms.

"Is this what I should wear because *shul* is a special place, a place where people are supposed to get a little dressed up?" I wanted to know.

"Umm humm," he said. "Yup, Mom. That's how come you gotta wear a dress and shiny shoes."

"Oh," I said. "I understand. Well, thanks for helping me. I really appreciate it. And now, I better hurry."

And off he went.

When I saw him next, he was wearing dress pants, a striped shirt, a sport coat and shoes.

I told him his attire was "particularly and indubitably appropriate for *shul*."

HE EARRING

My husband is the scholarly type. He is currently reading four volumes of history, three works of fiction and two collections of essays.

My husband enjoys these books. By day, he is a high school literature teacher. By night, he writes his doctoral dissertation. He thinks about authors, topics, themes. He analyzes, synthesizes, examines the words, the sentence structure, the vocabulary. My husband is a thinker. A student. And I say this with pride, because I consider scholarship a virtue. Just as plumbing is a virtue.

But my husband cannot plumb.

He is thoughtful, though. He bought me a pair of earrings last Saturday night, for no reason in particular except that we happened to pass an earring stand in the center of the local mall.

"Shall I try them on?" I asked, when we got home from shopping sometime after ten p.m.

My husband answered, "Yes." He said he'd make coffee while I removed the current pair of earrings and donned the new ones.

I complied by leaning over the bathroom sink and staring into the mirror to ease the new earring posts through the holes in my ear lobes. But alas, one of the new earrings slipped through my fingers and down the drain.

So I called the scholar. "Help," I said.

He came running, leaving the coffee to boil on the kitchen stove, eager to help me retrieve the earring.

"I think I see it down there," I told him. "Can you get it? You can get it, can't you?"

My husband knelt on all fours to study the pipes. He poked at the elbow-shaped metal piece that attaches the base of the basin to the outside world. "Soldered tight," he told me, with his lips pursed. He walked off to his workroom to get the pliers and returned with furrowed brow. Again he knelt to probe at the innards of the sink. "Soldered tight," he announced once more.

Then, pulling himself to an upright position, my husband pondered the alternatives. "I could use a wrench, but the pipe might break," he said. "Or maybe I could find something with which to scoop out the earring."

And here, I must take credit for the ingenuity. "Yes," I said, "you can scoop it out with this." I handed him our fish net, the very instrument we use to retrieve deceased pets from the tank.

The net and the stick to which it is attached are made of pliable plastic, easily bendable, perfect for fitting down the sink drain.

So he tried—gingerly at first—inch by inch, as the clock neared midnight. Inch by inch, he eased the net into the drain. "Maybe," he said. "Maybe this time . . . No, not yet."

He was perspiring slightly, but he was determined.

"I'll give it one more try," he whispered (my husband is very gallant in times of distress), jamming the fish net, handle and all, down the drain and through the pipe.

There was a rush of water as the pipe burst and a cascade of bubbles spilled to the floor. A small rivulet began to form under the sink.

Sheepishly, but with a certain amount of dignity, my husband turned to face me. And wearing a smile upon his lips, he uncurled his hand to present me with . . . my earring.

"Thank you," I said. The scholar nodded, and we adjourned to the kitchen for coffee.

In the morning, I called the plumber.

CHICKEN SOUP

Look, it's not the way it sounds.
And she's not either.

I mean she's in there, all right, chopping the vegetables and singeing the chicken. She's standing at my kitchen sink, wiping her fingers on the red plaid towel.

True, she's pinching the salt and dabbing the pepper and sprinkling the paprika among the root parsley and the knob celery, but she isn't only a chicken soup mother.

Not that there is anything wrong with plain chicken soup mothers. It's just that I want you to understand about my mother. She isn't plain.

She is sophisticated, intelligent, attractive. She is a career woman with an office and a secretary. She's got everything going for her, including my father.

So why is she taking five hours out of her day to stir soup in my kitchen?

Because she knows what's important—my supply of chicken soup.

I was out of chicken soup. The last of the containers housing my mother's homemade variety had been served. And both my mother and I understand that without the soup, my children will spend the duration of the winter catching colds.

So I phoned and asked my mother to make a house call. Naturally, she complied.

But it is more than that.

It is the whole ritual of her coming here to set my home smelling like my childhood. It's the fun of opening the back door and having my mother and father (who always helps with the soup) arrive with bags of fresh vegetables and chickens straight from the butcher.

Maybe it is unnecessary. Maybe I could make the soup as well if I really wanted to try. But I don't. I don't ever. I want my mother and father to make their periodic visits to my house for the express purpose of soup.

I want to continue calling them to report my depleted supply—to ask them, please, could they rearrange their schedules to fit in the broth? I want my kids to come home from school on certain unspecified days to find Grandma in her flat soup shoes and Grandpa in his comfortable blue sweater, standing over the stove.

I am not a superstitious person, but this is nothing less than magic—the fragrance, the sound of the bubbling liquid, the children flying through the door on a cold winter afternoon, flinging bookbags on the table to hug their grandparents—and the single spoon dipped solemnly in the pot and passed 'round the room from mouth to mouth spreading only good health and love.

EXASPERATION

Dusk. The weekend was nearing a close. We were taking a walk in the neighborhood. My husband and daughter were ahead, my son and I, a half block behind.

My son was dawdling. "I'll never get it done," he said, scraping his sneakers on the sidewalk. "It's too much. I have to memorize about one hundred words for tomorrow, and I still have to read eight pages in the book for the book report and you're gonna make me do about a million things for the extra credit project, maybe ten million." He pulled in his cheeks and accused me. "I'll never finish my homework tonight."

I felt the knot tighten in my stomach. Sometimes, I can tolerate whining. Sometimes, I can't. On that particular afternoon, I could not.

Here we were, taking a stroll in the evening air, a finale to a lovely weekend, and my son was griping about homework. His dawdle became an angry strut as he worked up a fury against the mountains and hours and maybe months of time it would take to finish the assignments for his second grade class.

I knew he was overdoing it. I knew his homework would be finished in less than thirty minutes. I also knew he'd been playing ball all day and hadn't wanted to stop the fun. I realized he was sorry the weekend was over.

But so was I. And I was sorry he was spending this last fifteen minutes of potential family tranquility with a tirade about homework directed towards me.

So I stopped in my tracks. I put my hands on my hips and yelled, "Why? Why are you doing this? What do you want from me? What am I supposed to do about your homework? Why are you always complaining to me? Hummm . . . just tell me, will you . . . *why?*"

And there he stood, looking square in my eyes, wearing an expression of total disbelief, nodding his head from side to side as if I'd posed a ridiculous question. There he stood, in his genuine Canadian army hat and his navy blue sweat pants, pursing his lips in exasperation.

"*Well?*" I asked again. "*Why do you always complain to me?*"

And he answered simply, "Because you're the mother."

ASHION

She was planning to wear the brown skirt with the burgundy and yellow stripes, the yellow fluorescent sweat shirt, twelve multicolored rubber bracelets, six multicolored rubber rings, two ribbons in her hair and the yellow fluorescent socks.

But the socks were in the wash.

"And the outfit is ruined," she complained.

I tried to be reasonable. "Can't you just wear a different pair of socks today? How about burgundy socks? Or red socks? White socks? Green? How about fluorescent green? They match, don't they?"

I was not being sarcastic. I was being honest. "Fluorescent green is very close to fluorescent yellow," I suggested.

But my daughter was hesitant. "I don't want to look like a clown, you know."

I tried not to snicker. Obviously, the multicolored rubber bracelets, the bright hair ribbons and the fluorescent sweat shirt were a sedate and sophisticated combination. The wrong shade of socks would change the entire look and make a mockery of style.

"Far be it from me . . ." I muttered, exiting the room. "I am simply not-up-to-date on fashion. You'll have to figure out the socks question for yourself."

And then I wondered, is that what they all say? Is that the standard line of all the mothers of all the daughters who are caught up in current fads? Is it what my mother said when I insisted on wearing white lipstick in 1959? I have a photograph of me looking like a ghoul, with the lipstick and small black lines extending the outer edges of my eyes.

At various times, I bowed to fashion and wore poodles on my skirts, four crinolines simultaneously and a large red and white plastic button which said "Skip" (the nickname I chose for myself when nicknames were in vogue).

Did my mother understand the significance of the button or the style? Have parents always muttered to themselves, backing away from the fashion scene, as daughters cast off pinks for fluorescent greens and select sneakers in place of sturdy shoes? Comparatively speaking, I suppose rubber bracelets and yellow socks are less shocking than the length one's son's hair might have been in 1968.

Still, my overall understanding of the change in fashion, my acceptance of the need for youth to rebel where apparel is concerned, does not alter the fact that I can't know for sure which socks match what skirt in 1985.

So lacking a reliable adult resident authority with whom to confer, my daughter sought the next best thing, a sibling within her generation (albeit a male sibling two years her junior). "But at least he knows what goes together, Ma."

And what did the eight-year-old male fashion coordinator select for his sister?

The fluorescent green socks. "Because," he said, "they're very close to yellow."

EXECUTIVE TRAINING

My theory is that mothers make more efficient executives than non-mothers.

I use the term mother loosely to mean man, woman or housekeeper who is in charge of the home front full-time for more than six years. I insist upon six years because until the child is in school all day, the caretaker cannot benefit from the full range of experience in organizing and coordinating after-school activities.

Naturally, a stint at motherhood does not automatically qualify one for the position of executive. However, I truly believe that, given the same academic qualifications, the mother will outrank the non-mother when it comes to efficiency.

It is my contention that the person who has had years of training in bed-making, breakfast-making, braid-making, lunch box-packing, shoelace-tying, jacket-zipping, bookbag-hooking, argument-mediating, all prior to eight a.m., has acquired a priceless ability to function under pressure. Most mothers (and/or fathers/housekeepers) who have rallied to the six-thirty a.m. alarm to dress, feed and dismiss the offspring have learned the meaning of deadline.

And what, in fact, is a deadline if not a yellow school bus? What, honestly, is the difference between the conference with the corporate head at nine a.m. and the yellow school bus at seven forty-eight?

If you have to be there, you have to be there. If you are late for the meeting with the corporate head, he or she may actually wait a minute or so. Someone might offer him a cup of coffee until you arrive. He could peruse his notes, stare out the window, ponder the impending merger.

If you miss the school bus, the entire schedule runs amok. Mother must regroup the children, readjust the mittens, start the car and drive everybody to the appropriate destination—which, mothers realize, is a vast waste of time and thoroughly inefficient.

It is the handling of time, particularly time divided into segments of fifteen minutes or less ("Comb your hair now, you have four minutes until the bus; zip your jacket now, the bus leaves in two minutes"), which gives the mother an edge over the non-mother.

A person who has never had the pleasure of orchestrating team toothbrushing after team vitamin-taking to a combined count of six minutes and two seconds, cannot understand the fine tuning required.

The married or single person who has never mothered lacks the pressure of responsibility necessary to the making of a good executive. The non-parent may arise with the seven a.m. alarm and doze again for twenty minutes if he or she chooses to miss breakfast. But the mother cannot doze, because she is responsible for the nourishment of her babes. It would, therefore, be both inefficient and unfair to oversleep. In addition, unfed children are poor representatives of the "company" a.k.a. family.

If the person who has never mothered sets up a two-hour luncheon for noon and stretches the two hours to three, she can most probably make up the extra hour by staying late at the office.

But is the staying late really necessary? Is it in the company's best interests? Is it expedient? Is it worth the company's while to keep the lights and heat on for the individual who never mothered and therefore spent an extra hour at lunch? Maybe lunch should have taken a total of thirty minutes. Maybe lunch should have been dinner. Is the company paying overtime for naught?

Does the non-mother know or care?

Does the corporate head know?

Perhaps—if she's ever been a mother.

STAGE MOTHER

It wasn't a big part—not much more than a walk-on, really. But I think she stole the show.

She was a rat. And she was my daughter. She wore black

cardboard ears attached to a purple headband, construction paper whiskers stuck on with tape, her own tights, my turtleneck sweater, her brother's socks and one leg of her Grandma's hosiery donated lovingly to the cause and stuffed with Grandpa's argyles to create the tail which trailed behind her on the stage.

She was splendid.

I was proud. Can you tell? I took eleven pictures of the rat during the forty-two seconds of her performance. I stood in my seat and craned forward, blocking the view of those behind me in order to record my star on film.

I was being silly. And happy. But I wasn't alone. There were instamatics and movie cameras in every shape and variety. I could hear people cheerfully introducing themselves as "mother of the bear" and "mother of the ant" and "aunt of the tree."

What self-respecting seventeen-year-old would endure a thirty-minute production by nine and ten-year-olds, if she was not related to the robin? What two-year-old would stay awake long past bedtime, if not for the chance to see her big sister wearing pajamas on the stage?

I believe there is, after all, a kind of internal mechanism which enables parents, even siblings, to cheer for the home run, the piano recital, the portrayal of a rat, as though the events were momentous. Maybe it is this same mechanism which jostles me sometimes, at unexpected moments, to the memory of a newspaper photograph with a mother clutching her starving child somewhere in the world. I can recognize "family," and see my own good fortune.

Anyway, the houselights went on and the rat rushed to me with glowing eyes, ready for the hugs, the kisses, the approval, the love and all those other warm things which keep us going from parent to child and into the future.

SAFE LANDING

I could feel the wheels skim and bump along the runway.
Touch down! Home. I allowed my fingers to release their
grip on the armrests, allowed myself a sigh. We were safe.

Funny that I should feel so relieved, since I'd never really
doubted that we'd make it. Long before take-off, I knew one
day I'd be sitting here writing about the trip. But I was
anxious nonetheless. "What if?" I kept thinking. "Not now,"
I would repeat, silently warding off a crash. "Don't let
anything happen now."

And nothing did. The flight was uneventful. Yet, with
every bout of turbulence, with every suggestion to fasten the
seat belts, I would check the flight attendant. (Her expression would tell me if we were in danger.) We weren't. Still,
I was tense. Mouthing incantations, "Please land, please
land, please land." Reluctant to look out the window.
Suddenly unable to believe that we could stay afloat above
the clouds. Uninformed as to how we were staying up in the
sky. Afraid to ask. Probably not wanting to know.

When I was eighteen, I suppose I knew. Or at least I was
certain the pilot knew. If I even thought about the pilot.
Actually, I don't believe I thought much about anything
then. I simply trusted. At eighteen, I flew back and forth
from college for weekend visits. I flew on small planes with
propellers. I flew on shuttles, on stand-by, in the early
morning, in the middle of the night. I flew with complete
confidence in the ability of the crew and a kind of blind faith
that I was indestructible.

Not long afterwards, as a young reporter, I tackled
stories with the same bravado. Rarely did I question my
ability as a writer. I was either a complete optimist, not too
bright or innocent. Perhaps all three. Whether or not I was

capable of writing a story was never the question. The question was whether or not the public would be capable of reading it. How egocentric of me.

But I think I have become increasingly less so with age—particularly since the birth of my children. I no longer take their existence or mine for granted. And further, my failed first marriage has made me conscious of my good fortune in this lovely second marriage. So soaring there somewhere above the wide Atlantic Ocean with my children and my husband, each buckled in beside me, I felt the weight of what there is to lose if we should go up in flames, nose-dive, if we should break apart in mid-air.

I was glad to have taken the trip, glad for the existence of airplanes. And I am truly thankful to be home.

THE CHILD

I was planning to write about that child left in the car. Shall I force myself to focus on such serious stuff when I feel so good?

This morning, I went shopping. I walked up and down the aisles of the supermarket, picking out corn and tomatoes. I hummed to the Muzak on the speaker system. I saw a couple of mothers pushing children in strollers.

It must have been about the same time last year, when we came across that baby in the car. We were in a small town near Boston. We'd taken my husband's high school class on a three-day trip.

From my window above the typewriter where I am sitting now, I can see the neighbors' yard. The two of them, husband and wife, are working in their garden. Bending, weeding, planting. They've got a bunch of beautiful orange flowers growing under the tree across the way. I wonder what kind of flowers they are.

Anyway, it was warm that day, too. It must have been noon. We had just finished a picnic lunch in the small park on the outskirts of the quaint town. I can recall regrouping the teenagers, counting heads and proceeding in single file along the narrow main street. We were headed for the school van. There were parking meters to our right and a small department store to the left. We stopped to look in the window.

My neighbor is digging in her garden. She has a huge metal shovel and a wheelbarrow. We haven't begun to plant our garden yet. I wonder if we're very late, or is the neighbor early?

I believe it was one of the smaller boys who first spotted the child. "Look at that poor little kid. He must be sweltering," the student said.

I remember turning to follow his gaze. And I saw the youngster, a year, maybe fifteen months old, asleep in the infant seat in the back of the old green car parked on the street. The car windows were shut, and I could see beads of perspiration dripping down the baby's face.

I stepped a little closer to the automobile. The baby looked awfully warm, uncomfortably warm. The other students in our group gathered around to see the little child.

"Poor kid," someone said. "Can't we roll down a window? He'll suffocate without any air. And what kind of person leaves a baby in the car with the doors unlocked? Anybody could take the kid."

But we told the students not to touch the car or the baby. A parent, we said, must be nearby.

There is a cool breeze coming through the screen now. I'm making barbecued chicken for dinner. It smells quite good. And we'll have homemade potato salad, corn and fresh strawberries for dessert. My kids like barbecued chicken.

We waited for the baby's mother to appear. We assumed she must be just across the street, keeping an eye on her sleeping child while exchanging greetings with a neighbor— or down the block making small talk with a friend. We scanned the sidewalk. There was no one in sight.

Five minutes passed. The baby was perspiring profusely. I ran into the department store. Perhaps the mother was there.

But she was not, nor was a father or a babysitter. I asked the store manager to page the person who had left a sleeping child alone outside. Ten minutes passed. No one answered the page.

The child was waking up. In tears.

One of the students in our group ran to find a police officer.

The baby had begun to scream.

Fifteen minutes had elapsed.

I must sweep the driveway when I finish writing this column. Small green and yellow castoffs from the trees have covered the pavement. If it is early enough, I can sit in the sun and read a book before the children get home.

Twenty minutes. Still no parent. The policeman arrived. Moments later, from the other side of the street, nonchalantly walking towards us, holding the hand of a toddler, came the mother of that baby.

"You ought to be ashamed of yourself," someone shouted at the woman. Her expression did not change. The police officer said nothing, as we watched the child's mother open the back door of the car. The baby continued screaming as the woman ushered her older child into the automobile and closed the door. Then, she walked around to the driver's side, got behind the steering wheel and pulled away.

Music

I used to listen to classical music. Until recently, I believed that the sound of violins gave purpose to a mindless task. I would, whenever possible, fold laundry to Vivaldi, wash dishes to Beethoven, drive to work accompanied by Bach or Schubert or Franz Liszt. I would hum along with the melodies and tap out the beat with a finger or a foot. Until recently, I considered classical music a vital aspect of my continuing education. And furthermore, I loved the sound of it.

But I have changed. During the past few months, I have relegated Chopin to a fond memory and loaned my ear to the likes of Avraham Fried. By tuning the radio dial to a particular station, I have discovered a nearly constant flow of Jewish music. I have heard Yiddish tunes in high-pitched whines, melancholy *shtetl* songs in baritone. I have listened to *chazanus*, to modern Hebrew words intoned in *Ashkenaz* and *Sfard*.

I have twirled solo around the living room with dust mop in hand as some *chassidic* band performed unseen within my stereo. I have become familiar with the works of men's choirs and boys' choirs and famous *klezmer* groups. I have begun to distinguish between the mediocre and the great.

Although my knowledge of Yiddish is scarce and my comprehension of Hebrew nearly nonexistent, I am beginning to hear the nuances of sound. Occasionally now, I find that I can understand a word or two, a phrase, a segment of a song. The tone and title often hint at stories told within a piece of music. And lately, I have found that I can grasp a concept or a thought. Words spoken to me by relatives long gone return sometimes in Yiddish lullabies sent forth on airwaves to my home. With eyes closed, I can hear my grandmother humming an odd little European ditty, the memory of which I thought I had forgotten years ago. And the sound of Hebrew music makes me dance—evokes images of desert sands and dark-eyed people I have seen in film clips of the Middle East.

Even if I learn little of the actual languages being sung, even if I never know the meaning of the work, I am convinced that Jewish music has found a place within my soul. What I hear and what I am seem somehow inextricably tied.

And so it is that I no longer have the time or inclination for Tchaikovsky or Strauss. If there is Jewish music to be heard, then I believe that I must listen.

FLEETING FRIENDSHIPS

We were on a tour bus in a strange city, far away from home.

My son and my husband dozed peacefully as the miles passed. My daughter rested her head against my shoulder, watching through the window. My mind drifted. I was being lulled by the motion of the wheels over long, smooth highways.

"Mommy." My daughter spoke gently, but I could hear her smile before I turned to see her face. "Mommy," she said a little louder. "I just made a friend."

I was confused. What? Where? Had I fallen asleep? I checked my surroundings. Nothing had changed. We were still en route, flanked by the same groggy passengers, yawning, stretching, nodding, dreaming their dreams.

"I made a friend," my daughter repeated excitedly. "There." And she pointed through the rear window to another tour bus riding next to ours.

"Do you see her?" My daughter was on her knees, waving.

It took a moment for me to focus, but then I saw the child, another girl, perhaps a year or two younger than my own, with black hair, huge brown eyes, olive skin and a smile as wide as my own child's. The girl pressed her face to the window and waved with both hands as her bus pulled ahead of ours. My daughter changed positions in her seat, craning forward to catch a glimpse of the girl. Waving frantically, smiling merrily, the two of them shared a silent conversation as the distance between the vehicles lengthened. Until, finally, we could no longer see the girl or the bus.

"Where do you think she lives?" my daughter asked. "Do you think I'll see her again? She was nice, wasn't she? How old do you think she was? Did you think she was pretty? Maybe I'll see her again."

"Maybe," I said optimistically. But I felt inordinately sad, overwhelmingly sad, for several reasons. I felt sad because my child's friend had vanished too quickly. Because these little girls, kindred souls with long, dark hair had sensed a bond despite the buses and the panes of glass. They had reached out to one another through the chaos. Because the likelihood of their paths ever crossing again seemed remote, the remoteness was so vast that I could not help but wonder at the number of people sharing the earth and the comparative few with whom we come into contact. Fleeting relationships. Distance which separates. Circumstances.

Sad, as I remembered a similar incident from my childhood. Drinking juice at a motel early one morning, on the way to the seashore with my family. A child my age, ten or eleven, with sandy hair and a freckled nose seated opposite me at the counter. A youngster I spoke to without words. A human being I saw, studied and remembered all these years.

Is it, then, the faces? The eyes which look about to wink? Is it these visages which serve to lock whole scenes within our minds? And is it these secret, abbreviated friendships which pinpoint our relative insignificance and force us to ponder greater things? It is curious how a nameless child on a crowded bus has caused me to remember with clarity (and a sigh) another nameless child in a crowded restaurant on one particular morning thirty years ago.

SEPARATE BUT EQUAL

When I was a child, I used to set the alarm clock early on Sunday mornings so that I could have an hour or two alone with my parents before my sister woke up. There was something special about the private breakfasts with my mother and father. Something important about the closed kitchen door (to keep our whispered conversations from rousing my sleeping sibling). Obviously, the time spent alone with my folks was significant and important. It gave me a sense of intimacy, a feeling of temporary superiority.

Recently, I recalled that feeling.

My daughter awoke at two a.m. from a hideous nightmare. I calmed her with milk and toast. We sat quietly talking in the dark of night, warding off her fears as her brother slept soundly in the next room. I lay next to her on the bed, whispering words of comfort, making her laugh with memories of my own bad dreams. She giggled into her pillow, asking questions, nestling her head into my hair. She wondered aloud at the frightening process of growing up. I held her hand. She said she is glad I am her mother. I hugged her tightly. We fell asleep together before dawn.

Two weeks later, with my daughter off to a friend's house for the night, my husband and I dined together with my son. The boy was suddenly talkative. He entertained us with new songs. He described some recent worries, his plans for the morrow, his evaluation of today. He seemed glad for the chance to take the spotlight, to be the "only child."

It was the proximity of these two events, and the obvious joy expressed by both son and daughter at the opportunity for some individual attention, that has caused me to reevaluate my method of parenting.

Although I have long recognized the importance of separate treatment for separate siblings, perhaps I do not practice what I preach. I believe I have too frequently addressed my offspring as a pair, a couple of kids, a package deal. "Will you two be quiet?" "Will the two of you clean up that mess?" "I'm proud of you both."

For good or bad, I fear I have lumped them together as a team.

But maybe team spirit is no longer in order. I think the time has come to institute a little personalized attention—the kind not grabbed haphazardly following a nightmare, or found solely by the absence of one child from the dinner table. I believe the time has come for me to deal directly (and separately) with the two distinct children living under one roof. And if I offer them both a bit of undivided attention, chances are I'll receive it back. In duplicate.

JUST DESSERTS

For as long as I can remember, my father has been on a diet.

Not a voluntary diet, but a diet designed and enforced by his wife (my mother). As legend has it, my mother agreed to wed my father forty-five years ago when he was a slim, athletically built young man. But, says my mother, shortly after the wedding, her spouse changed shape.

According to my father, it was my mother's cooking which caused his shape to change. My mother, however, claims it was his eating, not her cooking, which made the difference.

In any case, throughout my life, I have known my father to be a handsome but somewhat portly man on a constant diet. "A strict diet," my mother would say. "A diet he will follow to the letter. A diet," my mother has announced periodically, "which is bound to take inches off your father's middle." But the inches have remained. And all the while, I have known the reason why . . . My father cheats.

I have stood by in silence, through rain, sleet, snow and hail, through pineapple upside-down cake, through meat-balls and spaghetti. I, his eldest daughter, have served as mute accomplice to my father as he has snatched handfuls of cookies behind my mother's back. I have seen him down a collection of carrot sticks in full view of his proud wife only to turn around and swallow a mouthful of licorice when she wasn't looking. And I've never said a word. I have, in fact, diverted my mother's attention on occasion, so my dad could take a slice of pie, a bunch of salted nuts, a half pint of chocolate chip mint. And I've done this all with nary a hint to my Mom.

But last week was the clincher. Last week, with no help from me, my father blew his cover. After all this time of successful cheating, my father gave himself away in one mad moment.

There we were, enjoying a Sunday afternoon family get-together at my parents' house. The grandchildren were playing in the back yard, my sister and brother-in-law were reading the paper in the den, my husband and I were engaged in a conversation on the porch, my mother was on the telephone, my sister's dog was asleep in the dining room. And my sister's dog's food, looking remarkably like candy, was sitting in its Tupperware container on my mother's kitchen counter. No one had emptied the food into the dog's bowl because the dog was not hungry.

But my father was. My father, encouraged by the mound of "candy" in full view, cheered by the fact that the family was preoccupied, quietly stuck his hand into the Tupperware container and grabbed a dozen golden tidbits. My father, elated by the thought that no one was paying attention to him, placed all those luscious-looking nuggets in his mouth at once.

And then my father chewed. And then he coughed. And then he yelled. And then he sent the dog food flying, as the family came running from every direction to see my father standing there, shamefaced and apologetic, as my mother roared with laughter, mumbling something about "just desserts."

⌒ HE SOUP POT

You'd think I'd given him gold. But it was only a pot—a dented, old aluminum soup pot destined for the garbage can.

"Want it?" I asked my son.

The response was overwhelming. "Do I want it? Yowee! Hurray! Oh thanks, oh thanks, oh thanks!"

He took the old pot by the handle and banged his way through the back door to call for his best buddy.

I could hear the two of them whooping up a storm of glee over their new-found toy. And I marveled at the predictability of certain combinations—two eight-year-old boys, a pile of dirt, a garden hose and a big old pot. Within minutes, they had converted the dusty ground beneath the apple trees into a massive imaginary stovetop. Their pot held a brew of mud, water, stones and rotting apples. They took turns stirring their soup with a two-foot branch while sprinkling the creation with a pinch of grass, a dash of weeds.

I enjoyed watching them, enjoyed seeing their bony elbows streaked with mud, their sneakers water-soaked and filthy. I found it comforting, in this age of sterile computers, to know that a couple of kids can still get a kick out of good clean fun in the dirt.

During these few weeks, the soup pot has become a

symbol, a statement of values in our home. Since its arrival in the back yard, the pot has served as a catalyst for ingenuity. It has been used to house everything from bugs to rocks. It has been a drum, a chair, a pond for plastic boats. The boys have used it to collect wormy apples littering our yard (for which they were paid one penny per apple). The old pot is inspirational. I have seen it filled to the brim with water, being dragged to the center of the dead end street where its contents were mixed with sand to create mountains for the village of imaginary warriors.

Unlike their bikes which are sometimes left parked in the driveway until morning, unlike the bats and gloves which have been known to disappear in the tall grass, the soup pot is never taken for granted.

At the end of the day, my son and his friend can be seen on either side of the soup pot, each grasping a handle as they reverently carry their treasure to the shed behind our house where it is locked up for safekeeping overnight.

SWEET NOTHINGS

"What's in your mouth?" I asked him.

"Humming," he mumbled unintelligibly between partially closed lips, his left cheek bulging with the "nothing" he was trying to deny.

"There is *too* something in your mouth. Now what is it?"

He shot me a grin and scooted up the stairs, followed by his sister. "Nothing," they said in unison. "Right, Grandma?"

My mother shrugged her shoulders and turned away. I looked questioningly at her. We were seated around the dining room table in my parents' house. The adults had been lingering over coffee when the kids escaped to play.

"But, Ma," I said. "You know very well your grandson has candy in his mouth. What is going on here?"

"Nothing," my mother answered firmly.

I know I have described my mother in past columns as an intelligent, level-headed, reasonable person. She is usually honest, too. But not this time. This time, she was definitely not telling the truth. Grandma and the kids were in cahoots.

I pretended not to care, pretended it didn't matter that my son was chomping on something filled with sugar, even though he knows I don't allow junk food at home. Pretended I didn't know that my mother knew I knew.

But pretending never works. I wanted to find out about the nothing. I guess they wanted to tell me.

Here is the story. Without my ever suspecting it, my children and their cousins have, they tell me, for years now, been privy to Grandma's special hiding place—the top drawer of the dresser in the small bedroom on the second floor of the house.

There, it seems, Grandma has kept under wraps, a ready stash of chocolate bars, lollipops, licorice, mints, gum "and sometimes cookies," say the kids. "There's a whole bunch of stuff in there."

Stuff which I would obviously not allow at home. Stuff which has absolutely no nutritional value, but which, according to my mother, plays a vital role in grandparenting. She says it is not the stuff exactly, but the hiding place, the shared secret with the grandchildren and the "nothing" in my son's cheek which represents a whole lot of something called love.

THE TEACHER

Teaching is hard work. I am not sure I understood that until this summer. Now, I know.

On July 1, I began a part-time job as writing counselor at a county day camp. According to the camp brochure, mine is a specialty, classified along with arts and crafts, music and drama. As a specialist, it is my responsibility to convey the joys of writing to those youngsters attending this camp. Not too difficult a task, I thought.

I am, after all, the mother of two, and I've written for one publication or another for more than twenty years. Certainly, my combined roles as a parent and a writer would suffice as experience for the part-time position of summer camp writing specialist, would it not?

Until one month ago, I thought I could handle the job with ease. In my mental version of this position, I would be the central figure seated in a quiet room surrounded by a handful of children all hanging on my every word, each child eager to pen the great American novel or a radio jingle at the very least.

In my fantasy, I would, by sheer enthusiasm, impart my faith in the power of words. Since I would not affix a grade to their compositions, my students would undoubtedly learn to love to write. I had confidence. Until July 1.

Interesting how for twenty years I've pounded the keys of various typewriters knowing full well that someone would later read and criticize my words. But that critic has never had a face.

A scathing letter or two to the editor pointing out my faults as a writer has, on occasion, hurt my pride. But the printed page has fostered a kind of anonymity about my trade. The newspaper itself acts as a buffer between what I say and what "they" say about what I say.

Not so at summer camp. Suddenly, one month ago, I found myself seated in a quiet room surrounded by a handful of eager children waiting for me to speak. I felt myself wanting desperately to receive the approval of these young people—wanting to hear them say they liked what I was teaching, liked me, liked writing. Yet, without the typewriter at my fingertips to catch the thoughts which travel from my brain, with an audience before me, I was surprisingly speechless. A writer at a loss for words.

I understood, finally, that these youngsters were expecting me to know something, to say something, to impart a piece of knowledge. They are astute, wanting to absorb, always asking who, what, when, where, why, how. They are natural reporters, wanting to learn, questioning me, challenging me with their pencils in hand.

My part-time summer job has been more than camp—it's been a valuable experience. It has taught me a lesson. Teaching is hard work.

 ISCIPLINE

My father requested that I no longer discipline my children (his grandchildren) in his presence. He does not want me to "make an issue" of incidents when he is around. Unless the situation is a true emergency, he has asked that I leave all reprimands till later. He says there is a time and place for everything, that yelling at his grandchildren should take place later, far away from him.

He says this not because he is anti-discipline. In fact, he

quite expects his grandchildren to behave admirably in his presence. He simply cannot stand to see them cry. As a grandpa, he says he has a right to feel this way.

But discipline is a fact of life, is it not? A child gets mud on the new pants five seconds after you've asked him to stay out of the puddle, tells a rather large white lie without batting an eyelash; the child talks back, smashes his sister on the ear, taunts, whines, hollers. The child acts like a child, and I'm supposed to sit by and take it?

"Only if I'm around," says my father.

But why? Why would this man go soft on discipline now? What is a grandpa anyway if not a grown-up daddy? In this case, my daddy. As his daughter, I can recall an incident or two when he didn't wait till later to let me know his feelings. I can remember the morning I refused to eat my eggs, the night I didn't come home till four a.m. My father was pretty angry with me then.

Don't I have as much right to be angry with my children when they break the rules, push me to the breaking point? Aren't I supposed to have a fit, yell my head off, cause panic in the restaurant? Isn't it my prerogative, my duty, to inspire my son or daughter to the heights of temper tantrum to prove a point? And, after the tantrum, to feel mild pangs of guilt? What good is parenting if there can be no warm reconciliation following the battle in aisle three of the Grand Union or in the parking lot of the Sneaker Barn? Isn't discipline (and all its ramifications) an integral part of child-rearing, a necessary evil?

Certainly. But these are rhetorical questions, after all. There is no point in discussing the issue further with my father. He has made up his mind. He does not want me to discipline his grandchildren in his presence. He doesn't want to see them brought to tears. And he expects me to do as he says because he is my father. Which is not the same thing as being a grandpa.

VETO POWER

"Veto."

"Veto?"

"Veto," she said. "You can't print that column."

"But it's so good . . ." I wailed, lowering myself to her eye level. "And I worked on it all morning. You're really not gonna let me run it?"

"Really," said my daughter, holding firm (although I could see tears brimming in her eyes). "You promised."

I sighed. I could, of course, coerce her into submission by playing on her sympathies. I suppose I could bribe her. In fact, I could simply submit the article and hope she won't read it.

But I would not do that because of the promise.

Five or six years ago, when this column began, my children were too young to understand much of what was printed. Even then, I read them the rough drafts of most of what I wrote. And I gave them veto power.

From the beginning, my son and daughter knew they had the right to nix any ideas which they felt would cause them pain if put into print. Only twice has either child used this power, this morning being the second occasion.

So I really can't complain. Both son and daughter have, with knowledge and assent, allowed me to write intimate details about our personal experience with divorce, remarriage, stepparenting. I have quoted my children in tears, in fear, in tantrums, in varying stages of embarrassment and remorse.

Often, my offspring have themselves suggested a column which they felt would touch a responsive chord in some other family. "Write about the time I got the stitches, Mom." Or, "Tell about all the new relatives I have, now that you are married again." Or, "Say we miss Daddy sometimes."

And I have. With their cooperation and permission, I have put my boy and girl on display each week, fifty-two weeks a year, year in, year out. Not without worry. Not without guilt. Not without wondering if this honest exposure to the scrutiny of readers is fair to them. If, despite their approval, they will not be angry with me later for what I write now.

Still, I have proceeded despite my reservations. I have been rewarded with kind words from readers, reassurances from my progeny that what I say about what they say is fine. Most of the time.

But not this morning. "No, sir. Absolutely not. Veto. Veto. Veto."

Thus have I come to write this column instead. The original is neatly folded in two and filed away for posterity's sake. One day, my daughter may enjoy rereading the unpublished words. She alone may find some truth in what I said. But no one else will ever know.

URIM

I was charmed, touched, surprised, gladdened by the spectacle unfolding in the streets. There were queens and kings and clowns and gypsies, hobos and princes, bakers and brides. There were boys and girls and men and women, balloons and music and candy and fruit. And good cheer, high spirits, laughter, broad smiles. In kitchens and living rooms, on front stoops and back yard patios—everywhere in the clear cool air were the sounds of celebration.

Purim.

And we were a part of it. I was a part of it. Delivering *mishloach manos* on a sunlit afternoon.

"What a wonderful idea," I'd said when first my son and daughter had informed me of this custom to present a gift of fruits and sweets. The thought of treats brought back my childhood memories of Halloween. That holiday, so casually celebrated by assimilated American Jews, is famous for the concept of giving. In masks and costumes, children knock upon the neighbors' doors in quest of goodies to be carried home.

"But see, on *Purim*, Ma, Jewish children are supposed to dress in funny clothes and give out packages of candy and stuff to at least two friends," my daughter had explained. "And people might bring their *mishloach manos* to our door. But that is not what counts. What matters is the giving. That's the *mitzvah*," she had said. And I'd been touched by her words and proud of the ease with which she and her brother seemed to comprehend, to accept, to fit into this Jewish way of life.

In the days preceding *Purim*, both my daughter and son discussed the *Megillah* with me. They were thrilled when we accepted an invitation to attend a *Purim seudah* at a teacher's home. They made *hamantashen* with their maternal grandparents. They prepared for a carnival in school. They helped to wrap the packages of *mishloach manos*. And they included me. They encouraged me. They taught me. They enabled me to understand the concept of *Purim*.

And thus was I charmed, touched, surprised and glad-dened by the aspect of *Purim* overflowing in the streets and struck by the fact that I was a participant in this spectacle of joy.

HE SPIDER

Two mothers waited at our bus stop with the children each morning last week. I was one of these mothers. The other had a furry body and eight legs. She sat poised in the center of her gossamer web ten feet off the ground.

To the right of the web and several feet below stands a small rose bush with the remnants of summer blossoms. In the crevice between two adjoining branches we can still see a small cocoon, a tiny bag of silk, perhaps a spider's egg sac. Definitely an egg sac, we have decided.

While I watched for the school bus, kept my offspring company, protected them from harm at the street corner, I believe this mother spider was doing the same for her unborn young.

My children and I saw her pose, unmoving, in the center of the web as an early morning drizzle clung in beads to the thin threads surrounding her. We worried as she swung precariously from a newly-woven orb above the driveway between two fir trees near the bus stop. We thought a passing car could easily unhinge the flimsy supports of her intricate trap.

We studied the small pieces of debris and insects that unthinkingly attached themselves to the spider's design.

These items, we knew, would later serve as dinner for our friend.

We contemplated nature, remarking on the vast array of life within our world, the differences which make us each unique. Was it difficult to have eight legs? we asked. For people that would mean a lot of socks. And did a spider go to spider school to learn his trade or did he know it from the moment of birth?

Through our daily observation, we came to understand that this spider wove a new web nightly while we slept. For every morning her perfect creation would hang, gently swaying in the breeze, from a branch slightly to the right or left of the branch on which it had hung the day before.

We talked to our spider. Asked her questions. We named her.

Yesterday, she allowed us to watch her weave. Maybe we were earlier than usual, or she a bit later. Could she have chosen to delay her work until we arrived?

We stood quietly, afraid to talk lest we scare her. She dangled before us, like a parachutist clinging to transparent silk, swinging her body to the center of the web, attaching the thread, climbing once more, swinging down again. We encouraged her softly in our own language, wondering if she could hear our compliments, marveling at her handi-work.

By accident, we jostled her guide wire and watched her freeze as the vibrations warned her of possible danger.

Then the school bus came, and we left our friend.

At the day's end, we checked to see that she had completed her web. She had. We said good-bye and waved to her as we walked home from the bus stop. "See you tomorrow," we assured the spider yesterday.

But this morning, our spider was gone.

OPINIONS

"Can you see the indentation in her chin?" the orthodontist asked.

"Yes," I lied.

"Well, it shouldn't be there, should it?"

"Of course not," I answered, straining harder to comprehend the incomprehensible.

"Now turn to the side, and show your mother your jaw."

My ten-year-old cheerfully did as she was told, offering me a profile view from both sides and a front view of her apparently erroneously indented chin.

"The teeth look pretty good," said the orthodontist, "but when we adjust that jaw, her whole face will change!"

I know the comment was intended as an incentive, something positive for mother and child to envision for the future. A different smile and a better bite to boot.

"But I like her smile," I managed to say. I am always intimidated by medical people. However, in this case, my daughter's birthright was at stake. She has inherited my mouth, and nobody ever told me my bite was bad or suggested that our family jaw could cause headaches in the coming years.

Still, the orthodontist insisted that the malformation was genetic. "Turn to the side, Mother, and let me see your mouth." And, "Hummm." And, "Hummm . . ." And, "Hummm . . ."

So I paid for the consultation and left the office wondering whether in decades hence, my daughter would be furious with me for allowing this doctor to "change her smile" should I agree to the dental work. Or would she blame me for instigating jaw-related headaches should I nix the procedure?

I decided it was best to seek a second opinion. "Now, do not tell the new orthodontist that we have seen another orthodontist," I advised my child. "Just let him examine your mouth, and he will tell us what he thinks."

The orthodontist thought. And thought. He moved my daughter's chair up and down. He adjusted the overhead light. He searched within her mouth, checked her teeth, her gums, her jaw, her bite. He said "hummm" and "hummm" and a word or two about genetics. Then, finally, in the same serious tone of voice that the first orthodontist had used, he offered an entirely different diagnosis. Where the first had said the teeth looked pretty good, the second thought not. Where the one had said the jaw was off kilter, the other said the jaw was just fine. Naturally, their plans of attack to right the differing wrongs were entirely opposite. About the only thing the two agreed upon was the fact that "when we finish the job, her whole smile will change."

But I like her smile. Which is one of the reasons I have made yet another appointment to visit a third orthodontist for an opinion on those pearly whites.

THE CLOCK

The broken clock was my idea. Perhaps that's why it didn't work.

"Look at this," I said to the two eight-year-old boys (my son being one of them). "Here's an old clock. How would you guys like to take it apart?"

They looked at me with expressions of total apathy. They looked at one another and shrugged their shoulders.

"Okay," they finally said, as though they were doing me a favor, humoring me. "But why?" they wanted to know.

It was difficult to answer. You see, months ago, I had been present at a school function when the science teacher suggested "hands on" experiences for our offspring. She had touted the merits of real life experimentation with material objects. And I'd heartily agreed, promising myself right then that, should the occasion arise, I would rescue my children from the depths of boredom with some fabulous suggestion, such as a broken clock.

"It's yours," I told the two. "Better than a new toy. Enjoy yourselves."

They giggled, less in anticipation of the project ahead than at my apparently unwarranted enthusiasm. But they are good children after all, and they agreed to comply.

I left them happily, priding myself on the sure success of two boys, a broken clock and a screwdriver. Why, they'll have it apart and back together again in no time, I told myself.

But I was wrong. For several reasons.

First, these boys are not accustomed to dismantling objects, working or not. Maybe this is the fault of the parents. Have I been neglectful in not allowing my son to check the innards of the electric typewriter and the piano? Have I spent too much time on "don't touch that, please, you'll break it," to make exploration a possibility? Then, too, in retrospect, I suppose I should have mentioned that taking something apart is only half the fun. Trying to put it back together is the real challenge.

In any case, I failed on both counts. My son and his pal managed to disengage the face from the clock. And then they fought because there were two boys and one set of clock hands. They figured out how to unhook a variety of plastic wheels, screws and pins, but they argued over who would get to keep the larger items and who the smaller. Finally, they came to me in utter frustration and asked for a second broken clock. "Cause it's not fair to have only one broken thing."

Thus went the afternoon until, eventually, I heard them heading for their jackets and the great outdoors. I did not try to stop them. Instead, I placed the remains of their project in a plastic bag and threw it in the garbage can, wondering where I had gone wrong. Should I have given them a watch instead? Or an old radio? Maybe a bike with twisted spokes? An ailing car?

THE BAKERY

Empty. And dark inside although it was mid-morning. The door had opened easily to my touch. I entered, struck by the dinginess.

A black-haired stranger stood in the center of the floor. He held a broom.

"What happened?" I demanded to know.

"They retired," he said.

My stomach turned over. "Oh, no."

"Yes," came a small voice from the shadows. I turned to face an elderly woman in her oversized gray coat. Her wrinkled face was framed in a dark kerchief. She clucked her tongue against the roof of her mouth. "Tsk, tsk," she sounded, shaking her head from side to side. "A shame."

I could not answer. I followed the woman outside into the parking lot. The wind blew stray papers against the storefront as we parted ways, continuing to ponder our loss. I suppose we two were just a couple among the many customers who pushed their way through the glass doors unknowingly that morning a few weeks ago, expecting to be met by the usual fragrance of freshly baked bread, expecting Molly wearing her smile, anticipating business as usual, shocked to sudden realization by . . . silence.

Tears pricked at my eyes. I hadn't even said good-bye.

One wouldn't think the closing of a neighborhood bakery could have such an impact on me. I don't even possess much of a sweet tooth. Although I will sorely miss the cookies and the pies and the warm *challah* on Fridays, I will, in time, I suppose, adjust to other wares. No, it is not simply the edibles I will miss. It is the service. The kind words, the concern, the pleasant story, the attention, the taste of this or that, the special nod, the introduction to a granddaughter, the hand-drawn sign announcing a son's wedding. And overheard conversations between Molly and her husband, the baker, the man she calls "the prince." It is Molly's rosy cheeks that I will miss.

And the atmosphere inside the bakery. I will recall ducking in out of the rain to the good smell of rising dough and the sound of laughter bubbling up from customers as we waited in line for our muffins, cakes and Molly's advice.

I am glad my children had a chance to know Molly. She taught them a fine lesson in dealing with the public. She understands, perhaps innately, the value of a smile. For her efforts, I hope she knows how fondly we think of her.

I will miss the bakery for its fine sweets and for its sweet owners. I wish Molly and her prince the very best. A good life with all the icing.

$\mathcal{M}$EMORIES

A week ago, I said to myself, "Your file cabinet is a mess. There is not a hair's-breadth of space for one more manila folder. You can't cram another sheet of paper within, on top of, or next to your collection of paraphernalia. It is time to discard the extraneous.

"Self," I said, "get rid of your junk."

And I couldn't have agreed more. It is uncomfortable, probably unprofessional, to maintain such a disorderly file cabinet. "Therefore," said I, "henceforth, and until the job is completed, you will devote fifteen minutes daily to a perusal and purging of your useless papers."

But I cannot seem to comply.

For example, in the file folder marked *Directions*, I found the invitation and notes on how to get to Ruth's daughter's fourth birthday party. If my daughter is nearly eleven, so too must Ruth's be. How quickly the time has slipped away. I stared at the colorful card in my hand, remembering where Ruth once lived, wondering what has become of her and the daughter whose party my child attended. When the two girls were friends, I was newly separated from my first husband. I was frightened but determined to adjust. And now look at me, I thought. Married, with a house and kids growing up. I hesitated only momentarily before refiling the invitation in the manila folder—too many memories attached to throw that one away. The little card is a symbol of a bygone era in my life.

Nor could I heave the paper telling me how to get to the restaurant in New York where my present husband and I dined once, early on in our relationship. I could not discard the notations scribbled on torn napkins, the backs of shopping lists, old envelopes. The right turns and left turns, the stop signs and landmarks set down in ink and pencil during the past seven years to help me locate homes, businesses, apartments, relatives, friends. In most cases, it is not the information which is meaningful to me, but the images evoked. Somehow, the *Directions* seem worth saving.

In the folder marked *Letters*, I feel I must hang on to those written by friends I've known since arriving in the county. Letters I began filing when I purchased the cabinet. How could I even think of destroying a note from the elderly couple who lived across the hall from us before they retired to Florida? They taught my children how to make fudge on Sunday mornings when I was living in the small apartment with my son and daughter.

In the *Vermont* folder, I found brochures from a vacation the children and I took, in our life between two marriages. The printed advertisements conjured scenes worth retaining.

Old postcards from friends, old phone bills and doctor bills, old frayed papers gave way to intact memories encased in my gray file cabinet.

And this before I began to rifle through the more than two hundred and fifty columns I've written over the years, or the half-completed novels, the unpublished short stories, the reams of thoughts I've scrawled on pages at odd moments and tucked away for another time.

That time is now. The fifteen minutes, the thirty minutes, the hours I have spent this week poring over the words and feelings jammed together in this crowded two-drawer metal box, have given me pleasure.

Therefore, I have decided I cannot discard the extraneous because, for now at least, there is none. There appears to be just one solution to this problem. I will simply have to buy another file cabinet.

OO MUCH SOUP

"Are you nervous, Ma?" she said.

I was startled. "What makes you ask?" I needed to know. "What makes you think I'm nervous?"

My daughter said it was the soup. Her brother, sitting side-saddle on the kitchen chair, nodded in agreement. "You made way too much, Mom," he said, "didn't you?"

It would have been difficult to deny, considering the twelve plastic containers lining the counter, each filled with a quart of vegetable soup. And there was yet a half pot left.

But how had they known? Had my children overheard me muttering to myself about the overabundance of soup? Or had they simply seen the ludicrousness themselves? Had they realized that no six people could possibly consume twelve quarts of soup as an appetizer for one meal?

I was forced to answer, "Yes, I'm nervous."

A part of me cringed at my own admission. Wouldn't it have been better to pretend that the youngsters had misunderstood? Shouldn't I have told them I'd intended to freeze the soup? Maybe I should have said I was feeling fine, in total control, that they'd been imagining things.

But I couldn't pretend. It was too late to cover up. I had been caught in the act, ladle in hand. My children deserved to know.

Then they asked me why. "How come you're nervous, Mom?"

And I realized the time had come to tell the truth. So I said the words. I said, "I'm nervous because your grandparents are coming to visit. Because no matter how much I love them or they love me, they are still your father's mother and father. And your father is my ex-husband, which makes things awkward . . . at first."

My children mused silently for a while, poking gingerly at ancient wounds—seeing something they had not seen before.

"You want to make sure they still like you, don't you?" my daughter asked.

I answered, "Yes."

"And they probably want you to like them, too."

"Yes," I said. "And now you have a wonderful stepfather who is not their son. No matter how much they may like him, they probably will feel strange when we all sit down to dinner together and the man at our table is not their child."

"Yes," my children said.

"You want them to feel comfortable here, don't you?" asked my son.

"And I want my husband to feel comfortable, too," I answered him. "But mostly, I want you to feel comfortable with your grandparents. They live far away. You only see them once or twice a year. I want the four of you to have a wonderful time when you're together, and wanting that makes me nervous. And that's how come I made too much soup."

 EAR

"Can we drive to Chicago?" he asked, placing emphasis on the word "drive."

"Why?" I wanted to know. We had been discussing the possibility of a family trip to the Midwest this summer. We hadn't even touched on a mode of transportation.

"Because I don't think flying is too safe right now," my

son explained. "I wouldn't want to take a chance."

I was surprised. A year ago, he couldn't wait to try the friendly skies, and now this potential pilot was telling me he'd rather take the car.

Silently, I reviewed some probable causes for his sudden fear of flying. Maybe the Challenger explosion had jarred his faith in aircraft, or the widely reported number of mid-air crashes in 1985. Perhaps my boy had somewhat prematurely developed a sense of his own mortality. It could have been that all of these reasons helped to shape his current feelings. But my son told me there was something more. My child, by his own admission, told me he does not want to take a plane because he is afraid of terrorists.

And my distaste of the issue caused me to respond too briefly to his fears. I reassured him with a pat on the head. "We'll drive," I said, "but it has nothing to do with terrorism."

Now, in retrospect, I wonder if I ought to be more specific. Should I let him know that fright is exactly the result towards which the terrorists strive? That if we give in to fear, we are, in essence, giving in to terrorism? Shall I say that terror itself is a lethal weapon against which only right can win? That we must believe in the better side of humanity and not be cowed by the weaker side? Should I, while touting courage, admit that as a mother, I have envisioned myself flinging my body over his or his sister's body to avert a spray of bullets shot wildly, as we waited in line for a plane to Chicago, Rome or Israel?

Shall I let him know that more people are killed in automobile accidents daily around the world than are killed annually by terrorists? And yet, I find those statistics meaningless when I think of skyjackings and snipers.

As in so many other instances of late, I realize the simple

answers do not suffice. I am a parent; therefore, I have a responsibility to my child and his generation. I must let him know that terror cannot reign. And yet I understand his feelings, because I, too, would prefer to take the car.

SHOELACES

The salesman handed my nine-year-old his forty dollar pair of sneakers, two pairs of shoelaces and an instruction manual on how to tie them.

My son was thrilled.

I was less ecstatic. Not so much because of the price, but rather because of the manual. There is something absurd about following printed and illustrated directions on how to tie one's shoelaces. The pamphlet seemed to epitomize that old phrase about making a mountain out of a molehill.

I scanned the copy. It was, indeed, a complicated listing of six possible ways of shoelace-tying, involving anywhere from two to seven laces per shoe. How silly, I thought. How telling. Through the miracle of progress, we can now say, even the simple things in life are difficult.

One might have thought that the advent of Velcro would have eliminated the need for the shoelace entirely. But the lace-tying manual is proof that simplicity is not necessarily fashionable or easy.

As I read through the instructions, it occurred to me that a similar guide might one day be written about telling time. While digital watches are currently in vogue, it is highly possible that the old-fashioned hands and face variety of clocks could regain popularity. Then, as in the case of the shoelace, we might find it necessary to print directions for first-timers.

I wonder, if we work with calculators long enough, will we forget how to use a paper and pencil? Will we need a beginner's guide to simple addition? Have we gotten so used to detail that we are lost without our typed instructions?

Are we, by rapid technological advance, prematurely eliminating some necessary steps to progress—then back-tracking to pick up the pieces (and tie the laces)? Maybe we should learn to crawl before we walk. Or we could simply wait for the operating instructions to come out in print.

OYS

Bugs. Everywhere. Creepy bugs, ants, spiders, crawly black beetles. In the fruit bowl, in the dryer, behind the tissue box, in my daughter's pajama drawer. Waiting there for me to jump in disgust each time I see one where one should not be. Sitting there mindlessly, dumb to my gasps.

And I am not afraid of bugs, not squeamish about insects in their natural habitat. Spiders weaving webs among the branches of a tree. Ladybugs perched in the rosebushes. Ants beneath the rocks. I do not even mind a few, searching for crumbs on the kitchen floor. Ordinarily, I see these creatures as a part of nature's plan. Curious. Fascinating. Moths on a screen door in summer. Bees hovering near the clover. I like grasshoppers, turquoise caterpillars. I have held live worms barehanded to show them to my children.

But I cannot stand the bugs in my washing machine, the ones on the oranges at breakfast, the group on the dresser top. They make me suck in my breath and shiver. And they aren't even real.

They are plastic. Little black plastic bugs given to my nine-year-old son one week ago by his ten-year-old friend. Brought home from school in the pocket of his jacket, dropped en masse on the kitchen table for me to see. Displayed as a source of pride, that an older boy would bestow such a magnificent gift upon a younger schoolmate. A cluster of prizes to be treasured in and of themselves.

"Don't they look real, Ma?"

Days later, as I continue to find them placed throughout the house, as my son continues to deny any part in the act, I find myself smiling at the boy's antics. Where did he learn this game of ants and spiders? How does he know about toads and frogs? He reminds me of Dennis the Menace, Huckleberry Finn.

And I am not sorry, I'm not stopping him. I suppose, by condoning the game, in some sense, I'm encouraging him.

Would I tacitly encourage my daughter were she to plant bugs in my bed? I believe I would. But she has not. She is too busy combing her hair, giggling, telling secrets to her friends. And I am not dissuading her. I am allowing the insects and the secrets to flourish here as I become increasingly convinced of sugar and spice and everything nice and that boys will be boys, etc.

THE TRAIL

I have spent the morning thinking about Hansel and Gretel. You see, I believe they made a mistake. They never should have used bread crumbs. They should have used paint. Blue paint to be specific.

These last few hours of contemplation have made me realize with absolute certainty how misguided were those waifs. If the two had simply approached me for advice, I could have offered the ideal solution. Of course, they would have had to wait until today to speak with me regarding the matter of trail-blazing, since it is only recently that I have come to understand the significance of it. But now that I have seen the light, I am, literally overnight, an expert.

It began two weeks ago when, in homage to spring and the overflowing back yard shed, my husband and I commenced a seasonal cleanup. We bagged some fifteen piles of last fall's leaves, heaved a sack of ancient pipes and unwanted cabinet doors and emptied the shelves of half-used paint cans, the contents of which had come with the purchase of our house.

We piled the debris along the hedges in front of our home to await the monthly trash pickup. And there it remained, undisturbed until last night. And then, not realizing that the cans had rolled under the tires, I accidentally drove over these containers which, haphazardly sealed as they were, burst open in a flurry of color to adorn the shrubs, the lawn and the entire street in pastel shades of bluish-white.

Personally speaking, I like the color blue and might actually have left the paint to coagulate in a five-foot-wide puddle on the street. But I thought the neighbors might object.

So I borrowed a hose and a couple of extra children, two brooms and a bucket. With the help of my parents, who happened by, we cleaned the road by flashlight as the oil-based paint flowed ever onward towards the end of the road.

By ten p.m. and the light of the moon, the street looked acceptable to my eyes. I was cold, wet, tired and less than charmed by the stray dogs and squirrels which had stopped to watch the goings on. In short, I had had enough.

Thus, it was not until this morning, when I walked outdoors into the harsh light of day that I noticed the pale blue trail the size of a car tire leading from my driveway to the very top of the block and straight out onto Main Street.

And that is how I have come to remember Hansel and Gretel.

 ESPONSIBILITY

My fault. Again.

But this time, I accept the blame. After the whimpering accusations, the hostile retorts, the lame excuses to prove that it was I, not she, who had caused the problem in the first place, I finally decided to take responsibility.

My eleven-year-old daughter was, to put it mildly, in hot water because she had left her dirty clothes on the bathroom floor after her shower, had not put the games away after playing with them on the living room rug, had not returned her pocketbook to its hook in the closet, had not put her bicycle back in the shed for the night, but had left it, instead, to rust or be stolen in the center of the driveway. Had not, despite the late hour, brushed her teeth in preparation for bed.

So I yelled. I ranted. I threw her bulging plaid pre-teen pocketbook on the floor, muttering about its ridiculous contents. I removed four wrinkled shirts and two skirts from her closet and, clutching them in my hands, issued a spontaneous lecture on the merits of replacing one's clothes neatly on shelves, in drawers and on hangers. I said, to be exact, that "I have too much to do to iron clothes that are a mess because of the way you handle them." I said, "Next time you tell me something needs ironing, you can iron it yourself."

And do you know what she said to me?

She said, "Okay." She said, "I'm trying, Ma."

And I knew she was right. Ninety percent of the time, maybe ninety-nine percent of the time, I fold the shirts and skirts, I put the bike away, I clean up the bathroom after the children's baths, because it's easier. Somehow, I always figure it takes longer to ask or tell the children what I want them to do than it does to complete the task myself.

If one or the other of my offspring asks for a glass of milk, for instance, I usually get it. Not because he or she can't get it himself, but because it will be quicker if I get it. In that instant before I decide to run to the refrigerator, I envision the nine-year-old climbing on a chair to reach the cabinet to remove a glass (which he might break). I see him climbing on a different chair to remove the container of milk from the top shelf of the refrigerator. I hear him having to call me anyway to pour. Or worse yet, pouring it himself, and spilling the entire contents on the counter and floor.

But I am wrong. Wrong in not allowing him to try, wrong in always imagining disaster, especially wrong in doing things for the children that they could do for themselves and wrong in being angry when, suddenly, I decide they should have been doing something all along.

As I perceive it, the solution to my problem will require persistence on the part of the children and patience on my part.

When, as in the case of the rusting bicycle, my daughter tells me she did not put it away because I told her she had to come in for dinner right that minute, I must remember to hold the meal in favor of allowing her the extra time it will take to wheel the bike to the back yard shed.

And when, following her bath, she tells me she did not pick up her clothes just yet because she was getting into pajamas first, I must remember to give her an additional few minutes before swooping down on the sopping towels and socks.

On the night of my recent tirade, I ultimately told my daughter that I will accept some of the blame for her actions if she will accept the results of my solution.

"The fact is," I said, "I want you to be a responsible human being, and I guess the only way to insure that is to teach you responsibility. So from now on, I will tell you what I would like you to do and I'll try hard not to do it for you . . ."

And not unexpectedly, she said, "Okay."

ETTING GO

What's twenty minutes? No time. Or, forever?

A scant two weeks earlier, we had given her permission to peruse the neighborhood on her bike—providing she was with a friend and providing she followed the basic rules of safety.

Like getting home before dark.

Maybe we hadn't actually specified the coloration of the sky, but it was certainly implied. After all, the move from driveway and back yard bicycling to the run of the neighborhood is a major leap in faith. We trust her. She is trustworthy.

And proud. The newfound freedom had settled well on her slight frame. She had been sitting tall in the bike seat peddling hard up the hill, shouting bye with a casual wave of the hand. But I knew she was thrilled. Glad to feel the wheels turning rapidly beneath her as she and her friend turned the corner. Gone. Detached and moving forward towards independence.

And I, as always when bumping up against a milestone, felt the impact. The pride in having reared her thus far to be healthy and bright and capable of maneuvering a two-wheeler through these sidewalkless suburban streets. Pride, and a wariness at this much-used world impinging upon my daughter's innocence.

But I had begun to let her go. After school, on weekends and then, finally, one evening when the sky was still light and the air thick with heat.

I told her the hour I wanted her back. Perhaps she hadn't heard. I had named the time more for my sake than for hers, knowing instinctively that I would not worry (could not worry) about her whereabouts until the designated moment of her return.

And even then, even when the hands of the clock moved forward two, five, ten minutes, I did not give in to the fear. It wasn't until the sun had vanished totally, until a kind of chill settled in on the night or my imagination, that I began to panic—calling a friend at whose home she might have stopped, asking the boy across the street to check the blocks nearest our house, convincing my husband to drive in circles through the neighborhood. It wasn't until dark that I started to worry, and I worried brilliantly until she rode up panting, twenty minutes late.

And she apologized. Said she hadn't realized how quickly comes the night. Said she knew I'd be worried. Said she would never again stay out past dark. Said all those things which proved to me that she is old enough to ride her bicycle in the neighborhood, old enough to understand when she has made a mistake and old enough to sometimes make her mother feel very old indeed.

BOOK FOUR • REFLECTIONS

REFLECTIONS

INTRODUCTION

The balance began to shift. Little by little, *Yiddishkeit* weighed more heavily on the scale. I felt compelled to take the initiative, to make decisions. I was less self-conscious, more serious. I had discovered something.

"And the teacher said we should come for *Shabbos Chanukah*, Ma. The teacher said her kids want us there. And her husband wants us there. So can we go . . . oh please, oh please, Ma. Can we?"

"Go to the teacher's house for *Shabbos*?" Can we come in out of the chill December air to enter a home filled with laughter and warmth? Can we watch the teacher as she lights the *Shabbos* candles? Follow her into the kitchen as she scoops out the *cholent* from a crock pot? Listen to the lovely *Shabbos* songs? Share the *mitzvah* of *Shabbos*? Observe as her children light their *Chanukah menorah* on the window sill? And will we return home on Saturday night to light our own *menorah*, to hear our children with smiles in their voices and lights in their eyes ask if we might, "please, oh please, keep

Shabbos from now on?"

This was a time for positive answers. Commitment. Unity. A joyful, beautiful, somewhat pious, perhaps self-righteous time, and a time tinged with pain inflicted inadvertently by us upon those most affected by our sudden change in life style.

"Why?" however was no longer a relevant question.

We had become part of something magnificent and we were not alone. Suddenly, we found ourselves surrounded by friends we had not known before. We discovered the *shomer Shabbos* family around the corner, the couple with young children living just two blocks away, the elderly man who passed us weekly on his way to *shul*. With our decision to change the focus of our days came the realization that a *shomer Shabbos* community existed right within our neighborhood. We were thrilled and eager yet somehow not surprised. We simply opened our doors and a new world entered our lives.

HOME

To each his own.

Suddenly, the cliche has meaning.

We returned last night from a day in the city. A day spent with friends and relatives in living rooms and kitchens. A day of cake and coffee, children and traffic, honking horns and gritty air, city streets, congestion, people everywhere.

A day of brick houses, like upright humans with shoulders squashed against one another. No trees, few birds, no squirrels. Men and women in cars and trucks, on sidewalks, in shops, in streets. Shouting, nodding, muttering, moving. No grass, just patches of yard with solitary lawn chairs and single clumps of weeds abutting other yards on either side.

And me, watching the action the way I would watch a movie, an outsider looking in. Me, holding my children's hands, maneuvering through the congestion, perspiring in the heat, tasting the city in my mouth, feeling it in my head, smelling the smoke and the food and the dust rising from the sun-heated pavement, wondering why anyone would want to live in such commotion.

Yet, I know they do. They tell me in no uncertain terms that they find the silence of suburbia quite deafening. Better, they say, to hear the wheeze of buses spewing forth exhaust than to listen to the wind.

"Better to shop," they say. Far better to have, within a stone's throw, a half-dozen markets, clothing stores, bakeries. Better to look out the window at humanity regrouping endlessly.

Better? More fulfilling than the grass and the trees? (I have a bird's nest in my backyard.) Can their street vendor compare to the ant hill under my porch? Don't they understand the value of the purple flowers blooming near my window?

"But the pulse is here," they would tell me. In the people. The rich ones, the poor ones, the nameless faces parading by, each representative of the family, a culture, an entire generation.

And what about my bumblebees? My pine cones? I need the sounds of lawn mowers and crickets as much, I suppose, as they need the sounds of passing trains.

So we part friends, taking our leave in crowded doorways. And I drive away, wondering if the sun likes shining on the city streets—secretly certain that it prefers a different, less harried domain—understanding fully that phrase about no place like home.

THE JOKE

"No soap, radio."

Those were the words. The punch line to a joke which I no longer recall. Actually, the joke was a trick, a meaningless story with a nonsensical finale to which people either responded with gales of laughter (thereby proving their ignorance) or blank stares (thus showing they understood).

If one feigned comprehension of the humor hidden in that joke, one was obviously a fool. And, making one look foolish was precisely the point of the tale.

I was age twelve when I first heard the line, "No soap, radio." The speaker uttered the words knowingly at the small crowd of friends gathered 'round to watch me. Those already privy to the game winked slyly at one another. Several chuckled, egging me on, "Get it? D'you get it?"

I did not. I was embarrassed at my lack of comprehension, but I simply did not find anything funny in that line. I could not laugh. I was humiliated thinking I'd missed the point.

Later, when they explained the joke of the joke, I felt partially vindicated. However, none of them, neither the joke teller nor the crowd of friends, ever understood the depths of my dilemma.

This non-joke with its non-humorous punch line was, as far as I could tell, no more or less funny than the hundreds of other jokes I had heard previously. Or thereafter. With nearly four decades of knee-slappers lodged somewhere in my brain, I can finally admit that rarely, if ever, do I get the point. Or if, by some quirk of fate, I do get it, I never feel moved to laughter. I can never repeat the joke.

But I am not humorless. Always, even when the rest of them were howling uncontrollably at some inane quip which passed me by, I would find myself laughing at their laughter. I can usually see a joke—just not the same joke others might see. I have even found humor in my position on the sidelines, poker faced and uncomprehending as the jokes roll by. I seem to prefer life itself, unedited and constant, to the contrived one-liners of a comedian. And until several years ago, I thought I was alone in my view. I believed that I was destined to spend my days as my own best audience, my confidante, my own source of cheer in matters of humor.

And then, I met my husband. After all this time, I met a serious, studious, wonderfully funny individual who makes me smile and giggle and laugh until I cry. And joy of joys, he thinks I'm funny, too.

THE PICTURES

I cover my hair now when I light the candles. I do this primarily because of the pictures in the book. Even before I noticed the illustrations, I carried with me a vision of the way it would feel to be thusly clad. But the drawings gave me the courage to begin.

For months now, I've been reading the English version of the prayers and songs we recite on *Shabbos*. While the rest of the family happily wends its way through the Hebrew letters on the right hand pages of the little *bentcher*, I have had to rely almost entirely upon the left-hand side. It is there, in bold-faced type, that the author tells me when to stand and when to sit and what is being said or sung. And it is there on page ten, under "Kindling of the Lights," that I found my inspiration.

In shades of fuchsia and mauve against a background of white, she stands not two inches high, eyes shaded by her hands. Before her, candles glow. Above her shines a blazing sun, behind and beside her float glittering orbs—moons, planets, tiny stars. Her lips are pursed in quiet concentration as she contemplates the creation of the world. Perhaps she comprehends. I study her face and the face of the woman in blue on page sixteen of the little book. Here she waits at a clear high window, a child on either arm. Candles, *challah* and a cup of wine decorate the table in the forefront of the scene. And as the woman waits, looking out into the night, I, the reader, am invited to look in. And further, I am asked to see the husband as he arrives from *shul*. Against a fan of light, his *shtreimel* and *kapote* make a curious silhouette in the center of the page. He faces forward, while behind him and in silence hover two large angels with blue-gray wings.

I am captivated by these simple drawings which hint at breadth and depth. I am intrigued by the sounds hidden in the soundless page and the fragrance implied in the loaves of woven bread. The static images move in my mind. I feel more than I see. There is a warmth there. And a sense of expectation. Peace. And knowledge. Consistency and trust. And there is comfort in the timeless cycle. The pictures make me want to climb inside the pale blue room where the woman wears a look of serenity on her face and a clean white shawl upon her head.

CELEBRITY

She was sincere. Really sincere. She came up to me, arms outstretched, smiling. "You made my day," she told me. "Honestly. I feel as if I know you. I've been reading your column for years. You don't know how happy I am to meet you."

"Me?"

She nodded, beaming.

I was flattered and embarrassed. A part of me wanted to hug her for the compliment, another part wanted to hide behind the couch.

We were standing nose to nose in the home of a mutual friend, a friend whose party we were attending and who had, moments before, introduced us to one another.

"I sometimes cut out your columns and save them," the woman told me.

I grinned at that, trying hard to show humility, wanting to accept her praise graciously, feeling my head swell with pride as she called her husband over to meet me. "This is the one who writes the columns," she said

I nodded, feeling silly and elated. How strange to think that strangers know my name.

I have, on occasion, been noticed by local shopkeepers. "You're her, aren't you?"

The parents of my children's classmates. "I wondered if you were the one in the paper."

And strangers standing behind me in line at the check-out counter. "Loved the one you wrote last week, honey. It is you, isn't it?" (Staring into my eyes.) "Thought so."

I have even been told by a few people that my columns decorate their refrigerator when the topic is particularly appropriate. And of course, I have had my share of those who, upon first meeting me, feel compelled to critique my life. "What did you do that to your kid for? And why did you have to write about it?" Or the others who tell me in no uncertain terms that they have read and disagreed with every column I have written.

Yet even these critical sorts give me a lift. At least someone is reading, I always tell myself.

For the most part, however, my relationship with the reading public is slight. I sit here at my typewriter in the corner room of my house, looking out at the crabapple tree and the lawn I mowed yesterday. I peck away at the keys, having constant second thoughts, wondering at my audacity in setting things down in print.

Then, a column finished, I buy milk and eggs, watch the children play ball, start dinner. I carry on with life as usual until the next time someone picks me out in a crowd. Then, for a moment or two I gloat and soar and celebrate, because I enjoy being noticed, after all.

 RAINY DAYS

It was a ploy, a lure, a last-ditch effort to ward off the boredom, because I did not want to hear them say, "There's nothing to do, Ma."

I did not want them to damage my idealism, to explode my fantasy of tranquil summer afternoons. I wanted them to spend their days in perfect harmony with one another and nature. I wanted them to swim, play ball, jump rope, take walks, read books, paint, color, climb trees and dream. I wanted them to drink their juice, lick their ice cream cones and thank me for keeping them carefree and happy.

But happiness is relative. Last Tuesday, it rained. And they uttered the words. Before mid-afternoon, flanked by one friend each, my son and daughter in atonal unison said, "There's nothing to do, Ma. We're bored."

And I was worried. If they could not keep themselves merrily occupied for half a day, perhaps I have been wrong all along. An admission which I would be loathe to make. Particularly since I have been gloating so for the past month.

For years now, I have contended that camp is too often an unnecessary experience, a costly way to rid oneself of the responsibility of fostering fun for one's offspring. Having put those thoughts in writing, however, I was forced to eat my words last year when my own two children opted for four-week stints at separate full-time day camps.

But this summer, when neither child chose to return to his particular facility of summer fun, I smiled knowingly. "Just as I suspected," I said aloud. "Children need to spend more time unfettered and free."

I promptly signed them up for a town-run camp which seemed to offer the best of two worlds, structured activities three mornings a week and two full days of trips. It was certain to be the perfect blend, with all of those afternoons free to prove my point about unfettered time.

Children, I said to myself, need space in which to grow. Imagination flourishes when structure is removed, creativity thrives on the freewheeling day. Since my offspring were infants I've advocated innovation. Give them the chance, and they'll discover a wonderful way to fill their time.

But then came the rain and the admission of boredom and my fear of being wrong. Perhaps they need full-time camp after all, I thought. Maybe back yards are passe. Maybe only counselors can make suggestions regarding fun, mothers having no worthwhile thoughts on how to fill the hours. Maybe, in the end, I will have to submit to the blocks of time theory.

But not yet. "Not just yet," I said, as I mounted the stairs to our attic, forcing enthusiasm into my voice as my children and their friends followed behind me. "Come quickly," I said. "Let's see what's here." And they climbed to that musty, damp area above our kitchen, tripping over plastic-covered boxes filled with toys and books.

"Come see," I said. "Look, here are all of your trucks and cars. Do you remember this green one?" I asked, unearthing an old favorite from the pile of dump trucks and vans.

"Can we bring 'em all down?" asked my son.

I said we could.

Then, taking yet another precarious step, I chanced the question to the girls, my daughter and her friend, children who had, less than a year ago, placed their dolls in bags for safekeeping. "Remember her?" I held high the blonde in the beautiful silver dress. "I'd forgotten all about this one with the pink flowers in her hair, hadn't you?" I cajoled.

In the dim light of the single low wattage overhead bulb, I saw my daughter look knowingly at her companion. The two of them exchanged glances of rekindled interest, of recent memories not yet buried.

"Let's bring them down," my daughter said.

"And the doll furniture, too?" they wanted to know. "How about the stuffed animals? The action figures? The puzzles? The box of blocks?"

So we stand, a full week later, the girls, the boys and their good old toys having been joyfully reunited (if only temporarily) indoors during rainstorms, outside on the hammock, in the living room, the bedroom, the dirt pile out back. And summer has been set right once again.

LETTERS

I found myself there, beside a pile of musty letters sealed in a bag inside a cardboard box on a shelf in the basement of my parents' house.

Yesterday, while searching for some odd bit of memorabilia or other, I came across this collection of words. Handwritten missives mailed to me when I was eleven or twelve years old. As I sat there on the damp floor of the basement, straining to read in the dim light, I could feel myself shrinking, the innocence returning.

"Dear Annie, I made a new friend," read one letter. "She's kind of a snob." And, "I can ride my bike real good. Figure eights and all. Love and lollipops, Lois."

"Dear Annie, We're having a real nice time. The water is just perfect. On Monday we went to the boardwalk. As usual, it was crowded. I got a straw pocketbook along with popcorn, a jelly apple, pizza and ice cream. Love, Diane."

"Dear Annie, How are you? I'm fine. I hate school. Over and out."

Yesterday, while the sun shone brightly on 1986 and my children ate strawberries at Grandma and Grandpa's picnic table, I sat cross-legged on their basement floor allowing time to melt away. I read ten letters signed "Cheerio" written on blue airmail stationery and sent directly from my pen pal Mary in London, England, in 1958. I read six letters from Zina, a child whose exotic name was the sole impetus for my engineering a correspondence with her.

With a vague sense of shame, I reread, twenty-eight years later, the letter from Gwen, that bespectacled girl whose overtures to friendship I had not returned. Two years my senior, the girl had written to me from the boarding school she attended during the winter months. As I read between the lines yesterday, I believe I detected a loneliness there. "Please write," she had said. "It will really help me along a lot to pass these miserable days of tests, tests and more tests."

In the damp coolness of the basement, I relived school days in the wooden floored classrooms where I spent my childhood. I saw parks where I'd sat beneath tall trees to watch the fireworks on summer nights. With each letter, I remembered the homes where these friends and I had shared our thoughts, our hair ribbons and our fears.

Yellowed with age, but completely intact, were postcards from Niagara Falls, notes from Atlantic City, stationery festooned with glittered butterflies, kittens, and various other motifs.

For a period of sixty minutes, I resurrected the curly-headed girl who vacillated between dolls and the desire to wear makeup. "When is your Mom going to let you use lipstick? Does your bike have hand brakes?"

Through the words of my childhood friends, I felt again that vague anxiety which began for me at twelve and which has never quite subsided. Reality, I suppose it is. The onset of adulthood.

Within the letters from Joan and Diane, Lorna, Lois, Gwen, Zina and Mary lay a pattern, a blueprint for growing pains. I suppose I could not have seen it then.

But what was it, I wonder, that made me save the letters? What blind foresight had me store them away for such a time as this? When, in the midst of my reverie, my own eleven-year-old daughter would steal quietly down the basement stairs to find me there, suddenly, a peer.

Wordlessly, I handed her one letter, then another, until finally, she said to me, "They sound like letters from my friends, Mom. Just like letters from my friends and me. Just like me."

MOTHERHOOD

It was the apparent insignificance of the moment that surprised me. I had asked my husband to try to get the kids to quiet down. It was nearly ten-thirty p.m. on a school night, and I could still hear them whispering to one another from their adjoining bedrooms. I had been yelling at them to go to sleep for an hour—to no avail.

As I cradled a mug of coffee in my hands, my spouse made his valiant attempt at silencing the youngsters. They were quiet for a full thirty seconds before I caught the sounds of their muffled giggles as they hid their faces in their pillows.

And suddenly, a thrill of pride passed through me. At a time when I would have expected to respond to their antics with minor fury, I found myself smiling.

They are really in there, I thought. Two children, asking for trouble with their boisterous clowning, are in there, and they belong to me.

This momentary swell of pride, I felt, was less for the children than for me. In that instant of recognition, I saw myself as the partial creator of these two human beings whose personalities, appearance, intelligence, sense of humor and ability to infuriate seemed suddenly remarkable. This is not the first time I have experienced this unsolicited emotion. Once, while standing outside the ladies' room door at the rear of an airplane in mid-flight, I responded to a stranger's inquiry. "I'm waiting for my daughter," I said. "She'll be out in a moment." At the words "my daughter" my stomach suddenly flipped. I had wanted to add, "And I have a son, too. See him over there. I have two of them, two beautiful, intelligent, charming, sweet, maddening, wonderful children. And they are mine."

It is this possessiveness that fills me sometimes when I least anticipate it. Frequently, maybe too frequently, I think of my children without actually considering the thought. I accept my role in relation to this boy and girl as a matter of fact. But occasionally, the fact strikes me as incredible. I am their mother. They call me Mommy, Ma, Mom. They shout at me, cry to me, tease me, kiss me, hug me, challenge me and frustrate me. They know me. They love me. They trust me. They are part of me.

And at odd, fleeting moments, the concept of motherhood overwhelms me.

THE TEACHER

I was right. One hundred percent right. They do have a great deal to say and little hesitation about saying it. They have seen more, done more, thought more, lived more, laughed more, worried more than I have. They have opinions, ideals, aspirations and desires. They make me feel inept and inarticulate by comparison. Never intentionally, but by the sheer magnitude of their combined years, I am dwarfed and awed and inspired. Odd that they call me their teacher.

It began a year ago when I suggested and agreed to coordinate a writing course for senior citizens to be sponsored by a local college.

During a moment of humility one afternoon, I had suddenly recognized this weekly column for what it is, a comparatively youthful attempt at mirroring life. A bicycle with training wheels, an infant in diapers. A column with shortcomings, writing style being the least significant. I understood that it is experience I lack most. Life's experience.

And yet, I realized then and now that this column does have its loyal fans, faithful readers and followers who knew me when, who relate to my trials, my mundane chatterings. How fortunate, I thought on that particular day, to have this medium for my message.

But what if I didn't have it? Would I write my story anyway? Would I set down in words my impressions and feelings?

Of course I would. I always have, have I not? And isn't that how this column began some six years ago, with a collection of my insides spilled out on typing paper and handed over to a managing editor?

So now I am forty with a second husband, a house, a mortgage and a group of friends and acquaintances who tell me they recognize themselves in my words.

But what if I were sixty and writing? What if I were living on Social Security? What if I were seventy-two and widowed, eighty-four and arthritic? What if I had been born in Europe, reared five children, been grandmother to fifteen? What if I had traveled to China or Africa, spoken not a word of English when I set foot on the shores of America? Suppose I remembered a mother in tattered clothing running from the Nazis? Running from pogroms? Suppose I could recall World Wars I and II?

Who would I be with an overview of life born of age and experience? What would I answer if asked my opinion of love, marriage, family, children, housing, loneliness, happiness, friendship and health?

And what, I wondered, would happen if I passed out pens and paper, posed a question or two, suggested a topic and asked someone else to set it down—someone or ones who have seen more, heard more, done more, know more than I do? What would happen if I asked them to write?

They would call me their teacher.

And I would be the student.

GREAT OUTDOORS

I carry this image of the four of us out there in multicolored sweaters, rosy-cheeked and clear-eyed, raking leaves into huge piles under a blue autumn sky.

I see us working together, side by side, shouting and laughing as the leaves mount higher beneath the bare limbs. I see us stuffing plastic bags with crisp brown remnants of maples and oaks and willows.

I think of us stopping to examine the texture, the hue and the size of castoff prizes shed by ashs and poplars in our yard. Come here and see this yellow one, I want one of us to say. Or, look how perfect is the shape of this, what symmetry, what art! What beauty in the pretty leaves swirling to the ground on a breeze.

I picture us at day's end, returning our rakes to the shed, facing one another with good will—tired and hungry, glad that we have accomplished our task together in the chill bright sunlight. Then, I envision us drinking mugs of hot soup around a crackling blaze in the living room fireplace—warm and comfortable and satisfied.

But nobody shares my vision.

Except for the promise of steaming soup and the roaring fire, not one member of this household considers yard work a pleasant family pastime.

My daughter laughs at me when I suggest that she help me rake for enjoyment. She has actually agreed to practice the piano on a Sunday afternoon rather than don a pair of work gloves and toil a bit in the great outdoors. It is not that she is opposed to fresh air. She will gladly climb a tree or ride her bike. It is the chore of grooming the grounds which doesn't appeal.

My son will spend hours building huts and forts and mountains of leaves for hiding and jumping, but on those rare occasions when I request that he put the mountains to a different use and, further, that he cart the leaves to the front of the house for trash pickup, he develops a sudden and severe allergy to the autumn foliage.

Even my husband finds nothing charming in the concept of raking and bagging. Of the three of them, however, he alone is totally honest. Simply stated, he hates raking leaves.

Why I find this surprising is the surprise. Neither my husband nor my children enjoy mowing the lawn in summer, planting the garden in spring or shoveling the snow in winter. I am the only one to take pleasure in these activities, particularly if we do them together as a family.

Still, I suppose I can't complain. With comparatively little prodding, I can usually get them to join me out there for an hour or two of togetherness with the rakes and the leaf bags. But should I, by virtue of some lovely white clouds and the red and gold leaves, be tricked into thinking that my husband and offspring are sharing my thoughts, I have only to look at their faces for confirmation.

Deadpan, scowl and boredom are painted boldly across their eyes and lips, as they humor me in stoic determination, paying their dues to my personal philosophy of fun and the seasonal cleanup.

GENETIC MEMORY

"Step on a line," he said.

"Break your mother's spine," I answered. "Step on a crack."

"Break your mother's back."

My son and I repeated the incantation again and again—he, intrigued with the rhythm and the content, I taken by the flashback. The hardest segment of sidewalk to negotiate when I was nine was the one two blocks from school on the right-hand side of the street. I used to worry that my mother's spine would be bent in two by the end of the day.

And here, now, was my own son engaged in the same, nonsensical, age-old game, passed on from generation to generation for no apparent reason and with no obvious source. Who had taught my boy the rhyme? And who had taught me?

"Step on a crack," I thought, is similar to the kootie catcher, the spitball and initials carved in trees, ideas destined for regular reincarnation.

Expanding on that thought, I spent last evening telling my children how I had helped to plummet the back of Mrs. Root's head with paper airplanes when I was in the seventh grade. I described the time we placed a thumbtack on Mrs. Duncan's chair. I recounted the cheers we had shouted for a junior varsity basketball team, told of the pimples that had surfaced on my forehead and chin when I was twelve-and-a-half, and I admitted to spending hours on the telephone talking to girlfriends.

"And now," I observed, "you are doing it. You, my son, are breaking my back, shooting spitballs and making airplanes. You, my daughter, are on the phone. But how did you know? Who taught you?"

Could it be genetic memory? A chemical combination in the brain which carries the gene for perfect spitball-making and which appears with regularity in the fourth grade child? Is it something inside which tells you when you ought to know how to drive teachers and parents a little crazy and by what ancient means?

And if we as adults already know the scenario, why are we surprised (or maybe we are not, and I alone am shocked) by the cyclical turn of events?

"Who told you about cracks and lines and mothers' spines?" I posed the question.

But my children shrugged their shoulders and walked away from me, leaving behind a trail of sneakers, pretzel crumbs and crumpled looseleaf paper—landmarks I recognized as if I had passed them yesterday on my way.

COFFEE AND THOUGHTS

Lunch hour.

Interesting phrase, I thought to myself as I glanced around the room. The small restaurant was beginning to fill with customers. I sat alone on the plastic-covered wooden bench in a booth facing the door. I was waiting for a friend who had arranged to meet me during her lunch hour.

I was early—a quirk of mine, being early. It is not so much tardiness which I dislike, as it is rushing to make the airplane, the bus, the appointment. So I willingly sat there for a quarter of an hour, staring at the neat group of jars—ketchup, mustard, sugar, salt and pepper, nestled in a corner of the table.

The waitress, in her crisp uniform, stopped by to ask if I wanted coffee.

I answered, "Yes."

She said, "I take it you are waiting for someone," indicating the place setting opposite me. "I won't bother you again until your friend arrives."

And she left me then to enjoy my coffee and my thoughts. I sipped from the heavy white restaurant mug, wondering what the waitress thought of my life—if, indeed, she had given it any thought. Did she, for instance, think I was an accountant? An attorney? A secretary? An executive scheduled to meet a client? Or could she tell at a glance that I was none of the above? That I was, in fact, in costume.

I had specifically worn a dress and high-heeled shoes for this meeting. I had blushed my cheeks and lipsticked my mouth, both extraordinary machinations for me. As was this lunch hour.

Being a free-lance writer, columnist, part-time teacher, I spend the bulk of my day at home in front of the typewriter. My typical work clothes include a sweat shirt and sneakers. Between stories or interviews, I vacuum the bedrooms, wash the bathtub, take a walk. I never wear makeup. When I am hungry, I remove a container of yogurt from the refrigerator. The most inflexible moment of my day occurs at three forty-seven when my children come home from school. Nothing else is definite.

But could the waitress tell? Could she or the patrons of the establishment know by looking at me that I am unaccustomed to regular coffee breaks, company routines and schedules?

Would, for example, the group of lawyers lunching to my left be surprised to learn that I fit this particular hour in between the second load of laundry and a trip to the cleaners? Would the diners talking boisterously around me expect that I, like they, had another appointment at two and still another one at four-thirty?

The room, I noted, was filled primarily by men. All wore sport coats or suits and ties. They discussed sports, the stock market, underlings at their office and who had been caught using the company phone for personal calls. Their conversation was public, loud amidst their hearty laughter, offered between huge bites of corned beef sandwich.

I overheard. I watched while I waited.

Eventually, my friend arrived. She was precisely on time, wearing a tailored black suit and a smart blouse—looking like a working woman.

We caught up on one another's lives, shared news of our respective families, nibbled at our salads and left.

I watched her drive off in her sporty new car and felt just motivated enough to remove the crumpled tissues and the children's gum wrappers from the front seat of my own automobile before pulling out. Then, I sighed with relief and headed for home, feeling fortunate indeed not to be locked into a lunch hour.

SHABBOS

Shabbos came into the house—a palpable presence. *Shabbos* settled among the folds of the curtains on the living room window, above the satin cover on the braided *challah*. *Shabbos* hovered over the table, glowed within the cup of ruby wine. *Shabbos* lent its taste to the soup and meat, to the sweet desserts—brought its light to the children's eyes and the candle flames. *Shabbos* walked with us to *shul* and home again and filled the room with ringing songs of praise. *Shabbos* descended on Friday night with a tangible quietude and took its leave a full day later to the fragrance of pungent spices.

For the first time.

With the decision to become *shomrei Shabbos*, we invited this radiant queen to enter our lives, and she accepted. With grace and dignity born of the ages, *Shabbos* enveloped our home, surrounded us, made room for us, expanded the space and the hours, altered time.

And we greeted *Shabbos* as we would welcome a stunning bride, as we would meet a sage, a child, a father and a friend.

And *Shabbos* swirled towards the center of our days. All the thousands and millions of *Shabbosos* wafted through the dusk to arrive at our doorstep at the close of the week as though we were special. As though we were deserving. Entered our lives like a crown of jewels, moving waters, to connect us with a promise and a past and a future. And we received this gift of *Shabbos* at the very moment that we asked to make it ours.

THE SAXOPHONE

"Practice," my father would say. "Did you practice?"

And I would saunter off disconsolately to the old piano, willing my fingers to produce something, anything, without help from my brain.

I hated to have to think about playing. I loved to play.

"But it takes practice," my father would remind me.

"Now try it again."

And there he would sit on the edge of the chair, beaming at my tentative efforts, his blue eyes smiling with pride. "Good," he would say. "Again."

Why he loved my playing so, I couldn't imagine. I was unsure and unenthusiastic. I tried, but I was never really good.

Yet, he didn't seem to care. He appeared actually to enjoy my playing. "Some day you will understand," he would tell me when I questioned him. "Some day . . ." he promised, the way he promised that some day I would insist that my children zip up jackets in winter, tie shoelaces and perform other thankless tasks.

Today is the day.

Here I sit, in the brown and orange straight-backed chair in the small outer room of the music teacher's studio, waiting for my son to finish his lesson. On the other side of the door, I can hear the boy pushing melodies out of his newly-rented saxophone.

He stops, he starts, he plays a few bars and falters. He begins again. He hesitates and proceeds. I can hear him in there struggling, succeeding, struggling once more, and I am out here beaming with pride.

Alone in this waiting room, I feel my heart quicken as I recognize a song after the seventh saxophone lesson. "This one I know," I whisper aloud. "How beautiful is the music."

How much joy this boy will receive when friends, cousins, family, sing along to familiar tunes. How much fun he and his sister have already known with one at the piano and the other on the rented sax. And there will be more. There will be attempts at combos and bands, original compositions. There will be sheet music for songs with words unrecognizable to me.

Long after lessons have ceased, there will be sporadic returns to the piano and the saxophone where particular selections will forever evoke particular memories. The solo in the fourth grade *Chanukah* program, the number one hit of 1986, the time Uncle Carl brought his clarinet to play a duet, Grandpa's face at the first impromptu performance.

And years hence, there will be one moment when an adult child of mine will sit in the waiting room just outside a music teacher's door, listening to new sounds, remembering old, recalling a mother who suggested "practice" and wore a look of pride for any perfect or imperfect rendition of a selection heard less for the music than for the love.

THE COMPUTER

I think of it as an alien—seated there in stony silence on the desk in the next room, its row of green eyes shut against the world.

I believe it is accusing me silently of ignorance and fear, laughing noiselessly from its innards at my ineptitude. But I do not budge to meet it halfway, do not try to befriend it. I approach it periodically to stare icily at its face. I pace up and down before it until I decide, at last, to leave the thing in peace and return here to my typewriter and my admissions.

I cannot use the computer.

Will not use the computer.

It scares me.

I am old-fashioned and weak. I do not take well to change or challenge, and besides, I say, my typewriter has served me well. I am superstitious, too. Perhaps the columns will not emerge from my thoughts on a different machine—on a piece of equipment which does not clang and clatter with every touch of a key. Maybe I will be unable to create in a different environment, in another room. The setting, I say, is important.

But I lie. I don't truly believe in ritual and the phantom muse any more than I believe that the medium is the message. It is laziness above all which keeps me from the alien, newly installed within our home.

This monster item, hauled from the store in mountainous boxes with slick graphic covers, was a gift to our family from my parents. My mother and father and my son and daughter agree that the thing itself is somehow vital to existence in 1987.

And they may be correct. The children do not hesitate to touch the being, to press its various buttons and dials, to talk to it in one of several languages foreign to my tongue and ear. And I stand hesitantly over their shoulders, marveling at their courage and confidence, refusing firmly to communicate, refusing even to read the stack of manuals which would allow for such communication.

But I feel it is a losing battle against time, youth and progress. I must learn to understand this thing just as I learned to read and write. It is my responsibility to conquer the form feed and the disk drive lest I be accused of apathy or worse.

And I will, I tell my children and myself. Soon, I will look through all of the papers stacked neatly there on the shelf beneath the thing. Just wait a bit, I say, and I'll be spewing forth columns ad infinitum from the mouth of the alien and its accompanying printer.

But not just yet. Not now. How like a child I feel today,

a five-year-old left standing at a door, suddenly homesick and needing mother's hand.

And so it is that I have wandered back here to this comfortable typewriter to say that I will try the computer tomorrow. Maybe.

THE BUTTON BOX

I could just as easily have sewn the button back on when I got home. In fact, I told my mother I would do just that. But then, she reached for the button box and I couldn't leave.

It's not that I'm so fastidious about buttons. Chances are, if left to my own devices, I would have used a safety pin rather than needle and thread. Or I might simply have worn the coat minus one button for the duration of winter.

I remained at my parents' house to reattach the button because of Grandma.

Tiny and tidy, my grandmother lived to be eighty-five, wearing high, starched collars and smart gray suits. She would sit for hours sifting through the button box with her small efficient hands, determined to locate the perfect match for the button I'd lost or broken.

With precise, deft movements, she would thread the needle and, using a shiny silver thimble, she would sew as I watched in awe.

Using buttons from the same button box still owned by my mother, she would stitch and snip throughout my childhood.

Young as I was, I believe I understood even then that

much of this busy work was saved for Grandma as much for her sake as for ours. She loved being told that she alone could make things right. She loved sitting at our kitchen table on winter afternoons with the tea kettle whistling in the background and her grandchildren at her side.

My grandmother was less maternal than matriarchal, I think. She presided in a queenly manner over family functions. She was proud, intelligent, feisty and proper.

Grandma wore white gloves on all occasions, and brooches to clasp the collars of her crisp white blouses.

There was a cuckoo clock in Grandma's apartment, and her wingback chair was yellow and gray. She grew sweet potato plants on her window sill, and she sliced apples in geometric patterns.

Once, when I was six years old, she fashioned a wedding gown for me from old lace curtains and imitation pearls. My mother and I took a taxicab home from Grandma's place that day. My mother wore her dress and coat. I wore the gown with the pearls.

Grandma came to my college graduation, and I saw the pride in her bright blue eyes, the color of which she passed on to her sons and grandchildren.

Grandma loved to sing—operas, ditties, scraps of song in her high, clear voice. She fed pigeons in Atlantic City when the resort was yet a haven for families on vacation in summer. She belonged to clubs, read books, watched television, offered advice. She was pretty and pert, always perfectly groomed, always rather formal, I suppose.

As I ran my fingers through the button box, I touched some buttons her fingers may have touched, yellowed buttons from my youth, and I thought of Grandma and felt good.

EXTRANEOUS JUNK

I find them all over the house—little scraps of paper with cryptic notes scribbled across the top, unidentified telephone numbers printed in pencil on the underside of empty tissue boxes, official-looking forms peeking from partially opened envelopes, ragged-edged clippings torn from yesterday's newspapers, coupons for teen magazines, side panels of cereal boxes, stray socks, crumpled gum wrappers, inkless ballpoint pens, ponytail holders, empty glasses.

"And extraneous cups."

"What?" my husband asked, a half smile on his face. "What did you call them?"

"Extraneous cups," I repeated, pointing to the half-full mug with its now cold contents imprinting a stain on the night-stand near the bed. "You never put them in the sink. Nobody does except me," I remarked in an accusatory tone. "And it isn't fair."

I took the mug, with its ugly brownish liquid sloshing to and fro, and marched it to the kitchen sink, where it joined a half-full milk glass, an empty water glass and two cereal bowls with soggy corn flakes plastered to their sides—an impressive gathering, the first of this morning's collection. But a reminder nonetheless that my previous night's rantings had once again gone unheeded.

"Nobody listens," I muttered to myself, washing out the mug and glasses. Nobody cares, nobody notices, nobody helps. I could leave it all to pile up on the corners of tables and countertops—all the paper scraps, barrettes and dishes, and the entire gang of them would probably never notice— until they wanted a clean glass or a space on which to work— until they wanted the phone number scribbled somewhere for future use. And then they'd yell. "Where is it, Ma? I can't find the tissue box, and I wrote an important message on it about four days ago. Did ya see it?"

What if I said no? What if I said, "Gee, sorry I hadn't noticed it? Why don't you check under that pile of boxes with the other numbers?" What if, instead of asking about the numbers before heaving the boxes, I simply threw them away or left them to accumulate? Would anybody care either way? And is it really worth a battle to find out?

I've decided not. I've decided instead to temper my fury with reality and a touch of sarcasm. "Hand me that errant pony-tail holder, will you, dear?" "Would you mind removing the American cheese wrapper from the kitchen table, sweetie?" And, "Why don't you just give me your extraneous cup?"

And if they find me humorous—well, let them laugh.

THE BOOK

From the minute she said hello, I knew something was wrong. The usual lilt to her voice was gone. She sounded edgy, distracted.

I figured it was the recent move. "How are you doing in your new place?" I asked.

"Okay," she answered without spirit.

"All unpacked?"

"Almost."

"Do you like the house?"

"Yes."

Monosyllables. Not good. She's a talker, this friend of mine, a vivacious, energetic talker. These single word responses were a dead giveaway. Some kind of trouble was in the works.

"What is it?" I finally exploded. "What's wrong with you?"

She clucked and hedged for a moment or two and then, somewhat nervously, admitted the truth. "I can't find my book," she said. "And without it, I just can't function." Then embarrassedly, she added. "You probably think I'm crazy, don't you?"

But I don't. Not for one minute. Because if she's crazy, so am I. The book to which my friend referred is the one that holds her schedule of things to do. If it is anything like my book, it includes the dates and times of every work-related appointment or assignment necessary to her livelihood and furthermore; it details such vital information as when to pick up her daughter's coat from the cleaners, who is coming to dinner on which night and how many cupcakes she must bake (or buy) for the third-grade class party.

I think of my book as an additional brain. It is the place to put all the things about which I must worry. Once they are penned in black and white, I can breathe freely because I know if they are in the book they will get done. If not, I might forget.

My book tells me when to write columns, clean the fish tank, take the children for checkups. It lets me know whose class trip is on which day and whether or not I'm supposed to drive. At a glance, its pages enable me to tell my son and daughter where each will be at any given time. With the book at my side, I can coordinate car pools and interviews, piano lessons and haircuts.

This thin brown volume is my memory, my connection to reality. I think it is my sanity. If it were lost, I would be, too.

So I told my friend to hang up the phone and look again. "It has to be someplace," I assured her. "I know you'll feel better when you find it."

Which she did.

THE CAR

"The car is dead," he told me.

"How much will it cost to fix?" I asked.

But he said nothing. "No use," he finally explained. "She's dead. Finished. The car is gone."

I couldn't accept it. Refused to believe that, despite her age and work record, the old girl wouldn't be back on the road tomorrow. Yet, a fact is a fact, and the mechanic doesn't lie. For the moment, it seems, we have become a single-car family.

Once there was a time, not very long ago, when I would have considered the demise of an automobile a blessing in disguise. I like to walk, like the feeling of solitude and forced deliberation imposed by the absence of wheels. I like the necessity of strolling to and from the supermarket, to and from the pharmacy. Like not being called upon as chauffeur for the day. Once there was a time when I would have said, as long as my husband has a car to get to work, I can gladly do without.

And perhaps, I could have said that now, if all else were equal. But things are not—the children being the least equal of all.

Two, three, four years ago, had my automobile expired, I would have simply changed the rules of our lives. Instead of a distant playground, we would have visited the park around the corner. Had I been unable to transport my son and daughter to friends whose homes were five miles away, they would have had to play with friends next door.

The absence of the automobile would have simplified our lives. Choices would have narrowed. We would have adjusted. But life is less adjustable today. The second car seems less a conveyance for pleasure than it does a necessity, a functional appendage to our world.

Four wheels and an engine have become the key to saxophone lessons, gymnastic classes and birthday parties. Without a gas tank and steering wheel there would be no Little League or soccer practice, no trips to the shoe store, the clothing store, the mall. Restaurants and skating rinks would be out of the question, not to mention pools and camps.

But what does it mean? Have I simply succumbed to suburbia? Have these extracurricular activities I allow my children somehow become expected? Will I beg rides and borrow cars over the coming weeks lest I deprive my offspring of their due? Or will I put down my foot and stay close to home, hoping for a return to the basics?

Why is it that I feel suddenly crippled by the loss of an automobile—a machine which invariably complicates my life? And why do I miss my car?

JAMES

They make me yawn uncontrollably. They make my neck ache. They make me edgy and tired. Make me feel the need for snacks or drinks—anything to relieve the boredom imposed by board games, those torturous, family-fun creations guaranteed to find me periodically extolling the virtues of other entertainment.

I simply cannot stand them. Despite their colorful photos of Mom, Dad and Junior having tons of fun with pink and lime-green dollar bills, I never see the point and never have. I never care who wins. But my children do. My son and daughter want to reach the finish line. And furthermore, they want me to want to, too.

So I try. Periodically, when all else fails, when they've had enough of paint and clay, and books read aloud in the name of togetherness, they ask about a game. Sometimes, I agree. Not willingly exactly, but rather noncommittally, nodding my head in anticipation of the lethargy to come. And come it does, almost instantly—a wave of dullness spreading from my head to my feet.

"Your move, Mom," they'll nudge me, as I sit contorted on the living room floor.

And I'll say, "Huh?"

"Pick a card," they'll tell me, and I will pick and then they'll make me read the card. They'll even move my piece for me, my little yellow, orange or turquoise piece—watching me all the while to make sure I'm enjoying the game.

But it is hard. Even harder now than it was when I was a child. I faked it better then. Peer pressure, I suppose. What kind of kid would relinquish "Boardwalk" for a bath?

But I am not heartless. Today, as in my youth, I play to the end, even counting my money to find out if I've won or lost. Sometimes, though rarely, agreeing to a second match, my eyelids drooping, preparing for another round.

But fair is fair. I know I owe my offspring one or two for all the miles they've walked with total disinterest, as I pointed out the flora and fauna in our neighborhood. I play these board games on occasion, in return for the hours my son and daughter have spent visiting relatives they would rather not visit, eating meals they would rather not eat, doing homework they would rather not do. And I play because they want me to play. Because for some reason, despite my apathy, they continue to like my being there, head in hands on the opposite side of "Start." And I like being liked.

WINTER MEMORIES

It's a hiss. Not a hiss exactly—more a whistle or a sizzle.

Like an old steam radiator. Exactly. And that is what I love about the vaporizer.

No matter that my cold disappeared five weeks ago. Or that the noise itself is probably an indication of some faulty valve in the mechanism. The reason for using the thing is no longer relevant. What interests me is the psychological value of the sound of the broken vaporizer. That sound being the key to a childhood memory.

I am ten. I am in bed on a Sunday morning. The wallpaper of my room is blue and white. My curtains are organdy. Sunlight is streaming through the windows, bouncing off the snow outside. I smell coffee through the closed door. I hear my parents' voices in the kitchen. I snuggle further down under the blankets, soothed by the radiator's lullaby—steam. Steam heat, all through the cold winter mornings of my youth. A momentary bubbling and gurgling in the pipes and then, beautifully, the sound of steam.

It is not the same with baseboard heating. Today's subtle knocking or clanging before the rise in temperature does not fill me with a sense of well-being the way the radiator did.

But who am I to say what counts? Perhaps the Sunday morning sounds in our house will be as deeply imbedded in my children's minds as were the noises of my childhood planted in mine. Maybe when my son and daughter reach forty they will recall with joy the irregular banging of the water heater at the conclusion of their daily showers. They might find a sense of security in the memory of that old shed door which flaps incessantly just outside their window throughout the winter months.

For me, the cheer lies in the steam or a facsimile thereof. A simple sound which recalls a childhood of comfort in a home filled with love. I hope my children's winter memories will be as warm as mine.

THE REFRIGERATOR

The liquid butter pecan ice cream formed a puddle on top of the no-longer-frozen pizza box. The hot dogs were wreathed with transparent drops of moisture. Three individual quarts of homemade soup sloshed in their plastic containers. The ice cube trays were filled with water. Everything dripped, spilled or squashed to the touch, as we stared in disbelief at the ruined refrigerator/freezer.

Why? we asked, mopping pools of strawberry juice from the floor. Why tonight? Why not next week? Next year?

"It's uncanny," I commented, dumping eggs and cheese into a large green garbage bag. "If we hadn't gone shopping yesterday, this never would have happened. The refrigerator obviously intended to quit on a full stomach."

Still, we agreed, there was no use crying over spilled milk—literally.

We uttered several inane cliches, added a few less gentle words of our own choosing and set about calling every refrigerator repairman in the yellow pages.

But Saturday night, apparently, is not the optimum time for appliance whizzes to be on the job. Finally, we roused someone's wife, who assured us that her spouse would find his way to our home before midnight.

Which he did. Following a curt hello, he dropped to the floor, where, stretched to his full length, he prodded the underside of the refrigerator, mumbling and nodding all the while in much the same tone as the doctor would use when probing an infected throat.

The repairman suggested that the appliance might yet be salvageable. "If you can wait until Monday, I'll try to get the part," he said. He was implying, we presumed, that where there's life, there is hope.

But by Sunday morning, our hopes were dashed. Even the lettuce had withered overnight. The apples were turning brown in the fruit bin. The interior of the refrigerator was somehow warmer than the interior of the kitchen.

Pacing to and fro before the ailing giant, we weighed our choices: a chance transplant the following morning in an attempt to prolong the life of the ancient friend, or a trip to the nearest appliance store.

Finally, with heavy hearts, we decided to pull the plug.

With the help of a neighbor, a borrowed truck and a good amount of muscle and sweat, the old refrigerator was removed and a new one installed.

And now it is Monday. Admittedly, I like the quiet hum

of the modern almond-toned refrigerator gracing our kitchen. I like the fact that the ice cream is solid and the lettuce crisp. But I feel a twinge of pain when I look out the window and see the old fellow lying there on his side on the front lawn. With his innards piled neatly beside him and his door detached from the hinges, the refrigerator looks hauntingly pathetic—dethroned and demeaned. I do wish the trash collectors would hurry to take him away or I may find myself feeling the need to haul him back indoors just to alleviate my guilt.

ESACH

There have been many firsts. The first time I lit the *Shabbos* candles at dusk, the first time I walked to *shul* rather than taking a car, the first time I said no to a dinner invitation at the home of a friend whose kitchen is not kosher.

And with each of these firsts has come a sense of accomplishment and not a small amount of fear. Fear of offending my past, those friends and relatives who loved me and love me. And fear of offending the future by saying, doing, being something inappropriate to Judaism.

And so it was that this, the latest first, gave me a particular joy because I was quite alone when it occurred, and because my success arrived with no sense of fear.

Since my second marriage and my subsequent introduction to observant Judaism, I have made a grand attempt to encourage my children's religious growth. I have often marveled at their increasing comprehension of the history and customs and the language of our people. It is their facility of language, in fact, of which I am most envious. For while I am less than knowledgeable in many secular subjects, I can, at the very least, read the words in which these disciplines are written. If I cannot complete a problem in algebra or answer a question in social studies, I can turn to the appropriate reference book and I can learn. But where the subjects of religion are concerned, I have been helpless.

At my husband's suggestion, during the past several years, I have read the Torah once through, the Prophets once through and a host of other writings—all of these in English translation. And while I found the words beautiful, significant, meaningful, I longed to be able to do what my husband has done from childhood and what my children are learning to do. To look at the original. To open a book and read the Hebrew. To understand in some small way what has been written, what connects us to our very beginnings and to our brothers throughout the world.

Which is why, for nearly a year now, I have daily been working with this language. Little by little. Ten minutes at a time, using books given to me by my husband and borrowed from my offspring, with my young son at my side and my daughter offering encouragement, I have quietly, slowly made my way through the printed alphabet to the script and onto words—simple words—easy words, but words nonetheless. And it was just there, with a few dozen words to my knowledge, that I found myself preparing for this year's *seder*.

During my daily morning walk, taken as much for solitude and thought as for exercise, I found myself, just prior to *Pesach*, silently recalling the first of the four questions. "*Mah nishtanah halailah hazeh?*" The singsong phrase is among the few that I recall from childhood. And as I hummed, my pace quickened to the melody which hung tightly in my brain. "*Mah nishtanah halailah hazeh.*" The words were bunched together as they have been for more than forty-odd years since first I heard them. The syllables, a collection of sounds, the meaning of which I have always known solely from English translation.

Then, quite suddenly, as I began the song once more, a word separated out from the rest. "*Mah . . .*" I heard. "*Mah?*" What? What? "*Mah nishtanah halailah.*"

"*Lailah?*" Night. Night. "*Hazeh.*" This night. "*Mah nishtanah halailah hazeh?*" What makes this night different from all other nights?

And there it was. And there I was, alone, with chills running down my back and tears brimming in my eyes. I danced unobserved, thrilled by the knowledge that a door had opened for me—aware that this *seder* night would indeed be different from all others.

MATERNAL ADVICE

The phrase was more liberated, but the sentiment was the same.

"Remember who you are," I heard myself tell my daughter as she left the house. "You don't have to do everything everyone else does. If the kids get wild, you don't have to get wild, too. Say please and thank you and don't forget to help clear the table. Understand?"

She nodded, tucking in her lower lip and rolling her eyes slightly to let me know that I was overdoing the advice.

But I couldn't help myself. "Remember . . ." I yelled, as

she was halfway out the door. "Remember what I've told you."

I could see her cringe just as I used to cringe when my mother lectured me more than thirty years ago. But my mother's words were slightly different then. "Remember," she used to say, "you are a lady."

I still recall my annoyance at hearing that sentence—a piece of me always feeling cheated by the fact that, at twelve, I was more a child than a woman. Yet I took her warnings seriously. Time and again, the words kept me from squirting orange juice through my teeth at Johnny Kemp, from shouting nasty thoughts aloud at the girl next door, from wearing lipstick behind my parents' backs.

Just as that flicker of intrigue would cross my path, I would hear my mother's voice in my ears and I'd find myself thinking twice. "Remember . . . you are a lady."

I suppose I did remember. It is not that I never did anything wrong. I received my share of reprimands from irate parents whose sons and daughters I had taunted. I knowingly antagonized teachers. I was as catty and mean and selfish as any of the other kids. Yet, I wonder what I might have been without my mother's advice.

If she hadn't saddled me at twelve with all the responsibilities of ladyhood (as in sit like a lady, eat like a lady, act like a lady, speak like a lady) perhaps I would be a different woman today. Who knows what might have become of me were it not for my mother's admonitions and all their implications?

Which, I imagine, is the reason I feel compelled to offer parental advice to my own pre-teenage daughter. I have altered the words to suit the times, encouraging her to be a good person rather than a good lady, but the message is the same.

I want my child to be polite, to treat herself and others with respect, to be responsible and thoughtful, to represent her gender, her species—all of humanity—in a manner worthy of praise.

Now, is that too much for a mother to ask?

THE SWING SET

"My father took our swing set down," he said, standing in his driveway pointing to the pile of poles and seats and the rusted seesaw. "We got too big."

My children followed their friend's gaze to where it rested on the dismantled contraption. "We're getting rid of it," the boy continued in a tone of authority. He included his sister in the collective "we" of maturity. "We are too big," he repeated. (Too strong, too heavy, too old to play on the childhood thing.)

And my son and daughter nodded in agreement.

I sighed. Just yesterday, my daughter had hurt her leg on our swing set when the fragile plastic seat broke loose from the flimsy rope by which it was attached.

"You can't sit on that anymore," I had told her. And we'd removed the little seat.

And several days earlier, while watching the children balance on the top of the monkey bars, I'd yelled to them across the yard, to "get down before the whole thing tumbles forward. It can't hold your weight anymore."

In a moment of nostalgia during early spring, I'd suggested that we paint the poles for summer. But my daughter had laughed and asked me, "Why?"

My answer went unspoken.

To prolong their childhood, I admitted to myself. To pretend for one more season that they're small enough to find the top rung a challenge. To ignore his broadening shoulders, her lengthening legs.

I'd changed the subject to avoid the issue.

But my neighbor's acceptance of reality had pricked my conscience. I eyed the heap of equipment knowingly. Soon, soon, our set would endure the same fate.

Filled with somber thoughts of fleeting time, saddened by the passage of a phase, I wandered slowly to our back yard, casting a sidelong glance at the rusting swing set waiting for its certain doom.

And lo, not six feet from the boundary of our property, standing, in fact, on a patch of sunlit grass just behind the grass surrounding our own old swing set, was a brand new bright red and blue swing set with a slide.

My heart leapt. I was ecstatic, thrilled by the cycle of life continuing right before my eyes. I called to the young couple working there—hammering poles, adjusting the height of the swings.

"Enjoy," I said, waving from the doorway, smiling at their pre-school-age children, a boy and a girl, who are finally big enough to swing.

THE MOLD

There are some things about which my son is adamant. The mold in the piano bench, for example.

If it were my mold, I'd have preferred growing it in the

cabinet where the shoe polish is kept, or in the shed in the back yard, or in a box on the attic floor. But my suggestions were superfluous where this particular mold was concerned. My son had made up his mind. It would grow in a jar in the piano bench, and the sheet music would have to go.

Just as the shoes had to leave when the shoe boxes were needed for dioramas. Just as the eggs were evicted from egg cartons when art classes called for it.

Because some scientist, some researcher, some thinker long ago figured out the way that this or that should do a certain thing. And then, the teacher thought it would be "so much fun" for everyone to try a project of his own. She said "to gather materials, Mom, to get 'em from the house. She said, to bring 'em in. So this is what I need."

From nursery school on, how often have I removed the contents of cans and bottles before their time was up? How many sheets, pillowcases, blankets and towels have served as temporary costumes, never to resume their original roles?

And all for the sake of learning. All for the pursuit of knowledge. How many orange juice and milk containers have found their way to school with their innards left behind in spoutless bowls at the back of the refrigerator? How many pairs of perfectly good socks have given their lives to serve as stuffing for one puppet or another?

And what of the countless packages of uncooked macaroni, the bags of lima beans, the packet of seeds, the whole fruits and vegetables which have made their way from the kitchen to the classroom in the name of science?

And how happily have I submitted to the emptying of my shelves?

Quite happily, actually. Because, I believe that nearly anything which instills a love of learning is worth the effort. Even if it means a little mold in the piano bench.

$\mathcal{J}$EWELS

I never considered the value of my jewels until Great-Aunt Sara and Great-Uncle Jerry arrived from California.

Sometime during our after-dinner conversation concerning life, death, politics and war, my daughter found it appropriate to inventory her collection of baubles on the dining room table. While we adults sipped coffee and mused over long-forgotten ancestors, an array of bracelets, rings, earrings and necklaces was set out neatly before us between the cake plates and the fruit bowls.

Quietly, with nary a sound to disrupt our talk, the youngster made her way back and forth from the depths of her closet to the brightly lit room where we chatted over dessert.

Then, suddenly, by coincidence (or my daughter's design), the abstract banter ceased and we were confronted with reality. A half-dozen jewelry boxes of varying sizes and shapes, an assortment of rhinestones, seed pearls, silver chains and a smiling female eager to show her treasures.

And treasures they were. Neither gaudy nor ostentatious, the jewels were indeed an accumulation of feminine adornment—small gold hearts, pale lavender beads, signs and symbols of gender. No longer were they plastic and pipe cleaner imitations of jewelry, but real jewelry, gifts amassed during her twelfth year.

I was surprised by the quantity of things dangling, sparkling, shining before me, intrigued by my child's careful attention to the containers in which each item was housed.

The large wooden jewelry box with the oblong mirrors held necklaces with single ornaments, long velvet cases contained delicate bracelets. Plush cushions were the resting place for earrings with small posts. Each piece of jewelry had its home. The collection had an order. The exhibit was a source of pride to my daughter.

But the contrast with my possessions was striking. There in black and white, silver and gold, turquoise and yellow was a young girl's testimony to the jewelry industry of America. But I could not make a similar claim. Yet, my possessions are no less valuable for their lack of monetary worth.

To prove a point, I slipped away from the table and dislodged my own jewelry box from beneath a shoe box in my closet. Then, hurrying back to our guests, I presented the prize for scrutiny. My treasure chest is a former cigar box, spray-painted gold, adorned with macaroni shells, twists and elbows, given to me with love by my daughter nearly eight years ago.

Within this box are my favorite jewels—two crayoned plastic cups on faded ropes, gifts from each of my children on separate occasions, a glass pin in the shape of a rainbow, the duplicate of which I purchased for my daughter when we shared an afternoon outing six years ago, a plastic ring, two rubber bracelets and an assortment of priceless handmade items blinking, twinkling and glittering up at me from the homemade jewelry box worth more to me than all the diamonds in the world.

BEING THERE

I know why I'm there, wet and cold in the 'top of the third', on a rainy afternoon. I am there because I gave him a snack before the game, found the missing cap and batting glove and drove the car that got him there. I'm there because

I've packed his lunch for school, made his dental appointments and tucked him in through thick and thin, rain or shine, win, lose or draw, till the bottom of the ninth since the day of his birth. I am there because the pitcher is my son. And I love him.

And what about her? Why is she there chewing her nails, shouting encouragement through the chain-link fence? Why is she making all the calls before the umpire, snarling at the opposing coach? Why, without complaint or question, does she expect to attend these games as matter-of-factly as he expects her to be there? Because he has sat through every piano recital and play in which she has ever performed. Because they've ridden the school bus together, shared the breakfast table and said good-night to one another for a decade. She is there because the pitcher is her brother and she loves him.

But what about the man? The one behind first base wearing the light blue shirt with the word "Coach" printed in black across the front? What is he doing buckling the catcher's mask, putting ice packs on injuries, shouting "good eye" to the kid with the bat? What's he doing rushing straight from work to the mid-week game, skipping dinner to make it on time, hauling equipment from the trunk of his car to the playing field? Why is he standing there in the soggy outfield grass, warming up the pitcher? Why does he care about the pitcher? The team? The game? Why, with all the things he has to do, would he do this?

For the same reason he helped the pitcher with his homework last night, played catch with him yesterday, took him to a museum last week, taught him a song, told him a story, yelled at him to go to sleep, kissed him good-night and woke him up this morning.

Clearly, he does this because it is what he wants to.

Because he is my son's stepfather and he loves my son.
And I love knowing that.

THE DECISION

She will understand one day. She has to. I want her to.
Somewhere, at some time, my sister will know why I
couldn't drive to her son's *bar-mitzvah*, and she will forgive
me. But I don't know when.

As far as my children were concerned, there was simply
no question. "We'll walk," they had said. "It'll be fun." And
they'd meant it. They would gladly have marched the ten
miles between the synagogue and the hotel where the
reception would take place immediately after the Saturday
morning service. But on Friday, the older one woke up
feeling ill—too ill to make the hike. And we knew we'd have
to choose.

If we decided to attend the service, we would stay
overnight on Friday in a motel near the synagogue. If we
decided on the reception, we would sleep in the hotel where
that affair was to be held. In either case, we would bring
Shabbos dinner to eat in our room. And in either case, we'd
miss a part of something important to someone we loved.

With trepidation, we asked my nephew which he would
prefer. He said he'd rather we join him at the party. He said
it good-naturedly, gracefully. But behind his shoulder, I
could see my sister's eyes.

It is not that she hadn't taken my feelings into consider-
ation. It was I who had been short-sighted nearly a year ago.
It was then that she'd called to discuss her plans with me. She

was aware that we'd been moving to the right religiously, and she'd wanted us to know that there'd be kosher food for us. "But you'll have no problem driving from the service to the party, right?" she'd asked.

"Right, no problem," I had said. "Absolutely none at all."

But that was well before I understood *Shabbos*. That was back when I believed one could be sort of *shomer Shabbos*. Or sometimes *shomer Shabbos*. Or a little bit *shomer Shabbos*. That was when I thought *shomer Shabbos* was something one could occasionally choose to be. "Now it is no longer debatable," I felt compelled to say. "It's a part of me and I of it."

She nodded, accepting the decision. But I was certain that she did not truly understand. She was sorry, she said, and she was sad. I could tell she felt rejected, abandoned, deserted by her sister. And worse, she probably felt that I was judging her.

On Friday afternoon, we drove to the hotel where the reception would take place on Saturday after *shul*. We ate *Shabbos* dinner in our room on Friday night. We *davened* by ourselves on *Shabbos* morning. And then, when we knew the others would be arriving from the synagogue, we walked downstairs to the reception hall. Where there was a photographer taking pictures. Where people were dancing to a band. Where family members were lighting candles on the *bar-mitzvah* boy's birthday cake. Where friends and relatives understood that we had not been present to witness the rite of passage for my sister's first-born son. Where we were, comparatively speaking, fanatic in manner and deed—awkward and uncomfortable, set apart, unwilling and unable to participate in the festivities, aware of the discomfort we had caused, certain that our decision had been right for us . . . hopeful that one day they would understand.

THANK YOU

"Thank you, Mom," she said, hugging me tightly. "I love them. They're beautiful." Then, turning to include her brother in a broad smile, she added, "Thanks for being patient."

The two saleswomen in the small dress shop stopped in their tracks. "Did you hear what she said to her mother?" one asked the other. "No wonder she bought her three dresses. Who wouldn't for such a thank-you?"

The second salesperson gathered the garments and carried them to the check-out counter. "What a nice child," she told me. "And you're a nice mother."

I accepted the compliment, proud but not surprised that my daughter had thanked me, pleased that my generosity had not gone unnoticed.

Our shopping spree and my offspring's words of gratitude had been pleasant, wonderful even, but not unusual for most mothers and daughters in similar circumstances, I thought.

Yet the saleswoman said, "Not so. You wouldn't believe how mean some mothers are to their kids. The kids just can't wait to go home and hide in their rooms and cry.

"Some mothers tell their daughters how ugly they look in a dress or how awful a color is for them, how skinny or fat they are. Can you imagine how the girls feel?"

The saleswoman, not much more than a girl herself, carefully pulled plastic bags over the three dresses. "You were nice to your daughter," she said. "You told her she looked pretty. You let her make decisions. You didn't yell at her. You let her pick out the dresses she liked. You didn't laugh at her or make her try on things she hated. It's no wonder she thanked you."

"Thank you," I said.

Thank you . . . I thought about those words all the way home. Were we really so exceptional? I wondered. Don't most mothers think their daughters are beautiful? Don't they go shopping with plans to buy two new dresses and wind up buying three because their daughters smile so brightly or look so happy or seem so pleased with themselves? Don't they remember what it is like to be on the verge of womanhood, when the whole world teeters between security and fear? Don't they want their children to grow up feeling lovely and loved?

And why shouldn't the children say thank you? Isn't that what parents teach children to say in response to a compliment, a word of greeting, the purchase of a new dress? Isn't thank you something you must teach a child early on, if you expect to receive it later in life?

I would like to think that the saleswoman was misinformed. That a bad experience or two had altered her perception of mother-daughter relationships. I would like to think that on occasion, if there is enough money left over for the third dress, most mothers would give in to a whim because it is fun to make a daughter happy. I would like to believe that mothers want daughters to feel special and that both deserve a thank you now and again.

SPRING FEVER

Is this spring fever? The inability to concentrate, the vague feeling of restlessness, an almost irresistible desire to be outdoors? Is this a seasonal disorder, the condition of giddiness, of choosing to watch butterflies chase one another among the back yard trees, of knowing I should write a column, wanting to set words on paper and finding myself instead wondering at the forsythia bush still in bloom so late in the season, listening to the drone of an airplane high overhead, thinking about climbing the apple tree, contemplating moving my electric typewriter to the picnic table under the elm?

There are bugs in the air, fat black ones buzzing near the clover. I can hear them through the screened window. If I were to get up out of this seat and walk quietly to the side of the house, I could examine the insects more closely. That would be rather interesting, would it not?

Or I could get the mail. I might stand up, stretch, pass through the kitchen door, walk 'round the side of the house to the front where the crooked mailbox stands. On my way, I could check the birdhouse and the hydrangea bush.

Maybe I should walk to the store. I could call it exercise, just as I called this morning's walk exercise. Or I could take the same route once again this afternoon and look at the roses surrounding the corner house. They were so full and pink at eight-fifteen. Could they have blossomed further since I left them? Shouldn't I see?

If I wander around outdoors for a bit, an idea may come to me for this column. I might have a thought, a feeling to which readers may relate.

If I walk away from the typewriter this minute and look closely at the bark on the tree, I could determine if it is the bark itself or the sunlight making shadows which is creating such a fascinating pattern there. Mightn't that be an important subject about which to write?

I had wanted to say something serious today, to impart some vital insight. But the prospect seems less likely as the minutes pass. And I think I must be going now. I can smell the flowers through my open window. I can hear the birds singing through the screen. I can feel the breeze, watch it ruffle the papers on my desk.

I cannot, I tell you, sit still a moment longer. I really must find a bumblebee to follow . . .

SKINNED KNEE

It was the insult more than the injury, the feeling of having been tricked, fooled, taken unawares. It was the anger more than the skinned knees which brought tears to my eyes and made me want to punch the pavement.

My husband and I had been taking a walk, a casual stroll around the neighborhood. I was calling the excursion exercise. He was keeping me company. We were not more than three blocks from home, with me pointing out the sights—rosebush on the corner, yellow house for sale, dog, cat, someone's stray winter glove.

With no sidewalks to follow, we wound through the streets, staying near the right side of the road. Though some people complain about the lack of designated walking area, I've always considered it a plus. I equate the absence of sidewalks with country living. And I like to think my corner of suburbia is more rural than it is citified.

Thus, I was quite content, swinging my arms in the sunshine, totally unprepared for the vicious blacktop which rose suddenly to hit me smack in the face.

Or so it seemed. It happened in a matter of seconds. My feet got tangled in a castoff, rusty, wire hanger. I tripped and fell. My knees were scraped, my elbow skinned, the palms of my hands were mottled and bleeding, and my pride was hurt.

How dare this have happened to me?

My husband gallantly helped me up, chuckling quietly under his breath, pretending to be serious about my mishap but finding it difficult to conceal the laughter. I feigned bravery, shaking my head in contrived nonchalance. "No, no, I'm fine," I said. "Just a few scrapes, nothing major."

But I continued to fret, to pout, to check my elbows and knees. Like a kid, I thought to myself. You're acting like a child.

Precisely. And that is when I saw the point. Some things never change. A skinned knee at forty feels no different from a skinned knee at four. The injury always had been less painful than the shock of having fallen. The emotion I felt as an adult was the same one I'd felt at six and ten and twelve.

Suddenly, the stinging palms became a pleasant reminder of a childhood filled with cuts and scrapes, and a mother who hugged me and kissed the spot and gave me lemonade to make it better.

At once, the throbbing elbow was a link, a connection to the summers of my youth and a means of empathizing with my own children.

"Look," I purposely announced to my son as I walked through the kitchen door. "I fell down on the road and got hurt." I showed my battle scars with pride.

And my son responded with a grin. "Do you need a band-aid, Ma?" he asked.

"Yes," I answered. "And a dish of ice cream and a couple of cookies and something cold to drink. And someone to sit beside me on the couch a while and a kiss to make it feel better."

THE CHILD

He was not yet lost, but he might have been. He may have been lost in the past. He probably will be lost in the future. And I know why.

Because his mother leaves him alone.

In the checkout line of a large toy store with dozens of people clamoring for attention, among shopping carts and boxes and whining toddlers, this woman asks her son to "watch the packages" for just a minute "while Mommy checks something."

And off she goes—or went on the day I stood behind her waiting for my turn. And I was surprised to hear her tell the child to "stay . . . stay . . ." the way one would talk to a puppy in training. "And Mommy will be right back."

The boy, no more than two or three, did not glance up but continued to tinker with the small holes in the grates separating the cashiers from the customers.

I watched him, silently wondering where the mother had gone, how far she'd wandered in the store for the item she wanted to "check." As the minutes passed and the child stood fidgeting on little legs, it occurred to me that his lack of panic might mean he'd been left to wait like this before.

What if someone would just walk off with him? I thought morbidly to myself, as the woman finally returned with her item. "Good boy," she praised her son. "Good, good boy."

He didn't respond, but stood obediently at her side until she left once more—this time without warning, never bothering to tell the child she'd be right back (as if even that would have sufficed). She simply marched off to another counter to inquire or complain or comment while her son stood just in front of me.

The line moved, and I pushed the woman's cart forward,

nudging her child as I did so. "Here, honey, let's move this ahead just a bit," I said, talking to him gently, feeling uncomfortable as I spoke, realizing that he should not be listening to some stranger tell him where to stand and walk.

But the mother returned at last, smiling, laughing, patting "good boy" on the top of his head.

And I thought of saying something—anything—to her. I thought of telling her to please not leave the child alone for even a moment. I thought of saying, "You know, it's really not a good idea with so many people around and he's so tiny." I thought of suggesting that she take him with her, ask someone else to watch her packages the next time she felt the need to wander off. I thought of asking why a well-groomed, cheerful woman, obviously buying toys for her beloved son, would walk away without a word.

But I said nothing.

HEY

Who are "they"?

Who are the nameless ones we quote with confidence, when referring to the weather, the state of the arts, the nation, the world.

Who are the they of privileged information regarding the heat of summer, the chill of winter, the appropriate temperature for an infant's bath water?

They are the ones who say, "It may rain." They say, "Mud is good for bee stings." They say twos and teens are terrible and most divorcees remarry within five years or not at all.

I'm told (they say) they exist in Florida as well as New

York, and in Europe as surely as the United States.

But no one seems to know precisely who they are—or even if they are a single entity.

Perhaps the they of weather conditions refers first to the meteorologists of the world, those individuals whose scientific expertise is translated into clouds and sunlight in the newspapers, radio and television—to be read, listened to and watched by friends, neighbors and relatives who themselves become part of the they.

The they of doom—inflation, depression, a chicken pox epidemic—are not necessarily of the same primary group as the they of cold fronts and rain clouds. Yet the secondary source, they who spread the word, may be the same they as the they of the weather.

A grandmother, for instance, may foretell of a chill in the air while administering a warning to be pennywise—quoting they as the source for both bits of news. "They say the market's up." "They say we can expect a storm."

Although I question the validity of such a nebulous authority, I continue to quote it myself, as in, "They say hydrangea blossoms turn purple in acid soil." "They say women tend to outlive men."

And I am ever careful to credit my source, citing they as the giver of truth. This, despite the fact that I could, if I chose, be more specific. I could, in most instances, offer the names of those individuals who imparted the facts to me. The benefits of alfalfa, for example, were told to me by my father-in-law, who also offered advice on the use of vitamin C, vitamin E and bottled water, as suggested by "them."

My husband, a city boy himself, provided the information regarding the hydrangea bush. His source, I assume, was the nursery man from whom he purchased the plant. In relaying the facts, however, he said, "They say . . ."

The statistic on the longevity of the female of the species came in the form of an impromptu lecture by a friend. Her words of wisdom originated with "them."

I find it fascinating to note the diversity of subject matter gathered, absorbed and distributed by the selfsame they. They're incredible, I think. Or so they say.

THE SONG

We heard her before we saw her—the high-pitched voice ringing out in the still air of late afternoon, the words of her song a combination of current radio hits and phrases of her own creation.

We'd been out of the house for most of the day and returned just before dinner to this sound of music.

I was in the kitchen slicing tomatoes when I became aware of the lilting melody reaching me through open windows.

"Who's that?" I called to my son and daughter. "Who's singing outside?"

My children rushed toward me with fingers across their lips. "Shhh," they motioned and beckoned to me to follow.

From the windows of their rooms, each had a bird's-eye view of the performer—the little girl next door who, barefoot and wearing a pink bathing suit, crouched beneath her striped umbrella while a steady stream of droplets fell from the sprinkler which watered her gently sloping lawn.

Surrounded by trees and shrubs, the open area of yard formed a kind of stage for the performance being played out before the child's imaginary audience.

We watched in silence as she twirled to the choreographed number of her own design, dancing into the spray, singing of rainbows and love.

We were mesmerized by her theatrics, enchanted by her lack of inhibition, by her innocence and joy.

Watching her, I recalled in my own children moments of such wild abandon, times during which make-believe became real, when the outside world faded and only the moment would count.

While she hummed and skipped and raised her arms to the sky, other neighborhood youngsters joined us at the window.

A vague sense of dishonesty nudged my conscience as we continued to watch the child without her knowledge or consent. But I could not pull myself away, rationalizing that were she old enough to appreciate the gift she was giving, she would allow us to see this show.

Maybe one day, a year or three from now, when she is less able to shut out reality, I will tell her of this lovely summer's interlude. And then again, she may grow up to be one of those special individuals for whom, audience or no, reality, fantasy and *joie de vivre* go hand in hand—forever.

FIRST IMPRESSIONS

HOW? "We'll just do it, that's all," my husband announced. "I haven't been back in years, and it's time for us to go."

"Just like that? In the middle of summer when we need a new car and a new roof on the house? And the couch is falling apart, and the washing machine makes terrible noises? And I don't know the language? And your relatives there are so-o-o religious. What will I wear? And can we drink the water? Will the kids enjoy themselves? How can we possibly do this thing? Should we really just forget about the roof and the ailing car? Is it right to take our last penny, and to borrow on top of that, just for the sake of seeing Israel?"

But I didn't need an answer.

ARRIVAL. Eleven o'clock on an August night in the back seat of a cab, after a ten-hour plane flight, preceded by a four-hour delay, and suddenly, finally, we are here. In this taxi, on a smooth highway, with our eyes adjusting to the black velvet sky, the shadowy mountains lining the road, the sight of a full moon, a silver globe, a miraculous sphere suspended there before us in the heavens. Placed there to light the way this night, as I read the sign in halting Hebrew. Yerushalayim, it says. And my son leans forward to whisper in my ear.

"Mommy, Mommy. If this is all there is, if we have to turn around now and go home, this is enough, isn't it?"

DAY ONE. There are pink flowers outside our window and a white tiled floor in the kitchen. It is my first morning in Israel.

We walk to the Supersol to buy food for our little apartment. And the produce bears Hebrew names. "Hebrew letters," I say, crying at the sight of tea written in Hebrew script. Laughing with tears at the catsup and the cereal boxes and yogurt, adorned by the selfsame letters I read each week in a synagogue in New York.

And the sounds of the supermarket. People speaking a living language. With my untrained ear, I catch only melodies, few words, but I imagine the conversations. "How much are the berries?" she asks. And he gives her the price. Or, "We need *chalav*," to a small child. And the child says, "*Kain*." And I am thrilled. And my children, wandering through the store, gleeful at their mastery of this language, translate here and again for me.

"Mommy, look, olives," they tell me. "And bread and cheese."

Hebrew cheese, Hebrew juice, Hebrew customers shouting and smiling and conducting their lives in the land.

The land.

MASADA. "Everybody does it," he told me.

But I was skeptical. "Everybody?" I said. "At two-thirty a.m.? Are you sure?"

He answered, "Yes."

"Well, when's the last time you did this?"

"Fifteen years ago," he admitted. "But I'm positive it's okay."

I doubted him. Questioned his judgment, his sanity, even. But I acquiesced, finally, and woke the children. We gave them a hurried breakfast and hustled them into the car. And then, with my husband at the wheel and a cool Jerusalem breeze in the air, we headed for Masada in the dead of night.

The lone car on the road.

On either side of the narrow strip of pavement, I could see whitish plants, skeletal and ghostlike in the dark. Strange shadows played on the Dead Sea to our left, shapeless looming mountains rose up on our right. And an eerie sense of nothingness, emptiness, a heart-pounding fear of isolation rode with me as we followed signs to the site of a mass suicide committed nearly two thousand years prior.

And all the while, I marveled at the majesty, the desolation itself in the black, dead night was magnificent. How insignificant we are, I thought. How like a pinprick am I on this length of road, winding past a sea of salt through a colorless night.

Strange, wild-eyed animals—coyotes, foxes crossed our path time and again, and I wrung my hands in fear and anticipation.

"I think people do not do this," I said. "Certainly not people in a car. Maybe buses of people, maybe tours. Maybe a tour you took when you were a young man with neither a wife nor children. But who would do this with a family in tow?"

But my husband persevered, stubbornly refusing to be frightened by my skepticism.

And I had no choice but to trust him.

"The sun will rise," he promised. "Over Masada. You will understand."

We arrived in the dark, the children, bursting with excitement, each carrying a container of water on the monumental uphill climb with the Dead Sea at our backs and the cliff of stone ahead and the sky turning yellow in the dawn. Higher, we climbed, panting, perspiring, noting a handful of others just ahead of us, just below, as we followed the serpentine pathway upward to the very top.

And there, on the ledge of a fortress constructed in an age of kings, I saw a pink pearl sky with streaks of orange and gold and mauve.

And then, rising slowly out of the sea, lighting Masada, lighting the world anew at three minutes after six a.m. on that particular morning, came the sun. A golden, golden sun.

And it was good.

And it was desolate there. Mountains. High, brown, red,

forebidding mountains under a bright sun. And my son and husband joined a *minyan*, *davening* in the remnants of a *shul* atop Masada with Israeli jet fighters flying overhead, breaking the sound barrier. And people speaking ten different languages, scraps of languages flung at the still air, joined together to *daven* in one voice.

A THOUGHT ABOUT TREES. The trees—growing out of the hard rock ground, out of sand and pebbles, out of dry earth. Clusters of green. Small forests seen from a distance on hillsides and mountainsides. Growing on terraced slopes, watered by hand. Nurtured and nourished by man. Cared for from seedlings. Valued, appreciated, understood to be gifts, cherished prizes to be dealt with thoughtfully.

I think maybe this is the way G-d meant it to be. He and we, together, making the trees grow.

THE SHUK. The *shuk*. A man with no fingers and one clouded eye sells drinks at the arched entrance. An old woman with orange hair squats on the floor selling cactus.

Inside, it is quiet, dark, mysterious. We walk through winding, narrow stone passageways. I taste the smells, the sounds, the dark faces.

The *shuk*. Olives, silver, meat, fish, pink, blue and silver scarves, music, water pipes, a donkey, dark-eyed children, cats in corners, underfoot, lurking, cakes and cookies and bread and belts, leather, dresses of cotton and velvet, dresses cluttered with rhinestones, the smell of spices, purple grapes, green grapes, cactus fruits.

The *shuk*.

YAD VASHEM. The pitch-black room and the single candle reflected thousands of times in thousands of mirrors, as the names of the children murdered in the Holocaust are repeated in monotone, endlessly. And we move in silence along a pathway through this place of painful memory in a kind of stupor. The children's room, the last place we visit after hours at Yad Vashem. But the room is endless as the names are endless. Each child dead before he had a chance to live.

I grab my children's hands as we reach the door—outside at last in the light of day, standing with our backs to the memorial and our faces to the hills where off in the distance we see a new Jewish settlement, white and shimmering in the heat.

"And out of the ashes," we think.

But we say not a word.

PROBLEMS. Who would have thought one plum could cause such a problem? One little purple plum fresh from Israel's earth, and suddenly, I am stricken with stomach cramps. But they tell me the condition is mandatory for all first-time visitors. My initiation, I suppose.

They promised us a telephone in the apartment.

It never would have occurred to me to ask if the telephone worked. Telephones always work.

Except in Israel. In Israel, I have learned, telephones work only when the operators are not on strike, the lines are not crossed, the telephone company decides to open its doors for two hours after lunch or when, in desperation, we leave the apartment to look for a pay phone and find that we do indeed have an *asimone* or seven, depending upon whether or not the operator has decided to disconnect the call.

But it is life. No big deal. No matter of great concern. So the phone does not work, will not work for the duration of the trip, and no one cares.

"Oh yes, well, the phone is not working," a neighbor says. "*Kain, kain,*" she says, with a smile and a shrug of the shoulders. "Would you like a plum?"

I am dumfounded and delighted. A country which exists without working phones and people who do not mind.

And the paperwork to rent a car. Five copies, carefully printed in tri-colored ink by a young woman outraged at our attitude of impatience.

We try again. "You promised this car would be ready two hours ago."

"Sign here," she says, pointing to the dotted line, unconcerned by our agitation or by the growing line of people waiting for cars.

And the banks closing for a siesta from eleven to three, with tellers in no hurry to complete the transaction.

And road signs illegible or nonexistent. Toilet tissue like cardboard, ice cream like sugared soup.

Forcing me to realign priorities, take hold of perspective—a country coming to life after thousands of years. A country, our country, my country.

The rest—is meaningless.

SHABBOS IN JERUSALEM. Standing in a galley kitchen in a house with two rooms. Shelling hard-boiled eggs with Cousin Chava.

Cousin Chava with a shaved head under a black *tichil.* Her hands calloused and strong. Smiling with green eyes, wearing a blue dress. Helping me to help her serve the *cholent* and the fish and the *kugel* and the chicken and the cake and the compote and the salad. Talking to me in Yiddish in the galley kitchen in the foyer of the sunlit flat, with the windows open over the red-tiled roofs of Meah

Shearim. And the sounds of the children outside and the sounds of *Shabbos* in the air.

Carrying plates of food to the table. To Cousin Yosef in his *shtreimel* and *kapote* with his white curled *peyos* and his beard and his sparkling eyes. Carrying food to the smiling Yosef, smiling at the day, at the food, at the table, at my husband and my son and the sound of my son singing with Yosef at the *Shabbos* table.

And Chava scooping food onto dishes. Placing dishes in bags for her grandsons to give to the poor. To the poor who have less than the two rooms Chava has for her lovely, gentle life. And me, feeling awed by the generosity, the simplicity.

And the children and the children's children. Girls with dark stockings and braids. Boys with knickers and round eyes. Young men with straight backs and broad shoulders. And sounds of singing and *davening*. And children, babies, women speaking. Smiling, gentle, loving women.

And the *havdalah* candle and the spices and the two boys dancing. Little boys dancing in their great-grandfather's high-ceilinged room. And me, standing there holding my daughter's hand. Both of us with tears in our eyes on *Shabbos* in Jerusalem.

THE WALL. I don't like objects. I like people. I like words. I like mountains, the sun, the blinding blue of the sky, the fragrance of tahini paste, the bearded men, real things, living breathing things. Not a monument built by men.

I will feel nothing, I tell myself as the heat of day bakes the cobbled ground and the top of my head and my eyelids. When I see it, I know I will not feel.

We stand then, in the old quarter of Jerusalem on some pink and beige stone balcony overlooking the city with the red hills beyond.

My husband says, "Look down now and tell me what you see."

But I cannot speak—for there before us is the Wall.

OOK FIVE • CONNECTIONS

CONNECTIONS

INTRODUCTION

They were rapidly moving out of childhood. "Not so fast," a part of me wanted to shout each day. "Slow down, please." But I kept silent, watching one or the other outgrow a pair of shoes, a jacket or a game. "What's your hurry?" I wanted to ask. The question was rhetorical. I knew exactly what they were doing—careening headlong towards adulthood, while I was standing still at mid-life looking back.

The faster they matured the more I clung to vestiges of their childhood. While they advanced in thought and conversation, I reverted to the daydream. Often, during their pre-teen stage, I found myself recalling my own youth. Suddenly, I saw my mother in myself. Her words spilled forth from my mouth. And not surprisingly, people began to tell my daughter that she looks a lot like me. Connections. Bonds. Memories.

Sometimes, grandparents came to me in dreams. I would see my paternal grandmother standing at the top of an expansive flight of stairs. She gave advice which, in the morning light, I could not recall. I spent hours poring over photographs stored in plastic in my parents' house. The woman in the pillbox hat and the pin-striped dress was my mother at age thirty. The curly-haired man vacationing at Cousin Sonia's in the Catskills was my father at twenty-four. Aunts and uncles were girls and boys in sailor dresses and knickers, smiling through eyes and lips the shapes of which have been transmitted to their children and grandchildren.

"Where exactly was your father born?" I asked my father. "How old was your mother when she immigrated here? Tell me again about Great-Uncle Julius. Who's that man in the hat and the long black coat? Was he religious?" After years of apathy, suddenly I developed an interest in family history. I imagined the *shtetls* in Poland and Russia from which my ancestors came. I remembered with what determination my grandmother learned to speak English. Yet I could recall the sound of her voice only in the Yiddish melodies which she had hummed to me. Sadly, I realized that I'd never known the meaning of the Yiddish words.

As my children rushed sure-footed towards their destiny, I faltered, searching in my past for strength and guidance—dimly aware of my responsibility as a link in a fragile chain.

THE BLOSSOMS

I cannot stand that tree with its dark green leaves and its full white blossoms. Cannot tolerate the memory of those delicate petals clustered at the tips of slim branches, signifying school.

It is not that I disliked school as a child. It is simply that I hated seeing summer end.

In the town where I grew up, July and August meant endless hours of hide-and-seek, hopscotch, back yard wading pools and ice cream cones. Summer was fireflies captured in glass milk bottles, trips to the Jersey shore, block parties, barbecues, picnics and cloudless skies. Summer, as I recall it, was an endless vacation, carefree and happy.

Until the tree produced its flowers.

There, on the front lawn right beside the porch steps, the buds suddenly would begin to bloom, and I would despise their appearance.

It hadn't always been so. As a toddler, before I'd understood the meaning of the flowers, I had loved their appearance and smell. I had actually plucked them from the lower branches to play bride along the sidewalk leading to the door. But later, when social studies and algebra entered my vocabulary, I came to look upon that tree as a symbol of impending confinement. Daily, I would check the stems and flowers, marking the progression of color from pale green to snowy white, noting with dismay the approach of season's end.

And always, by the time I'd selected my sturdy shoes and my back-to-school dress, the branches would be heavy with flowers, and I would feel the butterflies in my stomach.

No matter what the temperature outside, I knew that once the school doors opened in September, summer would be officially over—and with it would go my sense of serenity and joy.

And so it is that even now I cringe each time I pass a particular tree growing in a neighbor's yard. I purposely have not taught my children the significance of the blossoms, in the hope that maybe, if my son and daughter do not notice the flowers, summer will not end.

THE DOCTOR'S OFFICE

Relegated to the waiting room. Watching the fish swim around in the ten-gallon tank. Studying the wallpaper, the carpeting, the faces of the other mothers sitting there. Feeling proud and old and glad and a little sad.

It was the day of the "well child" visit—a term attached to the fifteen minutes per year when the offspring are examined by the physician, weighed, measured and pronounced to be well.

Always, in the past, this particular excursion to the doctor's office had produced in me an unparalleled feeling of accomplishment. Year upon year, I would stand beside my youngsters, nodding my head with glee as each was given a clean bill of health. "How tall you've grown," I'd repeat after the doctor, taking full credit for the two inches logged since the previous year's well child appointment. "And your hearing is perfect, your eyesight is excellent." Even your blood is wonderful, I'd think.

Annually, during these checkups, I would find myself smiling uncontrollably, beaming with joy as the doctor would mark off yet another segment on the children's charts, marvelling at the accomplishments etched in increments of inches and pounds.

Somehow, on these annual visits, I never felt the need to be humble when the doctor issued a compliment. I suppose I believed that I was somehow responsible for the straightness of my son's spine or the arch in my daughter's foot.

You must be a marvelous mother, I liked to think he thought, as I would look over the doctor's shoulder with maternal pride.

Until today.

I was already through the door of the examination room when the doctor said, "You can wait outside." The doctor, in his gentle tone, motioned toward the room with the line of chairs flush against the wall. "We'll call you when we're finished." He smiled.

Just like that.

And then, seeing my face fall, he added, "Unless one of them wants you in there."

But of course, they didn't. At ten and twelve, there is no longer a need for me to hold a hand during a blood test, to retie shoes or button shirts or answer questions regarding what they've been doing this year and what grade they'll enter in the fall.

And so it was that I made my way toward the fish tank where I watched the bubbles rise—noting with a vague sense of sadness the speed with which we grow.

The Watch

I never knew my maternal grandmother. She died before I was born. But yellowed pictures show her to be a rather buxom woman with marcel waves in her steel-gray hair and a stern smile on her lips.

My mother tells me photos are deceiving. Her mother, she insists, was warm and sweet, intelligent and loving, the matriarch of a poor but educated family who settled in northern New Jersey to reap the benefits of the fresh suburban air.

Through the years, my mother, on occasion, has walked with me past the house where she grew up. And periodically, she has described a room or two therein—the icebox in the kitchen, cramped quarters where the children shared a bed. She's offered fleeting glimpses of a life within the walls of this edifice long since repainted and renovated. And rarely, except on these forays with her, have I wondered about this home where my mother was reared—even less have I thought of the woman who gave my mother life.

But today, my grandmother is on my mind.

At precisely half past eight this morning, I prepared to begin my daily walk, a ritual which purportedly gives me exercise and during which time my columns frequently are born. Until recently, I limited these neighborhood meanderings to thirty minutes, keeping tabs on the time with the help of a small gray watch given to me by my sister and her family. But I accidentally washed, and thereby ruined, the little watch. And I have been without one ever since.

To mark the minutes, I have had to borrow other watches for my walk—my husband's square-faced watch which hangs heavily on my wrist, the one-handed identification watch (given to him by his mother on his seventeenth birthday), a round-faced watch with foreign numerals etched in gold. Today, I was planning to borrow my son's plastic stopwatch when my grandmother's timepiece came to mind.

And I found it there, where it has remained for many years, at the bottom of a box filled with other little-worn pieces of jewelry. I set the time, wound the tiny knob and heard it tick.

Like a miniature heart, beating in rhythm while I walked,

the watch walked with me as it must have walked with my grandmother seventy years ago.

TEENAGERS

The girlfriends. Doing homework on the living room floor with books and papers, potato chips and sharpened pencils.

I can see them as I stand in the doorway, liking the fact that they look so like the twelve-year-olds they are. And all the old styles are back, I think. The heavy socks, the laceless sneakers, the calf-length skirts. And ponytails with ribbons, just like the ones I wore.

I want to join them there on the living room floor—want to hear what they're saying about this classmate and that, this teacher or the other. I want to be a part of that timeless sorority, the members of which join briefly, when adulthood is nearly attainable and childhood nearly past.

Their skin is clear, untinged by makeup. I observe the blonde with the large dimple in her cheek, a cheerful, optimistic child. She makes the others laugh. She sings, she talks. She folds her long legs beneath her and puts the eraser tip of the pencil to her lips.

The other, with the ponytail and the blue eyes, is a serious, pensive child. She writes poetry and thinks somber thoughts.

And then, there is my own. A dark-eyed girl with long dark hair who looks self-assured and happy on the floor with her friends.

And I have much to do, but I cannot pull myself away,

loving the sight of it—this cluster of girls so similar, I think, to other such gatherings throughout time.

And I want to tell them this. To make them see how alike we really are. How I can remember, as though it were yesterday, the chips and pretzels and the math and social studies books. I can remember the conversations. The secrets. And yes—yes—I can see the mothers now, standing in doorways, moving toward us, hovering with their plates of cookies and brownies and soft drinks. Mothers, edging nearer. And I can remember, lowering our voices lest these looming women overhear our private words. I can remember wanting them to go away. To leave us alone. To disappear somehow, so that we could whisper and giggle and tease.

I can feel the old annoyance when some mother or other would stay too long, interject a thought, interrupt our private world or, worse, stop and question us.

And so, remembering this, I back away to the kitchen where my son, his sister's younger brother, sits and says, "You know, Mom, they're almost teenagers."

BELONGING

It rained again last night and the plastic tablecloth and paper decorations were wet and dripping, but the sun shone brightly through the roof of the *sukkah* this morning.

I moved slowly in the little shelter, hesitating as I plucked the apples and green peppers from the threads which attached them to the roof. Finished, I thought and felt sad. And suddenly, I found myself wishing that the holiday was just beginning, that we were only now decorating the booth and filling it with memories.

I wrapped the soggy construction paper chain into a ball and threw it in the garbage can—then had a pang of guilt for the empty space left in the *sukkah*. But even the *s'chach* must come down, I reminded myself. And the walls and table must be stored away until next year. And then, standing in the *sukkah* door, I found myself calculating the days until the next holiday.

With the autumn leaves yet swirling through the air, I found myself looking forward to *Chanukah*, envisioning flickering candles on the window sill, imagining the dark skies and chill winds of winter. We will eat *latkes* then, I thought, and we will remember our history, and when the holiday is through, I will be sad.

I stared hard at the *sukkah* walls with their brightly painted dancing figures and scenes from Israel—creations annually drawn by my son and daughter and their friends. The beautiful little *sukkah* must come down. But there will be *Purim* with its costumes and its *shalach manos* and its *Megillah* reading. And there will be *Pesach* when our house is filled with guests. There will be a year's worth of *Yomim Tovim*, significant and special, and I will celebrate them all, I thought. I will contemplate, commemorate, participate from the inside. I will welcome these holidays into our home as surely as I welcome *Shabbos*. I will learn customs and laws. I will make discoveries. With each small effort on my part, I will find, as I have found during the past eight years, that I will receive far more than I give. With each step forward that I take, whole worlds will open up for me.

As I pack away the frame and contents of the *sukkah* the truth will be clear once again. The more I know that I belong, the more I know belongs to me.

MOTHER'S WORDS

"I am cold. Put on a sweater."

On a lovely autumn afternoon, with the breeze just ruffling my hair, barely fluttering the sleeves of my shirt, my mother would stop me in mid-game to hand me some outer garment lest I catch a chill.

And in summer, in the heat of day, under sweltering sun at ocean-side, her words would ring clear and true. "I'm shivering," she would tell me. "Wrap yourself in a towel."

And in winter, I'd be swathed in wool the moment she felt the first gust of wind.

While other youngsters ran bareheaded and sockless from one season to the next, I was protected year-round against the elements, pneumonia or worse.

All because my mother said she felt cold.

How infuriating it could be. How embarrassing, with crowds of children ("all the kids, Ma") running hither and thither in short-sleeved shirts, and me in a pink cardigan with pearl buttons.

"All the others in sneakers, jumping in puddles, Mom," and me in red rubbers to keep my toes and ankles dry.

Me, angrily donning the robe, the jacket, the towel, the blanket, the coat, the scarf, the gloves.

Me, protesting. She persisting—at the hint of a breeze, running indoors to fetch the proper clothing for her child.

And I would whine, "Why?"

"Because I am chilly," she would answer honestly.

"But I am not," I would pout, frowning as she fussed with buttons and buckles, hats and mittens.

Then, grumbling with less conviction, I would allow my mother to kiss me and send me off again to play, feeling fat, clumsy and warm in my "extra clothes." I would wonder why it was she always knew when it was cold. How it was she could predict this chill before the chill occurred. And I would wonder why no one else's mother seemed to care.

I alone, it appeared, was blessed with this parent whose sensitivity to the weather enabled her to predict rain on sunny mornings, snow in cloudless skies. I was chosen to reap the questionable benefits of this woman's gift. I was prepared with the umbrella and the raincoat and, inevitably, the extra-heavy jacket. "Zipped to the top," she would warn. "All the way up to the top."

She cared not one iota for current fashion but insisted on warmth against all odds. "For your own sake," she would say. "Now do as I tell you . . ."

". . . because I'm your mother," I heard myself complete the sentence, staring my daughter in the eye. "Right this minute zip it all the way up . . . because I am cold," I said.

And suddenly, my mother's words made sense.

Mother's Cooking

Breaded veal chops cooked in oil, baked beans simmered in brown sugar and fried flounder with mashed potatoes and canned peas and chocolate pudding for dessert. Dinners of my childhood.

Last night, my mother called to tell me that, as a birthday gift for my father, she had made a pot of beans with honey and sugar and marrow bones. "The kind I used to make when you were little. Remember?" she wanted to know.

How could I forget? On the back burner in the huge pot on the big stove in the country kitchen. The same kitchen where the fragrance of homemade stew greeted me at the door on winter afternoons and chicken soup was a mainstay on Friday nights. But much has changed. Concern over nutrition has altered our eating habits, and even my mother stopped making the beans.

Until last night. "I thought he'd like them," she said, smiling across the phone lines.

"Beautiful," I could hear my father say, licking the spoon. "Beautiful."

And that, of course, is how I remember those beans—golden brown and bubbly and very sweet. But sugar is evil, they say. And so is oil, salt, white flour and red meat.

So my children have been reared on a diet of whole-wheat bread, fresh vegetables and skinless, boneless chicken.

Quite bland, I would say, comparatively speaking. Health-ful, perhaps, but nothing to compare with liver 'n' onions or hot dogs 'n' sauerkraut as a meal.

And not nearly as memorable. Will they, at forty, recall bean sprouts on pita with any joy? Will they care that I have tried to prevent future heart problems by eliminating salt from their diets? That I keep sugar to a minimum and shun nitrates with a vengeance? Will it matter to them that their mother reads labels for additives and preservatives, discard-ing precisely those items which she loved as a girl and which, by sheer mention, can set her mouth watering?

Or will they chuckle fondly, saying, "Well, at least she tried"?

Will they think of the meals of their youth as something they endured?

Not if I can help it. While they are still here, under my roof, periodically, I must offer them a taste of real food—heavy, sweet, fattening, non-nutritious food. Because along with their dinners, I intend to feed them some memories.

TO KVELL

To *kvell*—to fill with pride, to feel the blood rush to your cheeks, to feel your heart pound in your chest, to feel the hairs on your arms and the back of your neck stand on end, to feel taller, brighter, better—to feel like bursting with joy and passion—to understand once again, to relearn the miracle of motherhood.

My son, up there on stage, singing his heart out. My son, *mein zonenyu.* If only my grandmother could be here now to see him—to hear him out there being a part of something special. Oh, she would love it. She'd call him her *zieskeit*, a word which would slip into the English vocabulary she'd so resolutely mastered. But she would be unable to hold back. For this occasion, only Yiddish would do.

"*Eibershter, mein Eibershter,*" sings the choir, and I mouth the words silently from my seat in the darkened auditorium, aware of the nearly tangible bond linking me to the blonde-haired boy in the second row.

My son, a member of the Tzlil v'Zemer choir—my boy, wearing the bow tie and the red vest, wedged among the twenty other boys in ties and vests, my sweet boy, singing with feeling. And I am ecstatic, not simply because his voice has been deemed worthy of selection, not just because the choir affords him the opportunity to gain confidence and poise—I am ecstatic because my son is singing songs in Yiddish and Hebrew—understands what he is singing in Yiddish and Hebrew—is bringing the message of those songs to a standing-room-only audience.

I make eye contact with another mother of a choir boy and we smile knowingly, sharing the essence of this thing called *nachas*, understanding instinctively how each of us feels when watching her son. Because we are our sons—as they are part of us. These children have taken something from us, something fine, something having nothing to do with their voices but rather with their actions and deeds. These are good boys.

And even if they are good for the moment only, even if, when the performance ends, they will talk too loudly, ask too many questions, argue with their sisters, even if they won't eat their broccoli, will forget to do homework, they are up there now, on stage in the bow ties and vests, being good and beautiful and sincere and special and ours. Mine. My son. *Mein zonenyu.* And I understand what it is to *kvell.*

FALSE ADVERTISING

My daughter pursed her lips, perused the menu once more and ordered. "I would like the delicious, homemade french fries," she said. "And the lightly seasoned vegetable soup."

My husband and I cast knowing glances at one another as the waitress put pen to pad. "Will that be all, miss?"

"No," answered the earnest young customer. "I'll have a refreshing fruit cocktail. Thank you."

The waitress nodded her approval and walked away. "To converse with the chef, no doubt," I suggested.

"Well, somebody's got to make sure the french fries will be delicious," my husband answered, laughing under his breath.

"What's so funny?" my daughter wanted to know. "What's wrong with delicious french fries?"

And thus began her first lesson in false advertising.

"It's not that they're lying, exactly," we tried to explain. "Whoever wrote this menu probably hopes the french fries will be delicious. Look, he even drew a picture of delicious fries. But only you can tell him how they taste. Don't you see? It's the words which make you order the fries. Nobody can guarantee deliciousness in a fast food establishment."

She wasn't convinced.

"Look here," we said, pointing to the word homemade. "Homemade by whom? After all, this is a restaurant, not a house, isn't it? Nobody's mother is back there whipping up a batch of spuds from scratch. They're probably precooked potatoes popped in a microwave. But homemade makes them sound good, doesn't it?"

My daughter nodded half-heartedly. "Sort of," she said, ". . . I guess."

"And lightly seasoned soup. Doesn't that sound lovely? The phrase is so alliterative. Seasoned soup . . . All those S's make you want to sip the soup. You can almost envision a Frenchman back there carefully adding rosemary to a simmering pot of delicately flavored brew."

"But it's probably some kid in a paper hat dropping a few plastic pouches into a pot."

She looked crushed.

"Oh, come on," we coaxed. "It's not that bad. You just have to be discerning. You've got to learn the difference between what is fact and what is wishful thinking."

"Well, how do you know?" she asked.

And that, we had to admit, was a difficult question. How does one know, after all? Is it simply a matter of price? If the restaurant is expensive, is that indeed a guarantee of taste?

Is it ambience, the clink of crystal, the dim lights, the piano bar, that make the soup in one place better than the soup in another?

Is it the candles on a table rather than fluorescent lighting that necessarily herald honesty in menus? Or might the burgers at a fast food place be better than those in the finest of the fine?

"And who's to say what's fine?" the young lady wanted to know.

But she's an optimist, forever seeing the best in people and events and menus. And so, we were not surprised to hear her declare, "Refreshing!" as she swallowed a spoonful of canned fruit cocktail.

In season, of course.

THE ASSIGNMENT

Grandma in black banana curls standing over the pickle barrel in the general store. Grandma practicing penmanship in the third grade. Grandma at the icebox, the coal stove, the swimming hole. Grandma playing marbles and jump rope, sewing dresses and catching whooping cough.

"Gram as a kid, Mom, like me." My son hung up the phone with lights in his eyes. He'd just finished the first of six interviews with Grandma and couldn't wait to tell the world.

"When she was eleven, there was no frozen orange juice," he explained. "There were no jet planes or computers, no video or tape recorders. She walked to school every day and walked home for lunch. Groceries for the family cost less than three dollars. She swam in a brook behind her house and gathered fresh eggs from the farmer next door. And she played baseball . . . like me, Mom.

""She sewed a lot of her own clothes. She helped her mother cook. And she worked when she was my age, Ma. She worked in her father's store.

"Her house was cold in the winter, hot in the summer, and they never heard of stereos or food processors. It was different when she was a kid, Mom."

As different as our world will seem from that which will exist two generations hence. Yet, despite the advances, some things will remain the same.

Which is precisely the point of the class assignment. Talk to your grandparents, suggested the teacher. Ask them questions, find out what it was like to grow up more than fifty years ago, learn about what was and was not yet invented. Discover how one got along without a VCR and microwave. And then, project what your descendants will say about our "old-fashioned" ways of the '80s.

"It's a hard project," sighed my son, jotting down his next set of questions for Gram and Grandpa. "But it's really fun. I think I'd like to ask questions even if I didn't have to do it for school. It's interesting, isn't it, Ma?"

I answered, "Yes. In fact, it may be more than interesting. It may be vital."

Once upon a time, grandmas and grandpas shared living quarters with sons and daughters and grandchildren. But longevity, mobility and Florida are putting an end to that. And with the physical distance between grandparent and grandchild has come a waning of the oral history, a weakening of the "when I was a girl (or boy)" tales of yore. And that, I think, is a shame, a loss we will regret. Therefore, I congratulate my son's teacher for foresight in assigning this task to the students.

"Because Grandma and Grandpa have a lot of really great things to say."

THE DRESS

I've never been quite sure if he was serious.

"That's a lovely costume," he would tell me with not a trace of a smile.

And off I would run in a fit of anger. "It's not a costume, Daddy. It's a dress," I'd shout, stomping to my room. There, I'd pull the garment over my head in a rage and throw it on the bed, muttering angrily at my father's choice of words.

"Costume! Costume!" I'd say, slamming doors and stamping feet.

When I was slightly older, I would model two dresses for him, one after the other, wanting him to choose the winner. Inevitably, he would choose my least favorite, calling it the nicer costume of the two, noting something about color or style, sending me into a frenzy of fury concerning his taste in clothes. "You hate the one I like," I would accuse. "I know you do. You think the one I like is ugly." And off I'd go, storming and brooding, into my room.

Never once did I see wit in his calm demeanor or humor in the knowing glances he and my mother exchanged. Never did I understand that the father of two teenage daughters could not possibly have won this game.

"That's an elegant gown," he'd say of my coveted tailored suit and I'd grimace in frustration. "How can you call this a gown?" I'd want to know. "Can't you tell it's not a gown?"

But he'd raise his eyebrows slightly and repeat his words of praise.

And so it went. He'd compliment the hairdos I found least becoming. He'd flatter me in coats and shoes I did not like. And worse, he would ignore those styles in which I thought I looked quite fine.

He'd label something "cute" when it was elegant and "nice" when I was certain it was grand.

And yet, I continued showing him my purchases, continued twirling and strutting and smiling my sullen, teenage smile for him through all those years at home.

I always favored forest greens and blues and blacks, the somber tones I thought would make me look poetic. And he kept urging cheer and color. "A little life," he liked to say.

But off I went to college in my blues and greens and browns, and later married and became a mother, still favoring earth tones and shades of somber hue.

And then, last week, for some inexplicable reason, I bought myself a bright yellow dress, an ankle-length, high-necked, canary-hued ensemble, the first yellow dress I've ever owned. And I came right home and called my dad. I knew he would approve.

 FRIEND

"Maybe she was just being nice during that time," he said gently. "Maybe she isn't interested in talking to you now."

I thought about what my husband was saying. He could have been right. When my world was falling apart, when my first marriage was crumbling, when the children were babies, I had turned to her, and she had held me up. She'd given me hours of time, shared her meals with me, talked to me endlessly, reassured me, listened to me. She'd been a true friend, a trusted friend. When I'd needed her, she'd been there.

But then, we'd moved away. The kids and I had settled

far from her home, and we'd begun life anew. My friend and I kept in touch regularly at first and then sporadically, and finally, we spoke to one another not at all.

But sometimes on rainy mornings or snowy afternoons or during the heat of summer, I find myself thinking of her in the days before my marriage collapsed. I remember the pot of coffee we would share at her kitchen table or mine, our youngsters padding around the floor in diapers and bare feet, the worries and insecurities we willingly admitted to each other, our fears of ineptitude as parents, admissions of shortcomings as people.

Over our infants' soft heads, we imagined futures. Pushing baby carriages on country roads, we saw birds and squirrels, streams and trees through the eyes of our offspring.

Before the demise of my marriage, prior to my preoccupation with day-to-day living, there was that space of time, those few years when she and I were young mothers together, marvelling at our sons and daughters—those mysterious creations so dependent upon us for comfort and happiness. And I believe that during those days we relied upon one another, too. Good friends amongst a group of acquaintances, like minds poring over Dr. Spock. Questioning. Measuring. Reassuring. Laughing at ourselves in the confines of her home or mine.

And so, one recent afternoon, when the rain formed beads on tree branches and the house was quiet, I missed my friend. And encouraged by finding her number in a dog-eared book, I phoned to say hello. But she was not at home. I left my name with the teenage child who said in a grown-up voice that she remembered who I was and assured me she would give my number to her mother.

But the days went by—one day, two, a week—when I

mentioned to my husband that she had not called. That I was, I suppose, disappointed.

It was then that he suggested the possibility of my having leaned too hard on her during that rough time of my life. He said that, although I may have buried all those sad and angry days and remember now the peaceful, happy times, her recollections may not be the same.

And while I knew he might be right, I hoped he would be wrong, hoped she could recall with fondness a jumble of plastic baby toys and teacups and hours of conversation when our children were small.

And then, the phone rang, and it was my friend.

WEDDING FANTASIES

"How was the wedding?" my daughter asked.

"Beautiful," I answered. "You were a lovely bride. Your gown was gorgeous—pure white with a wide lacy skirt and you wore a little jeweled cap on your head. The train was long and made of yards and yards of billowing tulle. You were absolutely stunning."

"I was?" she asked, raising her eyebrows.

"You were," I reassured her. "And the room was elegant, with glass tables and tall glass vases filled with flowers, and the lights were dim and there were pastel napkins . . . oh, it was so pretty." I sighed at the memory.

"There were plenty of guests. But not too many. Just the right amount. And they were refined. Yes. The entire affair was refined. Sophisticated . . . You know?"

My daughter laughed, shaking her head at my fantasy.

"Well, who was the groom?" she wanted to know.

But I couldn't answer. "I didn't see him," I explained.

She understood. It was, after all, make believe.

Sometime yesterday, about midway through the very real ceremony marking my young friend's wedding, I began to daydream. The bride, a petite woman in a tea-length cream-colored dress, became a hazy blur. In her place, I saw my own dark-eyed daughter in satin and lace. While the mother of the bride stood gazing at her child with tears on her cheeks, I envisioned myself in her place and cried with joy for the future celebration. When the music commenced, heralding the actual couple's state of matrimony, my reverie ceased. Yet, the image of my little girl as a bride remains with me today.

Despite my own failed first marriage, and even before this lovely second marriage, the dream of wedded bliss never faded entirely. For some years, in between my first and second husbands, I did profess to think the institution of marriage an unnecessary if not undesirable state of affairs. But even at that time, I never quite gave up visions of a wedding gown. Somehow, I guess the mystique of the blushing bride remains alive despite the times. And although I wore a simple knit dress for my second wedding, I did, I admit, harbor secret thoughts of gauze and eyelet lace. Which is, I suppose, the reason I found myself envisioning my daughter as a bride in a mist of purest white.

But she is only thirteen. There's time enough for her to pick a gown—and a life's mate, for that matter. And of course, when she decides to marry, she'll have the right to choose what she will wear.

But I may just have to remind her of the way I pictured her yesterday in tulle and lace with that little cap upon her pretty head.

THE COMPLIMENT

It was better than a gift. Better than a vacation, this compliment offered in innocence.

"I notice that you work hard in the house, Mommy. Thank you," he said.

Simply. Just like that. For no particular reason, as I kissed him good night, he whispered those words to me. And I melted.

For all the hours spent making breakfasts, lunches and dinners, for the years of vacuuming and dusting and changing linens regularly, for the scrubbed floors and the folded laundry, for the clean curtains and the polished mirrors, for all those mundane, boring, essential daily chores, a child of mine had seen and said thanks.

And it isn't the first time. Periodically through the years of parenthood, one or the other of my children has, unsolicited, commented on the cooking or the housework, and I have been especially grateful—and a little surprised.

Although I want my children to expect cleanliness and a semblance of neatness in their surroundings (traits I hope they will come to value in their own adult lives), the questions of how the shirt got folded or who washed the floor were subjects about which I was sure they never thought.

Apparently, I was wrong. Not only do the youngsters notice these things (which does not necessarily mean they offer to help set the table or take out the garbage), but they are aware of what is and what is not standard procedure in their friends' homes.

They make comparisons—not always to my advantage.

"My friends don't have to keep their rooms so neat, Ma. Why do I?" I'm often asked. Or, "Everybody else is allowed to have junk food after school. How come we're the only ones who aren't?"

And in those moments of reproval, I've been known to question my motives and methods. Occasionally, I have caved in. Still, I waver little on nutrition and cleanliness. I insist on baths and head-washes and combed hair. Things which require cooperation on the part of the children. I want them to make their beds and brush their teeth. If I thought about it, I believe I would consider these chores as much a form of training as homework, supposedly a precursor to responsibility in the workaday world.

Yet, the other requirements—the subtle chain of events which gets dinner on the table and grass stains out of jeans, the picayune details which are the focus of magazine ads—are realities to which I assumed the children were oblivious.

But, they are not. Or at least my son was not on that particular night when he snuggled into clean sheets in his warm bed and offered gratitude with a smile.

And his simple words of appreciation were enough to make the thankless tasks worthwhile.

COMING OF AGE

"Is that you?" she shouted, moving her mouth away from the receiver.

I heard a door slam somewhere in the background.

"Sorry," she said, returning to our phone conversation. "I wanted to make sure it was my son. He just got home from practice."

"Uh-huh," I answered, not surprised, imagining a son of

hers at fifteen or sixteen, maybe older, a hulking boy in uniform wearing huge white sneakers, bounding through her house.

From the moment she mentioned her son to the time she told me her age, I envisioned a boy nearing manhood, a son taller than his mother, a mother certainly older than I.

She had called to ask a favor. Would I, she'd wanted to know, be so good as to speak before a philanthropic group of which she was a member? Might I, she had asked, attend the annual dinner sometime hence and could I, on that date, say a few words, read a few lines—help the cause, so to speak?

And I said, "Yes, of course," feeling flattered by the request and vaguely intimidated by this unfamiliar caller, a poised sounding woman at the other end of the line.

She had introduced herself by name, mentioned a mutual acquaintance or two and proceeded to issue the invitation. All the while, I stood at my kitchen sink, twirling a pencil in my hand.

As she spoke, I pictured this woman—perfectly coiffed, seated at some elegant desk in a lovely, well-lit corner of the study in the home I imagined she owned. And while I conjured up her hairdo and shoes and the rooms of her house, I invented the height and age of her sports-minded son.

From the manner of her speech, from the tone of her voice and from her involvement in this organization of note, I assumed her to be an adult and I, by comparison, a girl, a cub reporter, a fledgling writer still new to the world of grown-ups and speeches.

I was proud and somewhat surprised to think that this individual, this organization would think of me as a professional, would think of me as someone capable of saying something important. Weren't speakers always more well-versed, more knowledgable, more impressive than I? You nust prove yourself worthy, I told myself. Sound interesting. Sound curious. Eager, but not too eager. Sound secure.

I asked about the estimated size of the group I would address and the average age of those expected to attend. (I felt sure that I would be the youngest in the crowd.)

She said, "Mature," in answer to my second question. "They are certainly not kids. They'll be about my age, I think, and I'm no youngster, after all. I'm forty-one."

And I was stunned.

Forty-one? This official, adult-sounding person, with the son I supposed to be nearly a man, was forty-one.

Why, so am I. I'm nearly forty-two.

It hit me like a blow to the stomach or a kick from behind. I felt the way I've felt when tripping or bumping into walls—disconcerted, maddened, shocked to know that I have come of age, that my daughter is a teenager and my son is eleven plus. That, had I wed earlier, a child of mine could indeed be sixteen or twenty for that matter, that the me I see when avoiding mirrors is twenty-six at most, that the me I think of when I think of me as a mother has children ages two and four, that that person is fiction now. The individual to whom the invitation was issued is known to be over forty. Quite possibly she was sought out to speak by virtue of that age and the maturity and experience it connotes.

"Oh no," I thought at first, and then, "Oh, well." And finally, "It had to happen, I suppose." And so I accepted the speaking engagement with grace, I think, feeling somehow changed and challenged by the deed.

They hadn't wanted a youngster for this job. They had wanted a woman, and they had chosen me.

"I can handle it," I said aloud. And added silently, "I hope."

CHANGING CLOTHES

Yearly, the dread comes upon me.

It begins with a gentle gnawing, a vague apprehension of the job ahead. It culminates with a seasonal knot in my stomach. Gotta get it done, gotta get it done, the knot implies. And I answer, please—not yet.

Like a child hoping the spinach will disappear from his plate, like a college student wishing away the term paper, I procrastinate from early March until mid-April, when I no longer can put off the inevitable changing of the clothes.

Would that this could be accomplished by a trip to the closet for a cotton skirt or a request that the children place their winter garments on a higher shelf. But that would make life simple, and simplicity is not the way of spring. Before the grass can be mowed, last year's dried leaves must be raked from the corners of the yard. Before the tomatoes can grow, the seeds must be planted. Before I can don the cotton skirt, I must find it.

I must pull down the overhead ladder and make my way gingerly to the attic where, through the long winter months, the summer clothes have been gathering wrinkles in plastic bags. Hung on makeshift racks and stuffed into ancient dresser drawers, the out-of-season garments have, this year as always, been stored away from October through April.

And now, just at the moment when the windows need washing, the yard needs tidying and the birds return, do the lightweight clothes demand to be retrieved from their hiding place.

If it were my wardrobe alone which required seasonal switching, I could handle the project with ease. The difficult part (the part that feels like spinach and term papers) is the children's clothing—the bathing suits and striped shirts and flower-print dresses which must be carried down and tried on and which most certainly will be too small, the winter coats and woolen sweaters which must be hauled upstairs to the attic to make room for the summer skirts and pants.

Then come the various piles of clothes which inevitably fill the chairs and floor as the children add to the "give-aways" that no longer fit and "throw-aways" that are no longer fitting and those "good enough for one more season" that must be refolded and placed on shelves.

And all this while the boy wants no part of the sorting and sneaks out the door to play baseball with his friends. And the girl notes that last year's wardrobe is out of style.

And I, in mid-April, suddenly become envious of those whose homes have larger closets, huge walk-in closets, closets the size of rooms, where down jackets and nylon windbreakers can share a common wall.

But then, I suppose, had I such breathing space, I would miss the changing of the clothes which signifies and certifies the onset of spring.

 EST OF BOTH WORLDS

It's all relative, I suppose.

"Can't wait to get away from here," he said, hedge clipper in hand, beads of perspiration on his forehead. "Gotta get out into the country. Gotta move up north away from all the hassle and the traffic and the noise. It's just too busy here for me, too much tension. I want to be where the way of life is peaceful."

Eyeing the narrow dead end road his home shares with

a dozen other houses in our suburban town, he described his dream society. It's a place where the corner grocery exists and fishing is a way of life. Where the "pace is slow and easy, the way I like it," he explained.

Determined to make this fantasy a reality, he told me that he and his wife have set their career goals towards comparative tranquility three years hence. In the interim, the two are putting up with tight schedules, extra jobs and additional schooling to ensure a different and more serene future for their young family. For a "future in the country."

"Which absolutely suffocates me," bristled the dark-eyed woman who sat opposite me recently during a totally separate, but somehow strangely similar, conversation. "I don't know how you stand it in the country with all those trees and birds. There's nothing to do. It's just boring . . . boring."

I had to laugh, correcting her error. "We don't live in the country," I explained. "We live in suburbia. It just seems like the country when compared with the city."

"It seems like the end of the world," she chortled. "And he" (here she nodded in the direction of her husband) "wants us all to spend the summer at the bungalow colony."

As she spoke, she pulled one or another of her five children onto her lap. "I'd much rather we all stayed in the city where there are things to see and things to do. You know, I love to leave the windows open at night so I can hear what's happening outside. It makes me feel as though the world is still going on while I sleep.

"If we have to go to the country, I'm going to take a VCR with me so at least I'll have something to do all day. You won't catch me wandering around on country roads picking dandelions. Give me Bloomingdales and Saks and a dozen different coffee shops, and I'll never complain."

I patted one of her children on the head, envisioning the little girl growing up a cab ride from the entertainment district, and a world away from lightning bugs.

To each his own, I thought and think once again as I sit here at my desk smack in the middle, halfway between city life and country life, an hour's drive from each. And as I sit, I find myself wondering if I am neither here nor there and lacking something by way of this dubious location.

But the hedge-clipping neighbor's description of nirvana leaves me vaguely nervous, I think. I am not certain I could stand the isolation of such solitude. And as for city life, my friend who hails a taxi for a quick fix at the Museum of Modern Art forfeits privacy for culture, I'm afraid.

And so I think I'll stay right here in suburbia which, for the time being, seems to offer me the best of both worlds.

A CHILD IS A CHILD

It's the miracle of the mundane which surprises me most, I think. The predictability, the normalcy, the extraordinarily simple realities of life.

Like his collection of plastic spiders, his shoe box crammed with baseball cards and his wicker basket overflowing with rocks.

Last week, he lunged through the back door after school with tousled hair, skinned elbows and pockets stuffed with rocks—not stones, not pretty pebbles, but huge, heavy rocks "filled with iron, Mom," as he told me, sprinkling dried mud and bits of moss across the kitchen table, holding the finds up to the light to "prove" to me that they did indeed contain tiny flecks of ore, that they were "special" and "beautiful and excellent," as was the place where he'd collected these treasures.

It had been a class trip to a now defunct iron mine located some thirty minutes north of the town in which we live, but it might as well have been in Canada or Europe for the mystery and magic he found there.

His eyes glittering with excitement, he continued pulling rocks from pants and shirt and jacket, as he told me of the cave he'd explored with its "huge hunks of ice in so many shapes" and the clean running waters "so clean you wouldn't believe it" and the "steep, steep mountain" he had climbed, which is how he'd gotten cut "here and here . . .," showing me the scrapes and bruises and other badges of bravery he'd earned on the journey. And how he'd gone "all the way to the top" where he'd seen "beautiful things," and how the guide had taught him to use a compass and a map, and how he'd "followed the course all the way to the road" and "how difficult it is, did you know, Ma?" How difficult it is to hang on to the cliff while you're climbing straight up or down and how sometimes "you have to kind of sit and slide part of the way" and how "that makes you laugh."

And then, with an old rag and a clean towel, he gently washed and wiped all of his rocks in the bathroom sink and lined them up to dry, and then he placed them in a wicker basket and set it on the table in the living room for everyone to see. And he called Grandma to tell her about the trip because "she likes that kind of thing" and she loves him and "she listened to everything and she said maybe sometime I could show her how to use the compass and the map and we'd go exploring the iron mine together."

And he waited at the door for his sister to get home from school so he could tell her the story in one long monologue before she even took off her jacket or put down her books or asked for a snack. And his joy was so contagious, so real, that she stood there listening in the middle of the kitchen, nodding as he recounted his tales of daring, and she followed him into the living room to see the rocks.

And then, he told the tale once again when his stepfather came home from work; the thrill of the day diminished not one iota by the passing of time, but rather having gained in importance with each repetition.

And now, a week later, I find myself smiling each time I pass the basket of rocks, recalling his boundless enthusiasm, marveling that exploration, adventure, earth, water, caves and stones have lost none of their appeal for a child of the '80s. Despite the computer and the VCR and the electronic football game, a collection of rocks is still a collection of rocks and a child is still a child.

DISK ERROR

"Disk error." Plain as day. Yet another time, the words spilled out across the screen as though this were a totally normal response to my question.

"What?" I found myself asking aloud.

"Disk error." The machine was adamant.

And I was near tears. "Why?" I pleaded with the printer. "Why is there a disk error? What is a disk error? Where is the disk error?"

In frustration, I punched keys I've never punched before, and still, with calm certainty, the words appeared to mock me. "Disk error," came the answer.

"It's unfair." I spoke gruffly, stuffing the Bank Street Writer disk into the disk drive and pulling it out again. "I know I am doing this the right way," I insisted, doubting myself even as I said the words. "So what is the problem? *What is the problem?*"

"Disk error," said the machine.

And I had to walk away—leave the room. I had to do something, anything, to keep from smashing that smug little screen. What did it know about errors anyway? And if it did know something, why didn't it just tell me? Why was it playing this ridiculous game, making me guess my mistake, like a zealous teacher forcing the student to learn by trial?

I toyed with the idea of calling my children at school— my daughter specifically. She's the one who taught me how to use the computer in the first place. She's the one who promised me that all the words I'd written last week were really alive and well somewhere on the special disk she'd saved for me. And I'd trusted her. I'd believed that although I could not see the printed words, nor the little people standing guard over them on the flat piece of material called a disk, though I could attest to nothing, I'd believed that somehow the column I'd written would be there, because my daughter had said so.

But I should have known better. What kind of an answer is "Because I said so," which is what she'd told me when I'd asked? How could she, or anyone else for that matter honestly believe that the printed word can exist on something other than typing paper? But what would the school principal think if I called and asked him to put my daughter on the phone because the column she'd said would stay put was somehow lost?

I pressed retrieve file again, and again the hated words appeared. "But you are in there," I shouted at the mute machine. "I know you are in there because I put you in there just last week. You are locked up on that little disk, and I want you to come out now. Do you hear me?"

"Disk error," said the screen.

"That is it," I told the silent house. "That was its last chance. Now I am calling the authorities."

Which I did—two of them, as a matter of fact, two computer repair shops with live people answering the phones and responding in condescending tones to my frantic appeals for help. The first young man, though sympathetic, offered useless consolation. He accused me of having inadvertently erased my words. "If you left the disk out in the sun or if it got too near a magnet," he explained.

But I said, "No. No magnet, no sun. My column was right there where I put it on that disk, stuck behind all the other disks, in that little plastic disk box on the table next to the computer."

Then, the man suggested that I perform some unimaginable operation having to do with boots and catalogues and initials. Finally, I hung up, feeling utterly dejected, but not yet beaten.

I called another authority who was less helpful, even, than the first man, telling me rather rudely that he thought I should wait until my "daughter gets home from school, since you say she is the one who knows about computers."

But I could not stand the suspense. I had to know once and for all if the column was in or on or anywhere near the disk. And so, again, I placed the thing in the machine and pressed a bunch of buttons. And lo and behold, there it was. There, for some unknown reason, was my story in black and white on the little screen right where my daughter had said it would be, with nary a disk error in sight.

 CHICKEN SCRATCH

"What does this say?" he demanded. "Tell me what this is supposed to be."

I stared at the letters scribbled in pencil in the lower left-hand corner of the column of words.

"Baked beans?" I suggested meekly. "Or brown bread?"

"Or bowling balls, or burlap bags or brillo brains," he guessed, only half in jest. "Tell me, will you, how am I supposed to read your handwriting if you can't read it?"

I grinned sheepishly. He was right, of course. Here I am, fortunate enough to have a husband willing to do the weekly grocery shopping, and inevitably, I give him a list which he can't decipher.

"Do you know what it is like to tap strangers on the shoulder every other aisle to ask them if they can decode your words?" he wanted to know. "Can you imagine how baffling it is to see, written beneath the heading of vegetables, such items as celery, lettuce, radishes and peacocks? Do you have any idea what a problem it is to try and find tadpoles and rocks in the frozen foods section?"

I grabbed the list from his hand and checked the items. Tadpoles? Or had I written torpedoes, or maybe it was taxicabs? "Tangerines," I shouted suddenly. "I remember now. I wanted tangerines."

And the rocks I'd asked for meant a box of rice. And, as for bowling balls, I think I'd hoped he'd bring me brown lunch bags. But even I could not be sure.

I find it hard to take this seriously. It's just a shopping list, is it not? So what if he brings home butter when I'd wanted bananas? Or peaches when I'd asked for potatoes? It's all the same, really. Food is food, I think.

But what if it were a prescription? What, I have often

wondered, if I were a doctor and the pharmacist mistook my peacock for penicillin when I'd really ordered something else?

What if the teacher, in writing on the blackboard, had scribbled Asia in such a way that the children read Africa and spent the entire lesson on the wrong continent? Suppose the mathematician substituted a three for a five because the numbers look a lot alike. Or the pianist played a B for a C based on poorly drawn notes. If the hairdresser dyed the customer's hair blonde instead of black because both words start with B? Or the mechanic fixed the muffler when he'd wanted the motor overhauled? What if everybody wrote the way I write? Would it be so funny then?

I suppose not. Nor was it funny in college when, because of my "chicken scratch," as the professor duly noted, my entire semester's grade was lowered one letter to remind me that he would not read if I could not write.

Which is why, from that time on, I have come to type nearly everything intended to be seen by others—everything, that is, but the shopping list.

SUMMER MEMORIES

It was the sight of a neighbor, standing there on the porch with her coffee cup in hand, that set the summer right.

It had something to do with memories, I suppose. All the years of seeing my mother posed just so—on the back stoop, surveying the yard, waving hello to one friend or another, cautioning us to be careful on the swings. All the hours of sunshine. And the picnic lunches under the oak tree and barbecues at the wooden table, with my father bending over the grill and my mother running up and down the stairs to carry out the ketchup, the lemonade, the knives and forks and napkins.

And my sister and I at play, dressing paper dolls, sitting on that stoop, our faces tanned, our hair pulled up in ponytails. Beetles clinging to the screen door. Fireflies captured in glass milk bottles. The distant sound of someone sawing wood. The chirp of crickets in the dark. Grass tickling bare feet.

The time my father helped us paint a row of huge rocks in alternating shades of red and blue and yellow. The swimming pool we visited on Sundays with all the relatives piling into cars for the drive upstate. And the baskets of chicken and potatoes and cakes we'd eat under leafy trees in groves beside the cool water.

The time my father stacked a pile of doughnut-shaped ice cubes on the automobile antenna so we could watch them melt as we drove home. The time he put a goldfish in the wading pool. The nightly drives to buy double-dip ice cream cones for everyone.

Weekends at the seashore when the sand was clean and the ocean clear. Shell collecting with my mother. My father in Bermuda shorts. Peaches and watermelons and cherries with pits. The hydrangea bush in my aunt and uncle's yard. The record player perched on the window sill, entertaining the neighborhood. Mr. Sweitzer and his zither performing for us in the heat of day.

My sister collecting birds with broken wings, stray cats, dogs with matted fur. Mosquito bites and bee stings. The sandbox. Mud pies. Coloring books. And crayons melting in the sun.

I loved it all. I love it still. I love the fact that my neighbor stands, coffee cup in hand, chatting with a friend across the overgrown hedge between their houses. Love being awake early enough to hear a different neighbor shout, "Mornin'. Great day for fishin'," as I walk past his door. Love the sound of children chasing one another through yards and up and down our block before they've had their breakfast or combed their hair. Love my son and his buddy dragging pillows and sleeping bags from one house to another all through the summer months, eating berries from bushes, skinning knees, playing catch in the back yard. Love my daughter reading in the lounge chair near the dogwood tree, munching pretzels from the plastic bowl, getting rosy cheeks and sun-streaked hair.

I love the summertime for giving me back my childhood every year.

AUNT MALKA

"Yiddish . . . Yiddish is *besser*," she admonished me, wagging an arthritic finger in my face. Stooped and wizened at nearly ninety, my husband's Great-Aunt Malka lectured in a high-pitched voice. From her perspective, Yiddish is the conversational language of the Jew. Hebrew is the language of prayer. And there I sat, the American and Americanized wife of her sister's son's son, unable to comprehend in either case.

She was insistent. "You speak Yiddish," she told me, as though her command would make it so. I took her hand in mine and squeezed it tightly. Offering, in the absence of language, an expression of the joy I felt at seeing her once again.

It had been almost a year to the day since I had first set foot in Eretz Yisrael. "We'll be back," we'd told our son, when he had cried upon leaving Jerusalem the summer before. "Somehow, we'll return."

And we had kept our word. Refusing to replace the old car, deciding against a new couch, we had chosen instead to save for this day when Aunt Malka would insist that we "*ess, ess mein kind.*"

The August sun cast its white light through the window of her two-room flat. I continued cupping Aunt Malka's hand in mine as she answered my husband's questions. "The children and grandchildren?" he inquired, in a combination of Yiddish and Hebrew. "The great-grandchildren? Your health? What *simchos* have occurred since last we met?" And then, finally, he asked her to speak of her life—the wars through which she has lived, the determination to survive, the changes she has seen, her steadfast faith.

I strained to capture her thoughts, but the few Yiddish phrases I knew could not hold the whole of her speech. She tried embellishing her tales with Hebrew, but I was hopelessly lost. Still, her presence, the humble wooden table, the feather bed where the Great-Grandfather (her father) had slept, the highly polished irregularity of the stone floors—these and the Great-Grandfather's timepiece hanging on one wall, the *Shabbos leichter*, the small pile of *sefarim*, the hand-baked cakes spoke eloquently where words were absent.

When at last we rose to leave, she walked with us through the door and halfway along the balcony which runs the length of the building's second story.

"Yiddish . . . Yiddish is *besser*," she intoned, kissing me good-bye. We descended the single flight of stairs leading to the street and turned to wave.

"*Lehitraot*," we heard Aunt Malka say.

THE BABYSITTER

"Everything okay? Kids asleep?"

The same old questions. The same moment of anxiety until she answers, "Yes." And, "Yes."

The same sense of relief in the knowledge that all is well.

The undeniable sameness—the repetition of events, the time of night that the call is made, the predictable inquiry, the expected response, a familiar and common happenstance of life—with one remarkable difference. This time, the children belong to someone else. It is the babysitter who belongs to me.

So I call her at ten to check on her to make certain that her charges have fallen asleep, that no one is hurt or sad or hungry, that my daughter has handled the situation well. I call to reassure myself that my little girl is fine.

And she answers, "Yes." And, "Yes."

But I hang up in confusion. My girl, my pigtailed child, old enough to cook dinner for some other tyke in braids. My daughter, tucking other mothers' infants into cribs and beds. My baby changing diapers, wiping tears, reading stories to little boys and girls who think she's all grown up.

Other mothers and fathers trusting my child with their child, thanking my daughter for her capable attentions to their sons and daughters, paying my daughter gladly for her expertise.

My daughter—washing other daughters' sticky fingers, giving nighttime bottles, holding pudgy hands.

My child—responsible for their children while they are out at meetings or dinners or weddings in another town.

And they, leaving phone numbers for my little girl—doctors' numbers "just in case," fire department numbers "just in case," numbers of police departments, poison control centers, nearby neighbors. They, leaving phone numbers, with the hope that my daughter will never encounter the emergencies for which the numbers are left. They, kissing their children good-night and saying, "Listen to the sitter. Remember, she's in charge."

And she—my daughter, being in charge.

And me, feeling proud and scared and thrilled and shaken by the sudden awareness that my little girl is someone else's babysitter now.

THE NEW HOUSE

Around the corner, yesterday, it seems, there were woods, squirrels, a groundhog or two, some poison ivy and a pile of rusty cans.

And now? A house—two houses really, sharing one common wall. A duplex minus entrance stairs and shutters. A structure nearing completion, standing where nothing save nature had stood before.

I walk by daily in the early morning, checking on the progress of this house, watching the roof appear, the panes of window glass, observing the arrival of garage doors and chimney tops.

Sometimes, the workmen wave hello from where they stand, waist-deep in planks of wood and cinder block. And I marvel at the speed with which their task is done, the building erected in a matter of weeks, a dwelling place sprung up amidst a stand of trees.

It intrigues me—brings back memories of sand castles and building blocks. It sets in motion that urge to create, to complete, to place one brick upon another until at last the project is done. Finished. And the builder can stand back to admire the work.

I am not alone in my feelings. Often, there are others watching just beyond the mounds of brown-red earth, staring at the workmen and the house—an adult or two with hands on hips, squinting eyes to try and see what's happening within the half-built walls, and clusters of children straddling bikes, dreaming dreams as huge green trucks deliver all the stuff of which the house is made.

And I dream, too. And wonder how. Wonder who is in charge, which one of the perspiring men with a bandanna wrapped 'round his head or neck has set this monument aloft? Who said, "First the trees must be felled"? Who gave the orders to remove the earth and determined where to place the excess dirt?

Which individual in jeans and heavy boots read the blueprint and told the crew to place the doorway here, the stairwell there? And when will the plumbers plumb? What color will the painters paint the outside walls? And who will pave the path?

Will there be shrubs and flowers on the lawn? An eat-in kitchen or just a dining nook? A fireplace in the living room? A den? A walk-in closet in the master bedroom? Where will they put the washer and dryer? What color will be chosen for the carpets and walls?

All this I ponder, watching workmen work. And then, I wonder, who will make this house a home?

THE OFFICE

It is a rainy summer evening. All the other kids are indoors playing games. And what are my children doing? They are in Grandma and Grandpa's office—naturally.

They're the heads of a major corporation, administrators of a large metropolitan hospital, editors of a thriving newspaper. They're something—anything requiring typewriters, telephones, reams of paper and sharpened pencils.

They're wearing name tags, opening file drawers, taking notes on legal pads. They're on coffee breaks, attending important meetings, coordinating promotional events. They are extremely busy, and they're having a wonderful time—at the office.

Which never seemed the slightest bit unusual to me until today when, contemplating the thunderstorm outdoors, I realized that, while other children are bored and whining, mine are hard at work.

But this is the way I was reared. With my parents' place of business attached to our house, the office was always accessible for playtime after hours or on weekends. From early on, my mother and father taught us to be careful when we used the office equipment. And they did encourage us to help them with "real work" when we were old enough. But for the most part, they allowed us to play. They would show us the supply cabinet filled with envelopes and pads. They taught us to be sparing with the glue. They pointed out where they kept the extra staples and pens. Then they left us alone to while away our time in a business of our choice.

And I cannot count the days I spent pretending to be a writer before I knew what a by-line meant. I am positive it was my parents' office which gave focus to my future.

I would sit behind one of the large wooden desks in a room bearing bookshelves and calendars and think myself an author of some note.

Now, on summer evenings or Sunday afternoons when we visit my parents, it is usually my son and daughter who dabble in professions within the world of fantasy.

But today it is I who have borrowed the corner of the office to write this column. And as I sit at my father's typewriter, I find myself wondering if I am really hard at work or if this is only make-believe.

FRUITY PEBBLES

I scooped out an extra portion of ice cream for my *Shabbos* guests and the memory of Fruity Pebbles made me smile.

"You let your children eat that stuff for breakfast every day?" I'd asked in an accusatory tone.

Her answer had surprised me. "Only on *Shabbos*," she'd said. "*Shabbos* should be sweet."

The phrase has stayed with me through the years as I've learned something about the truth of sweetness—not all of it in abstract form.

"Take the *Shabbos* party," I told my recent guests. "It's a wonderful time for ice cream and cake." (And clementines,

I might have added.)

Because that is what she'd served in mid-afternoon on the day of the Fruity Pebbles during my first weekend in a *shomer Shabbos* home.

"But why?" I'd wanted to know back then when, after breakfast and *shul*, and *kiddush*, and lunch and dessert, she had brought to the table yet another tray of cakes and sweets.

"To keep the children's interest," she had said. "To separate this day from the other days. To reinforce the lesson. Because it's good."

And she'd been right. So much so, in fact, that along with our decision to become *shomer Shabbos*, came our decision to serve sweets for breakfast and clementines and cake in late afternoon (necessary aspects of the magic, we thought, at one with the day itself).

Eventually, of course, the specific treats became arbitrary, but the rituals remained the same and the lesson grew in meaning with the passing weeks.

Now, as I dish out ice cream or slice a wedge of pie for friends and neighbors, I understand better the wisdom of the sweets—the shared taste for good things, for pleasant things, for conversation, company, rest and peace—for a space of tranquility within the week.

But I realized, on that first *Shabbos*, that it was more than the cereal. It was the library books borrowed on Thursday and saved for the children for *Shabbos* afternoon. It was the *Shabbos* shoes, polished each week for the special day, the *Shabbos* clothes set aside for the occasion, the *Shabbos* coats and hats, the flowers purchased especially to grace the *Shabbos* table.

It was the sense of excitement in an atmosphere of joy which I witnessed on that day, which I wanted for my family and myself. It was the treats and the books and the shoes and the flowers and the candles and the people seated around the table singing *Shabbos* songs together. It was *Shabbos* itself that I desired. And I wanted to help make it happen—which, I believe, was precisely the point.

So I bought a box of Fruity Pebbles to begin.

BOOKS

"And the Papa Bear said, 'Somebody's been eating my porridge,' and the Mama Bear said, 'Somebody's been eating my porridge . . .'" (And here the speaker's voice became a high-pitched squeak.) "And then . . . the little bitty Baby Bear said, 'somebody's been eating my porridge, and he ate it all up . . .'"

From where I sat on the lawn chair in the back yard, I could overhear a neighbor telling the tale of Goldilocks to his small children. The sound of his voice came through his youngsters' open window in a convincing imitation of the family of bears. I was impressed and pleased, glad to know that some things never change.

Like bedtime stories read aloud.

Too often lately, I've heard about poor reading skills among our youth. And frequently, I find, the blame is placed upon the teachers or on television, as if these forces alone would foster a society of couch potatoes, illiterates or both.

But I think the fault lies elsewhere. I believe the reason why children do not read has more to do with parents than with either television or teachers. It is because too few parents read Goldilocks to their children before kissing them good-night.

Though I have no statistics to prove my point, I would guess that a majority of American toddlers can repeat television commercials from memory well before they can recite a nursery rhyme. I would bet that most children have learned to focus on a flickering screen before they've learned to study an illustration in a book.

And I think we'll be sorry for this. We, who were reared on the printed version of "Snow White and the Seven Dwarfs" and "Cinderella" will have to contend with children for whom imagination is an anachronism.

Pro-television people tell me the potential for fantasy is just as potent on the screen as ever it was between the bindings of a book. But I cannot be convinced. I cannot believe that a talking Papa Bear in animated cartoon form prods the brain to creativity as surely as does the bear described in words. Even the static printed illustration of a talking bear insists that the child imagine such a thing in motion. I think the television demands too little of our youth.

And about the teachers? What of the kindergarten teacher whose students have had little contact with the likes of story hour but plenty of hours logged on the VCR? How dare we blame the teachers for the fact that kids can't sit still long enough to hear her tell a tale because they want to "see" what's happening instead?

But maybe we no longer see the worth of words ourselves. Which is why I was glad to hear a Daddy reading aloud to his children—reading in such a way that the children asked for more—reading to make them gasp and giggle and look forward to the time when they will be old enough to read all by themselves.

QUESTIONS

She called me "honest and sensitive." She said that she "learns from me." She thanked me for "sharing myself and my family" with readers. Just now, when I have been most doubtful about my abilities as a parent, this kind soul wrote to tell me she "approves of me." Her letter made my day. In fact, it made my month.

In this season of questioning, as my husband and I try to rear a teenager and a pre-teen, a stranger's complimentary note was the perfect balm for my deflating ego. Here, at last, was a person (albeit not a child of mine) who, through reading my columns, has concluded that I am a good mother.

And she was kind enough to put it in writing. On pretty blue stationery with a flower print border, she penned a vote of confidence for my ever-challenging role as "Mom." How thoughtful of her to let me know.

Because I've been unsure of late. Too strict or too lenient? I've found myself asking. Do my children have too much freedom or not enough? Is my daughter spending too much time at the mirror or is she not? Is my son staying up too late at night? Do I give in too easily? Not easily enough? Do I yell too much, demand too much? Do I smile as often as I used to smile?

Should I let her spend so much time on the phone? Should I buy her the clothes I do not think she needs? Am I giving enough time to each of them—or maybe I am giving too much time? Am I overprotective, underprotective? Am I analyzing everything far too much? Or am I not thoughtful enough?

Should I offer opinions about their friends or would that be considered interfering, hampering social growth?

Should I, at this stage of the game, stand back and observe the children as products nearly complete, or should I continue to try to mold and guide? Do I vacillate too readily or am I too rigid in my ways? Is it all right that my children are well-behaved in other people's homes and less well-behaved in their own? Do I trust them too much or not enough?

Why, suddenly, am I so unsure of myself? And is my own insecurity in some ways a compliment to the children whose opinions I've come to value? Should I be glad that my offspring are making me think?

Why do I utter "maybes" today where once I said yes or no? Why do the children's arguments sound more convincing than they used to sound?

Because they are getting older. Because I am getting older. Because we are a family grappling with all the forces with which parents and children have been grappling for years. Because no one said child rearing would be easy. And because of this, it was especially gratifying to receive a pat on the back for motherhood.

INFORMATION

Sometimes it is health and nutrition, occasionally it is psychology or sociology, often it is education, religion, the environment, women's rights, the economy, finances, morality and most recently—politics.

The topics of interest and the points of view vary, but the message remains the same. In today's world, one must be "informed."

I, in this case, being the one.

And to that end, I receive each morning a slim envelope containing neatly trimmed newspaper articles concerning issues of import on the local, national and international scenes.

From the time I left for college nearly twenty-five years ago, my mother and father have regularly let me know which subjects are of concern to them—and therefore may be of concern to me. To ensure the passing on of of ideas, they have used the telephone, the personal visit and, most often, the U.S. mail.

In this manner, I have received my daily dose of knowledge from the two individuals whose concern for my well-being began before my birth. But lately, the concern is getting out of hand.

Today alone, my envelope of information contained no less than eight items on the upcoming election—some being news stories, some feature stories, some columns by respected writers. Each piece was extracted from a different publication, and each carried a different message. All were worth the reading. A task which, when completed, left me more confused than ever.

Yet, I suppose that was the intention. Had I simply listened to the debates or confined my reading to one or two stories, I might be more certain of my choice today. But my parents have always insisted that thought precede choice. And they are, it appears, determined to make me think.

Their rationale for disseminating all this political information is that they, as senior citizens, have "less to do than you do, as a busy mother." And therefore, they say, "We can afford the time to read a variety of newspapers and magazines and to clip a sampling of material and send it on to you and your sister." (My sister also receives a daily packet of knowledge.) My parents claim their status as members of the older generation entitles them to the hours necessary for a thorough perusal of the media.

And maybe they are right. But I'm not sure. I am not convinced that age and hours are the sole reasons for my parents' quest for facts. Rather, I think it is their lifelong interest in the world at large, which keeps them ever searching for answers and raising further questions. I believe my parents are simply well-informed people. And if I'm lucky, I may learn something from them.

 IFTS

Some of the best gifts I've received have had nothing to do with practicality. So her selection of the beeping, screeching, siren-emitting sound box for her seventy-two-year-old grandfather did not surprise me.

"He will surely like it," she stated emphatically. "I'm positive."

Thus did I buy the beeping thing with batteries included, just as I have purchased singing coffee mugs, plastic necklaces and paper clip holders in years past. On the advice of one child or another, my husband and I have paid good money for everything from multicolored napkin rings to miniature music boxes to mark the birthdays of Grandma and Gramp.

And miraculously, the children's choice of presents has always proved correct. But who could doubt that Grandmas need baseball caps or that Grandpas must have footballs to mark the dates of their birth?

Isn't it obvious to everyone that a mechanical treasure chest is the perfect present for Grandpa, not to mention the fish whose tank Grandpa owns? Even the orange and blue ceramic fish to be hung upon the wall above the tank was selected with Grandpa in mind.

The fact is, everything chosen by the youngsters through the years has met with such success that the children have learned to take great pride in their taste where gifts for the grandparents are concerned. Grandpa has made them believe that he needed every pack of baseball cards he ever got, and Grandma has loved every dime-store ring and plastic necklace.

They have hung every hand-drawn birthday card on the walls of their home. They've worn every piece of jewelry, every hat and T-shirt they've been given. They have made sure to let their children's children know just how treasured these offerings have been.

Which is certainly the case where the sound box was concerned.

"Cause Grandpa said he could use it at the office and Grandma said she'd let Gramp use it in the house. And both of them liked the idea of attaching it to the dashboard of the car."

And it wasn't just the gift that Grandpa liked, it was the birthday party with the chocolate icing on the cake and the blue flowers and the candle and the birthday sign on the wall and the popcorn and cookies and potato chips. And that all the grandchildren and an assortment of neighborhood children came together to celebrate the day. Grandpa liked his birthday because his grandchildren like making him happy.

And the kids like believing that they know "what Grandpa likes best."

PROCRASTINATION

At seven fifty-five this morning, eight minutes before the school bus was scheduled to arrive, my eleven-year-old turned to me with fear in his voice. "You know that social studies test I told you about last week? Well, I just remembered . . . she's giving the test today, and I forgot to study."

I whirled on him with fury in my eyes. "What?" I shouted, ready to explode into my why-did-you-wait-until-the-last-minute-lecture.

But my son was smiling. "Just kidding, Ma," he said. "Just kidding."

I did not see the humor in the situation.

It's not that my son doesn't do his homework, mind you. He does it regularly (if not happily). And it's not that he isn't a good student. It's just that my son prefers "playing" to almost anything else in the world. Which means that when he says he's "finished with the homework and goin' outside to play ball," he really means he's almost finished with his homework and the little bit that's left he can easily do at seven fifty-five a.m., while looking for his sneakers, eating his breakfast and brushing his teeth.

An occasional pre-school homework attack is acceptable from anyone. But last week, when he "just remembered" something two mornings in a row, I had a fit. I stomped and shouted and raved and ranted. I told him (and probably all the neighbors) how irresponsible I think it is to think of something at eight a.m. which should have been thought of at eight p.m. on the previous night.

"And furthermore," I said, "if you take the time in the morning to do the things you should have done while you were playing ball instead, then there won't be time to make your bed or clear the table after breakfast, which only means more work for me. And then, of course, if you insist on doing (eight minutes before the bus arrives) whatever it was you should have done yesterday, you'll never make it to the bus on time, which will mean that either you'll have to miss school or I'll have to drive you there. And if I have to drive you, then I'll have to come back home and clear the table and make your bed because you were too busy doing the things you should have done before you went to sleep. So you'd better not 'remember' anything in the morning any more. And if you do remember something you are not going to be allowed to do it. And if by some chance you remember something and I allow you to do it, you'd better not make the rest of the family miserable by running all over the house looking for your sneakers and brushing your teeth and studying your spelling words and missing the bus. Do you understand?"

I think he did. Unless, of course, he had the social studies test today.

COOKIES

It was to be a routine cholesterol test—a nearly painless pinprick to determine the damage done to my arteries by forty-two years of sunnyside-up eggs, buttered toast and french-fried potatoes. I would give the technician my check, she would hand me a form for the insurance company, she would draw the vial of blood, and I would leave. A nine-minute procedure, all told. But I was second on line.

It was eight twenty-seven in the morning. I stood behind an elderly man who waited patiently for someone to open the laboratory door. And just as patiently, he sat in the waiting room as the technician turned on the lights, removed her coat and returned to the front desk. Only when she asked, "Who's first?" did he rise from his chair to hand her the tin of cookies.

"What's this?" she asked.

And the elderly man answered, "Just a little something for you."

The technician hesitated a moment, a look of surprise in her eyes. "For me? How thoughtful. How very thoughtful. How nice of you," she said.

"It's really nothing." The man grinned back. "I just thought you might enjoy having a cookie with your cup of tea."

Later, after the man had signed a sheaf of forms, after the technician had taken his blood, after he'd said, "Bye now and have a good day," a broad smile remained upon the technician's face.

"Wasn't that nice of him?" she asked me, as she poked my arm to find a vein. "Hardly anybody ever does things like that. Plenty of people give little gifts to their hairdressers now and then, but it's rare for anybody to say thank you to a laboratory technician.

"And yet," continued the white-coated woman, "we see so many of these people again and again. That man, for instance, he's quite sick. He's in here nearly every week for blood tests. Isn't it sweet that he brought me cookies?"

She placed a Band-aid on my arm.

"It's not that I expect to be thanked," she explained. "It's just so nice when someone notices . . ."

I agreed with her, wondering how often she has made small talk with men and women whose visits to the laboratory are connected with some painful illness or other.

"But this is a far cry from a beauty parlor," I ventured to say. "What you do for a living doesn't normally make people happy. Having one's blood drawn isn't the same as having one's hair curled. I imagine most people find it easy to say thanks to people who make them feel good."

But that's too bad, really, because even the thankless jobs must be done. And often the work entailed is tedious and difficult. Yet, it had taken so little. It had required one small box of cookies to brighten the technician's day. And the man who had presented the cookies had felt good about his gift. And I'd enjoyed watching the woman receive her humble prize. And the technician, I assumed, would spread the cheer farther still when, after work, she would return home to her husband and children and tell them of the bright spot in her day. And the elderly man too would no doubt relate to his own wife how greatly appreciated had been his gesture of gratitude.

Hence did my first cholesterol test have the makings of a very special memory.

THE TOY STORE

The two of us walked slowly through the aisles looking for a birthday gift for the son of a friend.

"You think he'd like this?" she would ask, holding up a shiny truck or a car or the latest gruesome monster for inspection.

"How about this?" I'd counter, presenting some puzzle or action figure or game.

Despite the rapidly approaching holiday season, the

large toy store was quiet on this rainy Tuesday evening. The damp and windy weather and the fact that it was the dinner hour had apparently kept most shoppers away. Thus did my daughter and I find ourselves nearly alone among the brightly boxed prizes lining the shelves.

Standing beside her as we examined a plastic dinosaur, it occurred to me that this child is nearly my height. Somehow, it struck me as odd to be facing, at eye level, the girl for whom I used to purchase toys. But I said nothing. After all, these waves of nostalgia are not uncommon, and they pass rather quickly. It was my daughter who spoke of it first.

"Remember," she began, "when you used to buy me doll's clothes here . . . And look at this," she said, stopping to examine a stuffed animal with pink fur and blue eyes. "Isn't this cute? Did you see these?" She pointed to the miniature boxes of food with which one might play house. "Remember when Cabbage Patch dolls were popular? Remember when I used to love to shop here?"

I nodded and put my arm around her shoulders. Of course I remember. How could I forget? All those years of Barbie dolls and baby dolls and doll houses and doll furniture. How I used to love purchasing the plastic ponies, the make believe makeup, the bicycle with training wheels. Why did I think that the toy phase would never end? How is it that, way back then, when she was a little girl, I somehow believed that I would forever be buying the most recent gadgets and trinkets designed to enchant the child?

How is it that until it stopped of its own accord, I never thought about the day when my daughter would no longer need a doll with yellow hair and I would no longer need to visit toy stores?

And so it was with some reluctance that, having selected

the gift for which we had come, we made our way to the cashier. Although it remained unspoken, I think the two of us, mother and daughter alike, had a mad urge to pile our cart with toys—little bathtubs for thumb-size dolls, little stuffed animals with beads for eyes, bottles and bibs and tiny blankets for games of make believe. As we passed the rows of children's books, the racks of tricycles and scooters, we left unsaid the words which might in a moment have set us to filling our arms with all kinds of toys—simply for the fun of it.

GROUP HOME

Not far from my home stands a white house with a wide front porch, a sprawling lawn, wicker rocking chairs and a group of residents, each with a different surname.

Tonight, as I drove past the place, I caught a glimpse of a tall, thin man smoking his pipe in the yellow light of the open door. Beside him in the shadows stood a shorter man. The two faced one another in animated conversation beyond my range of hearing. This, while within the curtained windows of the house, lamplight filled the first floor rooms and sent soft shadows to the chill outdoors.

"A pretty picture," I told myself, intentionally letting up on the gas pedal to drive more slowly past the house. A warm house, I thought, a happy, inviting sort of place peopled by a comfortable family. In a manner of speaking.

Of course, I cannot be positive about the residents since we have never been formally introduced, but on occasion, I have waved hello to several of the house's occupants.

Throughout the years, we have become familiar strangers as we've waited behind or in front of one another on line at the local grocery store, the stationery shop, the cleaners. We have learned to recognize each other as neighbors, everyday neighbors leading everyday lives.

And yet, the residents of this particular house are, I believe, somewhat extraordinary. One or two of them are deaf, several appear to have mental or physical disabilities, and most, it would seem, are mildly retarded. Their common tie is this home in which they live, this group home they share with one another and which, to some extent, they share with the surrounding community. Theirs is a dwelling place more noticeable than others because it represents a kind of triumph for the inhabitants, a success in suburban living.

In summer, this house, with its immaculate exterior, is the first to boast of freshly painted lawn furniture, white and cool against the neatly manicured lawn. This house, bordered by large pink peonies, looks nothing less than pretty in the summer.

In autumn, leaves surrounding the house are raked and bagged before they've finished falling. In winter, paths are shoveled and lights from frosty windows say something of the warmth within.

"A comforting scene," I've told myself each season as I've watched the men and women work to make theirs a family place. And I have always thought of it as that—a family place, an inviting structure where the residents seem frequently to be occupied in one task or another, one conversation or another. A family place where the folks can be seen sitting on the porch just after dinner, smoking pipes, talking or studying the stars. This is a group home which makes me glad that such group homes exist.

THE BIRTHDAY PARTY

A light dusting of snow fell from the gray sky. It was midday. I sat at the kitchen table, drinking coffee and gazing through the window.

Suddenly, the window changed shape. It no longer was the small, familiar one framed by hanging plants but rather a larger, more deeply set window abutted by two other such windows, each with diamond-shaped panes in their upper halves. And through the center window I saw the snow falling gently to the ground from a pale gray sky.

I was seven years old, still wearing pajamas on this lazy Sunday in winter. I could smell the coffee brewing in its pot atop the stove in the yellow-walled kitchen of my childhood. I could hear my father rustling the pages of the newspaper as he sat reading at the table. My sister was on the floor playing with her kitten, and I was watching the snow from the cozy warmth of the living room.

Then, the phone rang. I crossed the room to the small wooden stand upon which the black telephone was perched throughout my youth, and I answered.

The brief conversation which followed triggered conflicting emotions, carried with it one of my earliest lessons in embarrassment, disappointment and kindness. It left a lasting impression.

I can still recall her name. She was a none-too-popular classmate who sat beside me in the second grade. Her short brown hair was tightly curled against her scalp; she wore large eyeglasses with blue frames and her upper teeth were slightly bucked. She spoke with a lisp. She bit her nails. She wore dresses with ruffles, and she liked me.

So much so, in fact, that she had sent me a written invitation to her birthday party, to take place at noon precisely on the very Sunday of her call. She was, in fact, phoning to make certain that I was all right because everyone else was already present, but she did not want the games to begin until I arrived.

Of course, the moment she gave her name, I realized with horror that I'd forgotten about the party. I also decided in that fraction of a second between the question and the response that it would hurt her feelings were I to tell her the truth. And so, I said, "I'll be there in a few minutes."

And then, I ran wildly into the kitchen to tell my mother of this terrible faux pas. She helped me choose a dress, helped me select the appropriate lace-trimmed socks, the party shoes. She helped me brush my hair, and then, simultaneously, we realized that we had no birthday gift to give the child.

"You can give her the gift in school during the week," my mother suggested brightly. "It is more important that you be at the party. The gift isn't the reason she invited you."

But I was frantic. I knew the gift would count. I also knew that stores were not open on Sundays, and even if they had been open, it was too late to purchase something. So I did the only thing I could possibly do.

From the top of my closet, I removed the brand new clear plastic purse decorated with orange and yellow butterflies which had only days before been given to me. I fondled the prize lovingly, pained at the knowledge that this beautiful treasure, which I'd intended to save for spring, would now belong to someone else. Then, with my mother's help, we wrapped the present and attached the handmade birthday card.

My father drove me to the house, where I was just in time to play pin the tail on the donkey. I can remember exactly where I sat when the cake was served. I can remember the tall standing lamp in the corner of the room under which we guests had placed our presents for the birthday girl. And I remember that it had stopped snowing by the time the party was over and our parents came to take us home.

BUTCHER

I like the look of it. The sound of it. The ambience. It makes me happy to be there, makes me feel a part of something good—something warm and special and imminent. I like the fragrance and crowd and the clusters of children straining at mothers' hands. I like the combination of people, the young women, the elderly men. I like the essence of the place and the statement it makes. I like the butcher shop on Friday morning.

It is not the purchase of the meat which I particularly enjoy, but rather the reason for the shopping spree—the approaching *Shabbos* and that all of us standing there before the trays of chicken and chop meat and flanken are gathered together for a common reason. And I like knowing that many of us will exit the shop each Friday to hurry home, where we will cook similar meals.

Without having to say a word, those of us checking the chicken breasts understand that there will be a little *kugel* maybe and some soup and fish and meat on the table. There'll be salad, vegetables, interesting side dishes and, naturally, *challah*. We know this about our own *Shabbos* tables and about the tables of the others in the butcher shop. We will, all of us, welcome *Shabbos* with a meal fit for a queen.

Which is why we hurry there early Friday mornings just after the meat has been delivered to the store. And why we stand in line waiting for the woman at the checkout counter to bag our purchases and wish us *"Shabbat Shalom"* in her heavy Israeli accent.

But there is more than the imminence of *Shabbos*—there is the aura of *Shabbos* which precedes the day (and which lingers after). The sense of excited anticipation overheard in the Yiddish conversation between two women wearing white *tichels*, piling their carts high with meat and produce from the butcher shop.

It's the sound of laughter bubbling from the mouths of youngsters grabbing at brightly colored packages of candy lining the front counter of the store.

It's the rush of cold wind blowing through the open door as customers hurry through on chill December days. It's the hot summer air slipping by as men and women purchase meat in August when the sun bakes the sidewalk outside the butcher shop. It's the front window plastered with posters announcing classes or courses or speeches in local *shuls*.

It's the butcher himself making an appearance in his white apron, his sleeves rolled to his elbows—smiling at the customers checking the rows of meat, returning to the back room to bring forth the "special order" for someone or other who called yesterday about the family of eleven arriving in time for *Shabbos*.

It's the likeness to a meeting place—a community center, a club with a single goal. For all its sawdust and its mingled odors and its shouted orders and its harried patrons, for all its rushed and frantic pace, it is a happy place and a good place and a meaningful place.

I like the kosher butcher shop—particularly on Friday mornings.

FIRST TEACHER

I heard her before I saw her, and I guessed to whom she was speaking. By the tone of her voice, by the questions she asked and answered and by the very fact of hers being a one-way conversation, I was quite certain that the orator was a young mother and the audience was a baby.

And I was correct. As I rounded the corner of aisle seven in the supermarket, I came upon the two, a smiling mommy in a long gray coat and a smiling child in blue.

I watched for several minutes as the baby attempted to feed a rather soggy pretzel to his mother and the mother pretended to nibble the offering with relish.

"How sweet of you, you good, good boy," she complimented the child, wiping the corners of his mouth with her fingers. "What a generous boy you are," enunciating her words clearly. And the baby cooed from his seat in the shopping cart.

"How old?" I asked.

"Thirteen months," she answered, grinning.

"Adorable," I said, returning her smile and moving away to continue my rounds. As I made my way up aisle eight and back again down nine, I caught snatches of the woman's chatter as she kept up a running monologue for the benefit of her son. And for her own benefit, too, and for those of us in earshot, I suppose. Although I doubt if it was premeditated, I believe this mother and all other mothers of a similar nature find real satisfaction in talking to their offspring, both privately and in crowds.

It occurred to me as I listened to the mom, that she was aware of being watched, even judged, by the other shoppers. That she was, to some extent, asking for approval, silently requesting that we, her peers, stop for a moment to praise her progeny. But more importantly, I think she wanted us to notice her prowess as a teacher.

And I was not surprised by her secret wish. I've witnessed it before, wished it myself. Not quite as obviously, I hope, but with fervor nonetheless. In listening to this Mommy tell her baby not to eat "the yucky cookie that's all dirty now that you dropped it on the floor—here, have a clean cookie right from the box, see?" I wondered, as I have wondered in the past, how much sinks in, how much of the patter makes its way into the brain of the baby and how much gets absorbed into the cart filled with eggs, milk, bread and diapers?

Which, I assume, is a question the mother in gray may have been asking herself on the day of our meeting. Still, she dared not take a chance at silence with the opportunity for educating so evidently at hand. Could any thinking parent not take the time to explain why a dirty floor makes a cookie dirty, which means germs and possibly sickness? (An unfortunate thing in itself and always to be avoided, if possible.)

But sometimes even good people get bad colds and then "one must visit the good doctor to learn that yucky sickness is certainly not the doctor's fault, because doctors are helpful people just like babysitters and policemen."

I left the supermarket before the mother and her child had reached the check-out counter, before she'd paid for the groceries, replaced the baby's hat, tied the bow and no doubt explained to him the reason for zipping his snowsuit before braving the cold outdoors.

I was back at home and more than halfway through unloading the packages before, I imagine, she had him out of the car seat after reiterating yet again the necessity of safety on the roads. And I was in the midst of rinsing the fruit when I realized the simple chore would offer a follow-up lesson on the merits of cleanliness and color. "Take this shiny apple, for instance. Do you know what color this is? It is red."

Then she'd hug her baby for the smile on his lips, the twinkle in his eye, the look of intelligence she'd see or imagine on his face and for the joy and the privilege of being her son's first teacher.

THE LETTER

It was just a sketch. A pencilled drawing of a little flower pot holding one small flower and a couple of leaves.

"But she liked it so much, Ma. How come she liked it so much?"

"Because you are a good artist," I answered truthfully. "But more than that, she liked it because it showed that you were thinking about her."

"Then I'll draw another picture for her," he said.

And he sat right down to draw. This time, the picture was more elaborate. He took more time with the details and the shading. And when it was finished, he wrote a short note in the upper right-hand corner and signed his name on the bottom of the page. This time, although he'd created it for her, the picture held special significance for him.

This correspondence by artwork began several months ago when my parents told my son that an elderly friend of theirs had had a serious accident and had moved far away to be near her children. My son, who had met this friend on occasion throughout the years, agreed to send a get well card.

"But I don't know what to write," he'd complained after completing the salutation. "I said I hope she feels better. Now what should I say?"

Which prompted me to suggest a pretty drawing rather than words. "Something cheerful," I'd said. "Something that will make her smile. Something she might like to see while she is recuperating."

So he'd chosen a flowerpot with its single long-stemmed rose. He'd centered it on the page beneath the greeting. He'd signed his name, placed the missive in an envelope and we'd sent it on its way.

Neither he nor I had thought of the flowerpot since. Nor, sad to say, had we thought of my parents' friend. Until today, when the mail brought with it a handwritten note of thanks "for the beautiful picture by the wonderful artist." Praise for the drawing and for the gesture of thoughtfulness abounded in three paragraphs of tidy script written by the steady hand of this nearly ninety-year-old woman.

And between the words of gratitude she told of her frustration with the healing process. She spoke of the difficulties of adjusting to a new, less independent life. She wrote of the depth with which she missed her friends. She indicated her determination to get back on her feet, while grappling with the realities of broken bones.

She said, without saying, how good was this opportunity to write, to set some words on paper, to be forced to think, to spill out troubles in a little note, to reminisce about old times, to describe in brief her current, unfamiliar surroundings. She asked without asking for further correspondence. She implied the strong desire to communicate—to receive a letter, a card, a note.

"Another picture," said my son. "And when she gets it, I bet she'll write back."

THE MATH LESSON

It looked awful—rows of numbers, pages of rows, all with Xs and Ys and other equally intimidating letters.

"Algebra?" I asked.

"Polynomials," she answered.

"Yuck," I pronounced.

She smiled at me. "Wanna try, Ma? They're not hard."

I declined, shaking my head vigorously. "The last time I tried I was in junior high school, and I had to have a tutor to get me through the year. Forget it. I can't do algebra."

But she wouldn't take no for an answer. "It's not so bad, really. Let me show you."

How could I refuse her optimistic offer? So I acquiesced and allowed my daughter to write this terrible thing with Xs and Ys and a couple of Zs on a piece of lined loose-leaf paper. Then, I accepted the pencil she handed me. "Now, see if you can do it," she said.

But I could not. Not simply because the thought of algebra sent me into a panic, but because, the truth is, I could not for the life of me remember how to begin.

"I don't know where to start," I finally admitted, eager to give up the project.

But my teacher was determined. "I'll help you," she smiled.

And she did.

For the next thirty-four minutes, my eighth-grade daughter sat beside me at the kitchen table patiently guiding me through monomials and the like. With each success, she complimented me. With each mistake, she offered encouragement. She explained where I had gone wrong and suggested that I try again.

Which I did. For the first time in my life, certainly for the first time since 1959, I made an attempt at conquering math. And when it was time to prepare dinner, I put the math book aside with a real sense of accomplishment, thinking as I did so—better late than never.

Not better to have done the math—that, I suppose, is irrelevant. But better to have understood at last that I'm capable of understanding math. That even I, at forty-two, can come to a logical conclusion without breaking into a sweat.

Not so when I was just a girl. Back then, when algebra was part of my daily curriculum, the very mention of the word sent chills down my spine and contorted my stomach muscles into knots. I was afraid of algebra.

Or was I afraid of the teacher? Was I afraid that he would laugh at me, single me out? Did I worry that he would make a spectacle of me? Did he somehow make me feel as if math, social studies and science were boys' subjects, while English was for girls? Is that how I came to be a writer after all?

Maybe. But it doesn't matter now. What's important today is the fact that my female child feels equally at home with the humanities and the sciences, that her career options will be broader than were mine, that she is not afraid to tackle algebra and that she is willing to teach her mother, who may yet learn to balance the checkbook correctly—minus fear.

HOUSEWORK

Once, during a live performance, I heard a comedienne announce that any woman who does her own housework is a fool. "Do you hear me? A fool," she told the audience.

Occasionally, when I'm vacuuming the living room rug, or folding the day's third load of laundry, or washing the floor, I hear the echo of her words and wonder if I am.

A fool. Not just for dusting the furniture and cleaning the sink, but for the relatively old-fashioned style of life I suppose I lead.

Last night, for instance, while preparing dinner for the family, I found myself feeling content—feeling glad, actually, to be stirring and slicing. I found myself feeling fine about the prospect of cooking. And I wondered why.

How is it that in this era of microwave ovens and food processors, I do not own the former and prefer a sharp knife to the latter? Is it silly? Is it foolish? Am I, perhaps, at fault to be enjoying the mundane task of making dinner on a dreary winter evening? Should I want instead to have dinner prepared for me? And by whom?

By my husband? He would certainly do that if I asked. Or even if I did not ask. He would prepare dinner if I was not at home, if he knew I'd be late. If I wasn't feeling well. He'd slice and chop and fry and stir as well as I, but he'd enjoy it less, just as he does not like mowing the lawn or raking the leaves—jobs which belong primarily to me.

Because I do not mind them. I do not love scrubbing counter tops or grating carrots any more than most people love commuting daily to an office. But I do not hate these inconveniences. I accept them. They come with the job. The wiping and the mopping and the stirring are part of the responsibility which I choose over working in an office each day in order to earn enough money to pay for someone else to mop and stir.

And it is this element of choice, I think, which keeps me from feeling foolish.

Most of the time.

But not always. There are days when I admit to more than a mild twinge of guilt for doing what I do—or do not do. There are moments when I think I should be pounding the pavement looking for work, looking for a title to appear above my name on the door in some chrome and glass building somewhere.

There are quiet evenings when, with dinner dishes done, and the children doing homework at the kitchen table, I feel guilty for the peace. And then, I remember the comedienne, marching onto the stage in her silver gown, her face shining with makeup. I recall this performer with her entourage of helpers. This entertainer, the ultimate career woman, travelling from one show to another, one hotel to another, one town to another. And I realize that neither she nor I would trade places for the world, nor must we. That is, I believe, the whole point of liberation and the antitheses of playing the fool.

BUTTERFLIES

She wasn't really my aunt, and the butterflies were not made of jewels. Both of those facts I understood even at the age of six. And yet, in some vague way, I find myself still believing in the relationship and the precious gems.

The memory of Aunt Helen and the butterflies came to mind last weekend when, on a dismal Sunday afternoon, I read aloud to my son, a short story entitled, "The Artist of the Beautiful," by Nathaniel Hawthorne.

In this tale, a poor young watchmaker spends his every

spare moment creating an infinitely exquisite and terribly fragile, mechanical butterfly. The insect, with its glittering wings, evoked thoughts of Helen and the rhinestone butterfly pins.

I was a small child, and my sister even smaller, when first we met her. She had long, straight brown hair which she wore in braids wound 'round her head like a crown. Her ears were adorned with miniature wicker fruit baskets which danced merrily on either side of her head. She wore brightly colored flower-print dresses and shawls with dangling fringe. She kept with her always, and would show us with pride, snapshots of her dogs and birds. And inevitably, she carried an enormous woven bag, the contents of which were the makings of beautiful butterflies.

My parents introduced her as Aunt Helen—"Aunt," sounding less formal than "Mrs." preceding a surname. And thus did Aunt Helen's husband become Uncle David. Occasionally, through the years, Uncle David would join Aunt Helen when she came to visit.

And sometimes my sister and I would spend an afternoon or an evening at their house, where we could browse happily through the collection of trinkets and animals which made their home with this couple. But most often, Aunt Helen arrived on our doorstep alone, just before dinnertime.

My sister and I would, quite cheerfully, kiss our parents good-bye and Aunt Helen would proceed to serve us the meal—always with a song. I can see her now, scooping stew from the pot which my mother had left simmering on the stove. And I can hear Aunt Helen humming as she placed the food upon our plates.

I cannot say when or even if I ever understood that Helen was our babysitter. And I cannot imagine just how or where my parents found her. But for my sister and I, and perhaps for my mother and father too, Aunt Helen was a bit of magic.

When Aunt Helen came through the door, the whole world wore a grin and wonderful things were bound to happen.

Such as butterflies. Dozens of them. Maybe hundreds of them. Pretty little butterfly pins which sparkled in the lamplight as we whiled away the evening hours among small mountains of colored rhinestones.

With Aunt Helen as the teacher, I learned to place the stones just so in the tiny cups of glue which formed the insect wings. I learned to concentrate on symmetry, with blue stones facing blue and pink abutting pink. I made butterflies in crimson and gold. I made pastel butterflies and bright butterflies and butterflies whose wings were a combination of somber and gay.

Occasionally, when we ran out of glue or pins or stones, Helen would take us with her to the little crafts shop where she purchased the butterfly paraphernalia. Then, clutching small bags of rhinestones and frames, we would be dropped off at home to work on our butterflies until the next time my parents had to be away for an evening.

But it was never the same making butterflies without Aunt Helen. Never as good as having her there with her songs and her pictures, and her braids and her earrings and her bright red lipstick and her sparkling eyeglasses and her tales of visits to foreign lands.

Although I have spoken to her occasionally through the years, I have not seen Aunt Helen for a very long time. But I'm quite sure she has not changed. It is I alone who have grown older. Aunt Helen, I am certain, must still be making butterflies and magic.

THE TABLECLOTH

It is not so much the distance travelled by the thing, but the thought that what is mine today was held by someone else ten thousand miles away, a week ago or less. It is the connection with people different, remote, exotic and foreign which sets me to dreaming about labels on shirt collars and stamps on the underside of coffee mugs.

And sometimes, it is not the label but the thing itself, the garish plastic tablecloth I often use (despite the fact that I dislike the colors and the plastic) which sends me into sweet reverie.

Two summers ago, the tablecloth lay neatly folded in the bottom bureau drawer in the back room of the stone floored flat in Jerusalem where my husband's Great Aunt Malka spends her days. When I spread that orange and pink and yellow piece of plastic upon my kitchen table, a memory unfolds intact.

I see the tiny woman with her bright blue eyes. I follow her, tentatively, to the back room where two feather beds, a single table and a chest of drawers stand. She bends low to take the table cover from its hiding place, and graciously, she hands it to me. As she does so, she smiles. And I fall in love with her and with the funny tablecloth which I use so that I may continue to be in Jerusalem, in the high-ceilinged, stone-floored flat receiving the gift from my husband's great-aunt.

But not all the daydreams are familiar. Some—most, I think—are abstract, my connection to the person at the giving end, not really a relationship at all. But rather, a speculation which begins with a label—made in India. Or Japan. Made in Hong Kong. Made in Sri Lanka. In Mexico. In Taiwan. In Sweden. Imported from some distant land where some man or woman, some child, I suppose, sewed the intricate cross-stitching on the bodice of my dress, painted the small flowers in my dish and cup. Some mother, with dark eyes cast downward as she worked, held the cloth tightly in her deft fingers, dreaming dreams about her counterpart in a small suburban town in the United States.

Nor is it always labels which make me pause. Sometimes, it is foods which set me to wondering—about those who picked bananas in Brazil, the ones who gathered olives in Italy, collected the beans for the coffee, who chopped the cane for sugar, pressed the grapes for wine.

So many places, so many people, each with a particular face, a significant smile, a worry, a reason to laugh, with failures and successes to their names, with a heritage, a history, a future. And each a part of my life by virtue of the fact that I wear the shirt, eat the fruit, drink from the mug upon which they set their mark.

And all the miles the things have travelled, all the oceans and airways, all the mountains they have climbed, the deserts and fields they've traversed to come across my threshold, finally, to grace my kitchen table.

And thus, from my little house in Spring Valley, do I find myself daily transported to all the corners of the world.

MICKEY MOUSE

I will never forget her face. The look of shock, disbelief, pain. And then, an almost imperceptible nod of recognition as the inevitable registered, a vague narrowing of the eyes as reality set in. A coming to terms with the fact.

"Mickey Mouse is a person."

Just like that, she said it, standing on the linoleum floor, her brown eyes wide with the knowledge. "Mickey Mouse is a person." She repeated the truth once more. Then, she turned on her heels and headed down the hallway to find her friends.

Innocence lost.

In a matter of moments, with no warning, no build-up, the fantasy was shattered. And the five-year-old girl would never again be quite the same.

Nor would I.

It happened one bright morning several weeks ago when, as a class mother, I was serving refreshments at the school carnival. One among a dozen or so mothers and fathers, I had spent a pleasant hour watching the children at play. Song, dance, a lively band and food were among the highlights of the day. But the greatest treat, it seemed, was the honored guest and surprise visitor . . . Mickey Mouse.

Resplendent in red and black, he sauntered through the lunchroom waving to the audience, shaking hands with the youngest in the crowd, clowning with the students. Even the older children, my own among them, were not above posing for a snapshot with the star.

But it was the little ones in particular, the five- and six-year-olds who seemed mesmerized by the fellow with the gigantic plastic head and the enormous ears.

"We love you, Mickey Mouse," they chanted. "Happy birthday, Mickey Mouse," they sang.

And I sang with them.

When finally the party ended, cookie crumbs littered the floor, bits of candy crunched underfoot. Tired youngsters antagonized one another or whined and rubbed their eyes. A sense of ordered chaos prevailed as teachers tried to herd the students into groups. Here and there, a stray child had to be collected and returned to his appropriate classroom. Eventually, all were accounted for—save one.

One small girl had somehow managed to escape the eyes of the teacher, principal and classmates. One child had wandered unobserved from the lunchroom down the corridor to the lobby where she halted, finally, directly behind Mickey Mouse.

From where I stood at the base of the stairs, I had watched the child moving quietly in Mickey's footsteps. I had noticed how the top of her head barely reached the back of Mickey's knee. I had seen her staring solemnly up at Mickey's head.

I'd observed them approaching me, the costumed man in front, the tiny figure just behind.

A sweet picture, I'd thought to myself, wondering when the mouse would discover his little shadow. But I said nothing. And he never saw her there.

Which is why he felt safe in removing his head.

I gasped as he lifted it off his shoulders, and I shouted, "Oh no," aloud. But it was too late.

She'd already seen, and I watched her wince.

I watched her face turn white with fear. I saw her eyes widen in surprise.

And then I saw her shrug her shoulders, saw her cast away her infancy just like that. I saw a little girl accept the truth . . . Mickey Mouse is make believe.

And I thought that she must cry.

But she did not.

She puffed out her little chest; she raised her chin a trifle and she walked away.

It was I who shed the tear.

$\mathcal{S}$HARING

Sometimes, it surprises me—the overwhelming sense of joy I feel at the sight of the blue car turning in our driveway.

He's home. My husband is home.

It happens while I'm standing at the kitchen sink, slicing vegetables for dinner. In winter, through the steamy windows, I can see his headlights brightening the trees. Through the tumult of food sizzling on the stove, one or the other of the children asking incessant questions having to do with homework or a missing pair of socks or tomorrow's social studies test, amidst the sounds of someone practicing saxophone or piano, above the noise of music and the telephone's inevitable ringing, when my hands are covered with raw chop meat or egg yolk and my eyes are tearing from the onions, comes the sound of the tires on the road, and I feel my heart leap a little.

This is happiness.

A smile through the glass as I unlock the door for him. A rush of cold air and a sense of warmth. Reassurance. Security. Stability.

This is what it was meant to be, a feeling of rightness in the mundane acts of life.

"Hi."

And, "Hello."

And, "Did you remember to drop off the cleaning? Pick up the prescription?"

"What time is your meeting tonight? She got an A on her English report. Can you drive him to school tomorrow? How was your day?"

"And yours?"

And, "Can you help him with the math problem?"

"Have you seen my yellow socks, Ma?"

"Did you remember to pick up the juice?"

"What's for dinner?"

"Somebody please set the table. Turn off the stereo. Get the basketball off the kitchen floor."

"I think we're out of ketchup."

"Your uncle called from Brooklyn. He says to call him back."

"Anything good in today's mail? Why's the water bill so high? Stop teasing your brother."

"Go wash your hands for dinner. Somebody bring drinks to the table. Dinner's ready. Welcome home."

And then the spill. The funny story from the office. One of the children reciting a part from the school play.

And, "Please pass the rice."

". . . the string beans."

"Sit up straight."

"How's the burger?"

"Don't annoy your sister."

And my husband, sitting opposite me throughout the meal, a part of all this gentle chaos, this chattering and squabbling, this clutter and the laughter, sharing the happy turmoil of family life.

This second marriage feels good.

BOOK SIX • REALIZATIONS

REALIZATIONS

INTRODUCTION

So this is it, I'd find myself saying, still trying to pigeon-hole observance. This sense of anticipation I feel while polishing the silver *kiddush* cups, the aura of peace which descends when I light the candles, the almost shy pride which comes over me when I *daven* each morning—this, then, is Judaism.

"And this, too," I'd acknowledge, greeting my husband and son at the door on their return from *shul* on Friday night. "This," listening to one then the other child discuss some point of interest, relate some anecdote, "and this," as we would share a *Shabbos* meal. Judaism is family.

"But what of this?" I'd feel the need to ask. "What of the *minyan* on *Shabbos* morning? What of the wives and daughters seated on the women's side of the *mechitzah*? What of *Simchas Torah* celebrated with friends and neighbors? What of *Sukkos*? What of *Purim*? What of the gatherings? The sense of togetherness? "Ah yes," I would say, "Judaism is community."

Judaism is delicate—the knots on *tzitzis*, the braid in the *challah*, the *mezuzah* on the doorpost.

Judaism is strong—voices in unison, the *Kosel* in Yerushalayim, *chassidim* and *misnagdim*

Children—singing the *Birchas Hamazon*, infants at birth, the *bris milah*, the *bar-mitzvah*.

The elderly—with failing eyesight, chanting by heart, speaking Yiddish, passing this down to the generations—through the generations.

Judaism is hopeful. Forgiving. Remembering. Accepting. Demanding. Personal. Communal. Unfathomable. Obvious. Mundane and exquisite. Eternal, immediate. Judaism is ours and mine.

PESACH CLEANING

What a mess. And it took too long. And not a whole lot was accomplished—practically speaking. But in the end, they said it was worth it. I think I'd have to agree.

It all began as it does each spring with my request to the children to clean out their "junk drawers." It ended with the realization that junk is a relative term.

I had forewarned them days in advance that Sunday was the date. That they should be prepared to rise early, to eat a hasty breakfast and carry their respective "junk drawers" to the living room where I gave permission to dump the contents on the floor. In the center of the carpet, I placed a large brown garbage bag "for anything you want to give away." Next, I handed each child a detergent-soaked cloth and commissioned them to "clean." Then, I wished them luck and left the scene.

That was at nine-thirty a.m. It was after two when finally, they were "done, Ma." It's what happened between that I find worthy of note.

From where I stood, working at the kitchen counter, I could hear them sifting through their collection of "stuff." A silver rattle from my daughter's day of birth. A rubber duck from my son's first bath. A magazine from his initial plane flight. A blue glass bowl from a cousin in California.

Occasionally, as I went about my business, purposely staying out of their way, one or the other would call to me to "look, Mom." Or to "listen" to the seven-year-old letter written by my daughter's first grade teacher in praise of the then six-year-old child. At ten forty-five a.m., my son discovered an old harmonica which he found necessary to test before continuing his job.

From the depths of their two separate "junk drawers," the children unearthed pictures of classmates who have long ago moved away and bibs from their infancies kept safe for sentimental purposes. They found postcards and foreign coins, stamps from exotic countries, pamphlets on rock collecting, a pair of green earrings, a small gold locket, fourteen pencils and a China doll with pale brown braids, five Slinkys, two lace handkerchiefs, a skein of ribbon and the birth certificate for a doll.

As they worked, they reminisced, recalling when we visited Canada and they couldn't make the soldier in the photograph crack a smile. Remembering when we took a trip to New Orleans and bought the necklace as a souvenir.

Tucked away in my son's drawer was his first attempt at fiction (which he read aloud to his sister after he finished his harmonica solo). In her drawer were scraps of poetry she's written through the years. Both had bits of artwork, odd pieces of stationery, baseball cards and playing cards and loose change. Both found unused wallets and sheets of paper with friends' phone numbers scribbled in corners.

Buried in envelopes and plastic bags were magic tricks and hand-held toys and plastic dinosaurs from distant games of make believe. From the times before my daughter had a younger brother, days when she and I lived with her natural father in a different life a million miles and years away.

Hidden beneath the recent collection of things and items and gadgets were those which the two of them had kept from the apartment where we lived when my son was a baby and his sister was a toddler and I was the only parent on hand.

Kaleidoscopes and magnets, balls of twine and bags of marbles, a jumble of the frivolous and the serious.

Most of it impossible to throw away.

THE ASSISTANT

My right-hand man is a girl. Who was standing to my left when the thought struck home.

We were peeling potatoes at the time, preparing for the twenty-one guests who would arrive for the *seder*. I shouted orders to my husband to set up the folding chairs, to remove all the furniture from the living room (except for the extra tables we'd borrowed), to buy more vegetables and fruit. I told my son to rake the yard, to sweep the driveway, to take out the garbage, to vacuum the carpet and make his bed. I directed, I announced, I demanded; I insisted that they do what I said when I said it.

Which they did. While in the center of the turmoil, with tablecloths being unfurled and silverware being counted, my helper and I peeled potatoes at the kitchen sink. And it was there, amidst the chaos, that I turned to face her, noting with surprise that the two of us see nearly eye to eye.

That somehow, suddenly, she seems to read my mind, anticipate my needs, act, react, think and plan in a way I understand.

"Onions next?" she wanted to know.

I nodded. "Yes."

"And then, I'll bake the cakes," she said.

With little persuasion, with no coercion, with hardly a hint or a word, my teenage daughter had become my right-hand man.

For years now, she and her brother have been helping me when asked. They've been clearing the table, making beds, feeding the fish, raking the yard, cooking or baking when the mood or their mother insists.

But somehow, one day last week as we stood at the sink, the elder of my progeny outgrew the need for direction. Her help became automatic. Yet "help" itself implies the need for authority. She did not help. She did. And she continued to do throughout the day and into the evening. She stirred and mixed and served and carried platters to the table and removed platters and cleared the dishes and returned clean dishes to their places. She checked to see that everyone had eaten; she dished out food when she saw the need. She conversed when conversation was appropriate. She listened when listening was right. Side by side, she and I controlled the goings on in the kitchen. Four hands working together, two heads leaning over the huge pot of soup. Both of us distributing jobs to the others who offered to help. And she did it all with ease and poise, with a calm demeanor—as though she'd been doing it always and quite happily. As though she was enjoying herself.

And maybe she was. Perhaps she was feeling a sense of accomplishment in the knowledge that she'd helped to orchestrate a rather complicated domestic feat. That among the other things—the more cerebral things—she is and will be capable of doing, there will be this annual event of a *seder* for twenty-one or more. And, in such a situation, she will be prepared.

I was proud of her. And I suppose, proud of myself for having helped to produce her. And I told her so. Early the next morning, I thanked my daughter for all that she'd done to help make the previous evening a success. But she raised her eyebrows in surprise.

"It was nothing, Ma," she said.

Which meant something special to me.

THE LEGACY

"Look at that. A pretty little polluted stream."

I leaned over the embankment, following my son's finger as he pointed to the jumble of soda cans, beer bottles, cardboard boxes and assorted garbage which swirled among the weeds.

"Gross," he pronounced sentence upon the scene in a monotone. There was no surprise in his voice. No outrage. At twelve, experience had already taught him to expect the worst. "Pollution," he stated flatly, turning from the path. "Yuck."

And suddenly, standing in the warm spring sunshine,

beneath an umbrella of newly grown leaves, I was embarrassed—ashamed of the bottles and boxes, disgusted by the desecration and the legacy of disregard for beauty that I seemed to be offering my son.

It is not the first time I have felt this wash of guilt. Just last week, I recounted to my daughter the days of summer fun when, in my childhood and early teens, we'd head "down to the shore" for a week of swimming in the ocean along the New Jersey coast. I told her of the clean white beaches, the soft sand, the sparkling waters. The way we'd jump waves for hours on end. Of how we'd awaken early to walk barefoot, collecting shells.

And as I spoke, I watched her face, the expression in her eyes not unlike the one I'd expect to see if I were recounting the era of the horse and buggy.

"No ailing plant life," I told her. No sickened birds. No worries about distruption of the food chain, the ozone layer, the earth, the sea, the sky. We thought the lakes and rivers would remain forever blue. Back then we didn't understand how quickly things could change.

"No aluminum cans in the ocean then?" she asked ironically. "No oil spills? No debris? No junk?"

No barges of garbage with nowhere to dump their cargo, no medical waste along the shore, no page one pictures of diseased and dying fish in contaminated waters. No thought of the greenhouse effect.

Instead, there were more screen doors and fewer air conditioners. There was more homemade fried chicken and fewer fast food restaurants. There were fewer cars and more family picnics. And little chance that a casual walk on a warm spring day would culminate in the sight of a polluted neighborhood stream with me feeling sick about the state of nature to be faced by the children who will inherit the earth.

ANOTHER YEAR

I removed the dishes from the shelf, and the echo of the *seder* filled my thoughts.

A wave of sadness washed through me. Finished.

Pesach was over, and the mismatched dairy dishes and the glass meat dishes and the pretty *seder* plate and the jumble of pots and pans and platters would be packed into boxes and stored in the attic for another year.

And the house would be relatively quiet again. The sounds of guests would cease. Work would resume. Life would go back to normal.

I was sorry.

I studied the serving bowls. Less than a week ago, they'd been heaped with chicken and potatoes and vegetables and compote. They'd been placed on the table after the first two cups of wine and before the second two. And now, they would be hidden away upstairs in a dark corner behind the suitcases and the old hobby-horse.

As I set cups and saucers into cartons, I could hear the memory of guests laughing, talking. I could hear them singing at our *sedarim*.

I could see my children standing by my side helping me serve the soup and the meat and the salad and the fish. I could see them in their lovely clothes—my son in a dark blue suit, my daughter in a white cotton dress. I could envision my husband in his white *kittel* at the head of the table.

I lifted the *Pesach* silverware from the drawer and wrapped it in plastic. How I hated to see the holiday end.

One a.m. and I lingered, staring at the *Pesach* cookbook, the leftover boxes of *matzah* and potato starch, the scribbled list of items I'd planned to serve at the *sedarim*—the pencilled clutter of foods and drinks, the names of the guests to be squeezed around the living room table—a scrap of notepad representing hours of cooking, cleaning and celebrating.

Regretfully, I folded the sheet of paper in half and placed it carefully atop the lists I've saved from *sedarim* in years past—knowing as I did so that next year the sight of these memories will make me happy when, once again, I will prepare for *Pesach* in our house.

THE VISITOR

Listen. I'll tell you something, but I'd prefer that you not tell my mother. I'm afraid she'll think it's a reflection on my housekeeping. But the truth is, that's not the case. The house is clean. Very clean. And neat. But it probably doesn't matter.

It began during *Pesach*. In the middle of the week, after the *sedarim* were finished, after the company had gone, after the extra tables and chairs had been put away. After everything was back in place, that's when it happened.

It was just about five a.m. when we heard the sound. I suppose it was quite loud, because the two of us jumped up.

"What's that?" I mouthed the words. "Go check," I said, afraid to leave the bed.

My husband raised his eyebrows and headed for the bedroom door. I cowered, vacillating between visions of a robber and my son during a pre-dawn refrigerator raid.

"But there's no one out there," he said when he returned. "The kids are sound asleep. Did you move the *matzah* cover last night?"

"You mean the cover covering the plastic *matzah* holder?"

"Yeah," he said. "That one."

"No," I answered. "Why?"

"Well, someone moved it."

"The *matzah* cover? Why would anyone move the *matzah* cover?"

"To get the *matzah* in the plastic bag inside the plastic *matzah* holder," he said. "That's why."

"Someone did that?"

"Or some . . . thing."

"Thing? What do you mean . . . thing?" By this time, I was standing over the table, upon which lay the rumpled blue and white *matzah* cover exposing the plastic box and *matzos*.

"Where did those crumbs come from?" I demanded, following the trail of *matzah* tidbits across the tablecloth down the chair to the corner of the carpet near the piano. "A mouse?"

"A mouse," my husband said.

A mouse who found the macaroons at the end of the holiday week. A mouse who, after *Pesach* had passed, left donut crumbs across the floor. A mouse who has managed to steal cheese and peanut butter from every trap we've set. A mouse who came for the holiday and decided to stay. A mouse who has been eluding us at every turn. A hungry mouse. A smart mouse.

A mouse I hope my mother never meets.

AMP

No one warned me about the name-tags.

Or the trunk.

Or the twenty-four pairs of socks.

Nobody mentioned the flashlight, the soap dish, the laundry bag and the cot sheets when I said it sounded okay to me.

But that was months ago, when the trees were bare and we were all wearing woolen coats. Back then, in December or January, summer seemed like something in the distant future.

So I said yes. And my husband said yes. We said fine. Sure. Why not?

To be perfectly honest, I had my doubts that it would actually come about even after we'd given permission. This is not, you see, the first time she's mentioned the idea. For the past few years, she's considered it for a week or two each winter when the other kids discussed their summer "plans." But in the past, she's always dropped the subject and opted for the home front.

This time was different, though. She meant what she said. The application arrived. We filled it out. We paid a heart-stopping sum of money and signed a half-dozen forms to ensure our progeny the joy of sleepaway camp for the month of July.

For the cost of a two-week vacation for four, we agreed to send one child to a cabin in the woods so that she can battle ticks and mosquitoes, sleep on a mattress the size of a doormat and return home with twenty-eight days' worth of wrinkled clothes.

But they tell me she'll have fun. They say she'll enjoy every minute of it. She'll get used to camp food or become accustomed to a diet of bread and water. They say she'll make new friends and learn new skills and be a better person for the experience.

So how could we refuse? Never having gone to camp

myself, I cannot say whether or not I missed a vital phase of growing up. Perhaps I would have had greater self-confidence or a broader range of interests had I but given camp a try. In any case, I'm willing to see the possibilities for my daughter—despite the cost and number of socks and sweatshirts we have purchased for the trip and the trunk we had to borrow. I'm willing to weigh the positives against the sneakers and bathing suits we have bought and the countless name-tags I have sewn to every item folded now in preparation for the trip. I am eager to view the bright side, the sunshine and fresh air and camaraderie my daughter will come to know when she's away from home. I'm glad to give her this chance to test her wings and her hiking boots and her rain poncho and her calamine lotion and her tick spray and her new canteen. I am confident that she will have a lovely time.

But I will miss her while she's gone.

ROSES

There it was. Catching the yellow sunlight on its pink blossoms, looking fresh and beautiful in the clear morning air.

The stillness enveloped us as we stood reverently before the rosebush in someone else's yard. "It's perfect," I whispered fervently, "isn't it?"

My husband and children nodded in agreement, rolling their eyes at one another and suppressing laughter. Still, they humored me. "Oh yes, Mom," they said. "We can tell that it's special." They were teasing me.

Nonetheless, I began to explain.

"You see," I said, "when I was a little girl, I lived in a big green house. Each spring I'd run outside to play in the huge back yard with its sandbox and swings. I'd rest in the chairs on the wraparound porch. I'd hide in the shade beside the cellar door. By the middle of June each year, I'd have explored every inch of the great outdoors surrounding my house, every inch save one.

"And it never failed. For all the years I lived there, from birth until the age of twenty-three, I never remembered the rosebush until it was in bloom. And even then, it wasn't remembering, really. It was more a kind of discovery, a sweet surprise, an 'oh how lovely, and to think I'd forgotten it would be here' revelation.

"The bush grew directly under one of the large, many paned windows in the room I shared with my sister. It hugged the stone foundation so tightly that, had I tried, I suppose I could not have seen it through the organdy curtains. Nor would I have noticed the flowers from the rock-boarded walkway dividing our yard in half, nor from the far end of the front porch.

"I did see lilies of the valley, though, and buttercups and pansies. I saw the other odd and sundry flora in the yard. But never did I see the rosebush until one day each spring when I would, by some internal spurring-on, take it into my mind to walk once around the house at dawn. And there it would be.

"My rosebush in full bloom, pink and bathed in droplets of dew in the silence of early morning. I would smell the blossoms individually before plucking a few to bring to the house, always wondering to myself if the taking of its flowers hurt this living thing. From the yearly point of discovery until the last of the flowers had withered on the vine, I would visit the rosebush every day.

"And then, one summer, I got married, moved away and never thought about the rosebush again. Until yesterday when I saw the flowers in full bloom in someone else's yard."

REALITY

"It's perfectly normal for your age," he reassured me. "There's nothing you can do about it. It's only going to get worse." Then, pausing for effect, he added, "Welcome to the club."

I smiled half-heartedly at his joke. "Some club," I remarked.

But I knew what he meant.

Along with cellulite, gray hair, varicose veins and teenage children, farsightedness is apparently a fact of life at forty-plus.

So now I own a pair of spectacles, my first pair of pink-framed eyeglasses through which I will view the world a little differently henceforth.

However, I'm sure it's not my lenses alone which have changed with age but rather my perception in general. It's hindsight, foresight and insight which have altered over time—functions less tangible but equally as significant as the physical condition of my eyes.

As I head towards half a century of life, I find that concepts, philosophies and realities which once seemed crystal clear are out of focus now. The blacks and whites are shades of gray, the rights and wrongs and goods and bads are simply points of view. And while the words in books are sharper than they were before the glasses, the concepts which they represent are increasingly less clear. The certainties of youth have become questionable at middle age.

Yet, there are some truths I seem to note with greater comprehension today. The rapidity with which we move through time, the importance of laughter and love, the facts of old age and death. Some causes and effects, some results and consequences appear to be sharper despite the aging of my eyes.

And it is these altering and altered perceptions of the world which have colored the way I view myself.

The glasses? Perhaps they change the way I look, but other things have changed the way I see.

THE REUNION

Every few days, I make a note to answer the invitation—and when the day I'd marked arrives, I move the note ahead again. Because I'm still not sure of whether or not I want to attend. Nor am I sure why I won't, if I don't. It is truly a case of mixed emotions—the intensity of which I am surprised to feel. It is, after all, only a class reunion.

This is not a fiftieth reunion or even a thirty-fifth. It is simply a gathering of the one hundred and fifty-odd members of the high school class of 1964, among which I was counted.

Is it the realization of all that has occurred over the years? Is it that I like to think of myself as a different person now? Is it that I prefer the me of late to the me of early? But am I not being ridiculous? Aren't we all different from the people we were at seventeen? (And aren't we all basically the same?)

And isn't it that sameness which frightens me most? The knowledge that they will remember who I was back then and that, hard as I may have tried to be more cosmopolitan or more earthy, more worldly or more arty, they will see right through the facade and know that I am me.

Plain. And rather earnest. Trying hard to do it right. To get the good grade. To be the good mother. To find the answers without causing too much trouble, too much pain.

The good girl. The nice girl. The model student. And rather boring. The girl who spent her childhood and one whole marriage doing what she felt was right rather than what she felt was fun.

The one who somewhere, at some point between eighteen and forty-three decided to change her image—to wear larger earrings or higher heels, to be more open and honest, more knowing, insightful, more introspective and (simultaneously) extroverted.

The girl who became a woman who, despite the earrings and the introspection, is still essentially the same as she was twenty-five years ago.

But so will they be—for the most part, I imagine. Grown-up versions of the way they were—older, grayer, heavier versions of the athletes, the class clowns, the student council members we used to be—with adolescent children of our own.

And why does that disturb me? Why does any of this bother me? Why am I wondering whether I can lose ten pounds before the reunion date? Why will I worry about what to wear if I decide to go? To whom will it make a difference?

To me. I think.

 WELCOME BACK

She's back.

Along with her trunk, her baseball mitt, her used can of tick spray and eight loads of laundry.

She's back, and the telephone, which had hardly rung since her departure, is once again in constant use.

She has returned.

Her room, which remained tidy for the four weeks of her absence, has within the last forty-eight hours resumed its previous lived-in look. She's here. With a deep bronze tan, a dazzling smile and a three-inch gash on her knee from a hockey game she had to win.

Like a candle flame, she flits through the house, lighting on the kitchen chair, the couch, the countertop, telling stories of overturned canoes in the lake, late-night snacks, skunks which surprised the campers at dawn.

She speaks of orange and purple sunsets across the placid water, and I can imagine her at dusk among her friends. She tells of whispered conversations with the girls, and I envision her under her blankets, her eyes wide open at three a.m.

As she talks, a world unfolds for me, a piece of time in which she lived among her peers in a wooded enclave in the mountains. I see her eating lunch with the others, singing songs around a campfire, laughing into the early morning hours. I envision her playing softball and basketball, taking walks along the mountain paths. I sense the solitude and the community, the supervised freedom she must have felt. And I am glad for her.

Despite hours of preparation, the labels sewn on every sock and shirt, despite the shopping and the packing and the exorbitant cost, the past four weeks were worth everything.

She has grown. She has made friends. She has had an experience which she will remember for years to come, perhaps forever. She eagerly seized an opportunity, and she appreciated it.

She loved every minute of sleepaway camp. And we love having her back home.

MY VIEW

The windows wouldn't open. Literally. The clear, tall panes of glass were soldered to their rims, shut tight against the elements and outside sound, allowing for the view alone.

And that, admittedly, was spectacular. The Empire State Building, minuscule automobiles and even smaller people, the Hudson River and New Jersey beyond were all within my line of vision as I sat behind the desk in the hermetically sealed room on the thirty-third floor of the modern Park Avenue skyscraper in New York City.

I had been asked to arrive at nine a.m. for an informal meeting—which had meant my arising at six a.m. to catch the seven-thirty bus. And then, I'd taken a cab from Port Authority to the appointed destination.

For one brief morning, I'd run through life the way I might if I were a commuter. And I've decided that it's not for me.

Because the windows would not open. Of course, I really didn't give the city half a chance. I did not ride the subway, didn't eat lunch in a classy restaurant. I didn't shop or catch an exhibition after work. I didn't experience the gamut of advantages and disadvantages abounding in the place. I simply left my cozy home on a tree-lined street and headed for the land of neon and steel.

But I did not like the latter very much.

As far as I'm concerned, the city's great for cultural events, for occasional visits, for a shot of excitement or intrigue. But on the whole, I find it rather confining. Where there are those who would consider the bustle of city life a sign of vitality, I experience a sense of claustrophobia when I'm there.

Some, I've heard, love the honk of horns, the spew of exhaust fumes on crowded streets. I prefer the solitude at the bottom of the dead end road on which we live. And while I recognize a kind of beauty in the scene from the thirty-third floor, the controlled environment at that level disturbs my sense of freedom.

I like to feel the heat of summer through a screen. I like being able to reach outside to touch the snow in winter. I think it would bother me to work in an office where the temperature remains the same throughout the year.

And so, in case some wealthy New York executive is planning to offer me a high-paying position in a plush office with a panoramic view, I'm afraid I'll be forced to decline.

I simply could not function in a room where the windows are permanently closed.

On RETROSPECT

With these words begins the first week of the tenth year of this column.

My column.

Not unlike my arm, I think, or my leg, this weekly vehicle for an expression of my thoughts has become an appendage, an extension of myself—I count on it.

I rely on its presence to help me put my life into focus, to gain perspective on the scheme of things. I use it as a form of therapy—to get thoughts out, to set the record straight.

I see it as a diary, a calendar, a photo album, a good old friend. I know the whole of it the way a mother knows an adult child from infancy. I remember its beginnings as it recorded mine. I am at one with it, and yet, I am a separate entity.

I appreciate it for its silent counsel. It encourages me to speak but remains mute. It takes my words the way a mirror takes my face. It holds me to the light and lets me study who I am or who I was and who I am becoming. It keeps me searching.

It allows me to regress—to the days when it came into being and I was recently divorced and living in a small apartment with two toddlers. It was then I stated how sometimes, I felt "sorry for myself" for having "left so much behind."

In those first years, I spoke of life as a solitary parent, of the weight with which I leaned upon my mother and father and sister and brother-in-law. I shared my fears of the life ahead with anyone willing to read. I worried in print about my children's psyches and the wounds I thought would never heal. I fretted over my offsprings' runny noses, coughs, first days of school and first homework assignments. I thought about the possibility that one day they would choose to live with their father rather than me. I cried at weddings, tried to make ends meet. I had a host of other solo-parent friends.

Back then, as now, I wrote because I needed to write,

because I wanted to put things down in black and white and then read the words aloud again to study how I felt. But through the years, the columns changed as I have changed. My early efforts showed a heavy dose of anger. In later works, when I was feeling self-assured, I said so, and the saying gave me confidence. And then, I met my present spouse and penned a sense of disbelief amidst the joy.

And today, as I sit here reviewing the past, I find that I can read between the lines.

With the columns in hand to trigger the memories, I can relive the days when the children were small and riding tricycles or learning how to swim or crying because they missed their father or crying because they were children, and children cry. By scanning old words, I can remember both the writing and the incident which was the inspiration to write.

And so, today, I submit this column for those who would care to read what I have to say. But as I've done for the past nine years, I submit this column primarily for me so I will know what it is that's been on my mind today.

A SUMMER SON

Some people aren't suited for organized activities. Like school, for instance.

My son, for example, is quite sure that he could get along without the structure imposed by math and history.

What's necessary in life, he says, is time to play and think, time to paint, draw and read, time to listen to music and ride one's bike, time to swim and climb the trees. What counts, he feels, is studying the way worms work and who can eat more ice cream on a summer afternoon.

From his perspective, school cuts out the part of life that feels like wings. It makes you sit in chairs that have no wheels and forces you to concentrate on algebra when what you really need to figure out is how to build a better skateboard ramp.

And it does something to the fingers and toes—it makes the former grasp pencils and forces the latter into socks and shoes which take away the tickle of the grass.

School puts lunchtime at an hour when you might not necessarily be hungry, and it removes the option of standing before the open refrigerator door.

It makes you get out of bed before the dreaming's finished, it puts you on a bouncing yellow school bus before your breakfast has found its proper place.

School, according to my son, may open the mind to the wonders of the world, but there's more than enough to do in one's backyard.

Which is why he feels that summer should not end. Or if it must, then vacation should linger, since kids need hours to examine properly the color of the leaves in autumn and weeks to figure out just how a football should be thrown and what to do with pine cones which have fallen to the ground. And then, when winter comes along, it's almost vital for a kid to stay at home to watch for snow and all that stuff which makes it possible to ski and sleigh ride. It is necessary to be outdoors to understand precipitation, which cannot form within the classroom walls.

And so I send him off this season feeling torn by what he'll learn and what he'll leave behind. There's something to be said for his philosophy of freedom and more than a little truth in the benefits of play.

Still, I expect that a month or so from now, when he's settled into the routine, he'll come flying through the door one afternoon to report some wonderful theory he just learned, to show me a grade on his English test, to recount an event in history just the way the teacher told it to the class. And I'll be glad for him. And I'll be thrilled by the light in his eyes as he grows and learns.

For now, however, I am sorry that vacation had to end.

THE BRACES

"I'll never look this way again," he said. "Say good-bye to my smile."

He was kidding me, of course, both of us aware that the braces would not truly change his face. In fact, his teeth are really rather straight. It's his bite which needs adjustment (so they say). When the braces come off two years from now, the correction itself will be barely noticeable to the untrained eye.

But I'm his mother, and I can see something happening already. After one week, I can spot the difference. But then again, I noticed the change before the first wire had been cemented to his teeth.

"This will take a couple of hours," the receptionist had informed me when we entered the waiting room last Tuesday morning. "Parents don't usually wait here."

They don't? I said silently. How come? I wanted to know. But "Should I go?" is what I asked my son.

And he said, "Yes," flashing the smile to which moments before he'd suggested I bid farewell. In no uncertain terms, he said, "You can pick me up later, Ma. G'bye."

And that was that.

A noticeable change. Having nothing to do with the braces per se but occurring in the orthodontist's office nonetheless.

When I returned for him two hours later, there were indeed wires on his teeth. He said, "Hello, Ma." And, "What's for lunch?" And, "Will you drop me off at school?" And later in the day, he said, "It doesn't hurt much." And, "Here's how you're supposed to brush your teeth." And, "May I have a snack now please?"

A difference I could see. An adult attitude I hadn't known was there. A sense of perspective. "So I have braces now and a social studies test tomorrow and maybe it will rain next week. And I can't chew gum or eat raw carrots or taffy, and I'm going outside to ride my bike now, Ma."

A rational approach. But when did it occur? And how? Had it been waiting in the genes? Did it happen in the middle of the night? Did he wake up suddenly more grown up than he had been the day before? It must have been coming on for years or months or weeks at least—this ability to see life as a continuum rather than a series of events. It must have been happening before my eyes, and still, I was surprised to find behind the braces and the smile, a mature young man where before there'd been a boy.

Mezuzos

"Look at the doorposts," I whispered. We were sitting in the hallway just outside the ophthalGmologist's examining room waiting for the eye drops to dilate my daughter's pupils.

"What doorposts?" she asked, squinting in my direction.

"All of them," I answered. "Do you see the *mezuzos*?"

She nodded, curving her mouth upwards to one side. "Yes . . ." she said. "I see them. What about the *mezuzos*?"

"Well, don't you think it's sort of incredible?"

My daughter looked confused. "What do you mean, Ma?"

And suddenly it was clear. What appeared extraordinary to me was rather typical from my daughter's point of view. That the ophthalmologist is *frum* is a matter of fact, as far as she's concerned. Our accountant is *frum*, the owner of the pizza shop is *frum*, and the history teacher is *frum*. From my daughter's perspective, *kipos*, *tzitzis* and *mezuzos* on all the doorposts are a way of life—as common to her as they seem uncommon to me.

"You know it isn't like this everywhere," I felt compelled to say. "There are towns—some less than an hour from here— where hardly any Jewish people live. And there are plenty of places with no observant Jews at all."

My daughter nodded knowingly, but I could see that she did not really comprehend—any more than, at her age, I would have understood the concept of an Orthodox community.

The most religious Jew in the town where I grew up was the rabbi of the lone *shul* on the well-groomed street. There were, of course, Jewish doctors, lawyers, accountants and businessmen, but none, to my knowledge, wore *tzitzis* and a *kippah* to work and none placed *mezuzos* on all of their doors.

"You know," I told my daughter, "there are towns with no *yeshivos*, no Jewish bookstores, no *mikveh*, no *eruv*. There are places in America devoid of Jewish life."

"I know," she responded, in the same way I would have replied had anyone told me about the existence of vibrant Orthodox communities within a half-hour's drive from my childhood home. "Umm humm," I would have answered, without ever having really understood.

My daughter is growing up Jewish in a community of Jews. She feels a part of something large, something tangible, something inherently correct. Her frame of reference is different from mine. She sees *mezuzos* as the norm. She is thoroughly familiar with her Jewishness. Although she understands that there exists another way of life, she has not lived within its bounds. Of the outside world? She is aware. But I am glad to say, she does not really know.

SIMCHAS TORAH

Midnight.

The sacred scrolls have been returned to the arks. The singing and dancing have ceased. Tired parents and children have gone home to rest and sleep.

Save for those of us who know about the special place. We fortunate ones don coats and gloves for the one mile walk in the chill night air. We knock on doors along the way. "Are you coming?" we whisper. And one or two join the small band which tumbles excitedly through the back streets. Almost there.

Our pulse begins to quicken as we reach the village, tucked away in the corner of the county, shaded by trees. All is quiet as we enter the little community. Not a sound issues forth from the windows through which we see *Yom Tov* candles still aflame on table tops.

Silence.

Here and there a man or two, a group of boys round a corner, heading at a brisk pace towards the center of the town, towards the tall, stately building with its several entrances.

We part ways with the men to walk up a short flight of stairs where celebration greets us at the door.

Women in colorful dresses, some with white aprons and white *tichels*, teenage girls in starched skirts and white tights, children in their *Shabbos* shoes and babies in arms await the moment when *hakafos* will begin.

"This way," says a lovely mother, gesturing to us with her workworn hands. "I see that you are guests. Come. You must have a good view." And she takes us to the front row of the rough-hewn bleachers. "You are guests. It is important that you see." And she smiles broadly, proud of this community to which she belongs.

Excitement, like electricity, fills the women's section as we settle into place.

From my vantage point behind the white grillwork on the balcony, I observe the room below, which appears to sway as hundreds of men in black coats and hats join hands to sing aloud, standing ten deep or more on risers lining all four walls of the bright and airy *shul*. I watch their feet keep time to the single syllable intoned in a myriad of phrases, repeated endlessly in swelling sound. "Dy de dy dy dy dy," they sing, filling the *shul* with their *niggun*—reaching the high blue ceiling with the intensity of their joy, touching the crystal chandeliers with human light. Touching me.

I watch the little boys with curling *peyos* sway in time, following their older brothers, who follow their fathers and grandfathers, who follow the generation before and the one before that, each separately, all together, moving to and fro in rhythmic motion to a sound which personifies joy.

On *Simchas Torah* eve.

I press closer to the grill as the Rebbe starts to dance, inscribing some significant message with the work of his feet upon the floor. His long coat flutters, his high boots shine in the center of the room.

"It is beautiful, no?" whispers the woman beside me in an Americanized Yiddish.

I nod, afraid to speak lest I break the mood.

How fortunate for me, I think, to be a part of this. To live within an easy walk of New Square, the celebrated, self-contained community of *chassidim* descending from a place of similar name in Russia.

To think there are those who would belittle this. Jews who would deny their Jewish link to people such as these. To think there are those who would never dare to let their souls fly as the sound swells to become a tangible thing, a gift of celebration, reverberating, undulating, resounding and continuous—reaching the air, the walls, reaching beyond the walls to something which cannot be seen, reaching the eyes, the ears, the heart. Carrying with it a history, the voices of Europe, the music of the *shtetl*, a vision of the past, a commitment to the future. In a crescendo of sound, the voices ring of permanence, reality, trust, the sacred covenant, significance, unity. And I feel a part of it. It moves me. It opens something deep inside. It gives me strength. It connects me and bolsters me. It sweeps me with it and carries me forward. It belongs to me and I to it. It tells me that I am a Jew.

MUSIC

There is something reassuring about the sound. Something safe and recognizable. Something I love despite the wrong notes and the absence of a beat. It is the essence of the music, not the music itself, which makes me stop and listen when they begin to practice as they do each autumn with the start of school.

It is then, a week or two past opening day, when first I see them lining up at bus stops in the morning with their flute cases and sheet music in their hands. The little ones, it seems, always choose to learn the tuba or the bass. And I notice them with autumn leaves swirling about their heads, clutching their instruments with pride.

Another year, I think. Another generation of elementary school bands and midwinter concerts. Another season of homework and weekends and practicing, practicing. And the thought makes me smile.

And then comes the sound. Sometime just past dusk in mid-October, I will find myself outdoors attending to a necessary task—emptying the garbage, shaking out a mop, checking to see if there's rain in the air, and I will hear it in the still, quiet night.

The scales. Played by the boy practicing his trumpet across the street, or the girl at her piano two houses down. I'll hear my own son with his saxophone and I'll be forced to stop. To stand there silently, grinning at the vision of the children in our neighborhood struggling with some bit of song in the comfort of their homes.

And maybe that is it. The security of routine. The thought that these youngsters have spent their day in school, have played some, have eaten dinner, done a little homework and are practicing an instrument. Yes, the thought that these children are part of a cycle warms me. The way a Norman Rockwell painting warms me.

And then, as I wait in the dark for the next tune to waft through a window from somewhere on the block, I find myself thinking of other blocks in other villages and towns and cities and states. I envision little girls in pigtails playing violins in Idaho and boys practicing drums in Chicago.

I imagine something familiar, something sweet, something which I often worry will be lost. For the moment or two when they start to play the scales, while I listen from just outside my kitchen door, I imagine innocence.

The fear of hatred, the knowledge of poverty and hunger, injustice and pain are momentarily lost as I am transported to a time before I contemplated weighty things. The sound of children playing instruments on autumn evenings takes me back to my own protected childhood. It touches on nostalgia and borders on hope.

THE SWEATER

It was a sixty-five dollar sweater. Far too expensive, I thought. And he agreed. But he tried it on anyway just for fun.

And he loved it. I could tell by the look in his eyes and the way he kept touching the material that he really thought it was special.

"But the price is crazy," he admitted, pulling it over his head.

I felt a momentary pang of guilt before rehanging the sweater. There are some mothers, I know, who would not have thought twice about the cost.

"Pick something else," I finally said. "Any one of these." And I directed him to a rack priced at twenty-three dollars and change. He chose a perfectly acceptable sweater in aqua and black. He smiled and thanked me as I paid, and we headed for home. But the incident bothered me for several days.

You see, he is twelve years old. And he hates shopping. Rarely does he agree to accompany me to a clothing store. And when eventually I manage to get him there, he almost never shows excitement for an item on display. He usually is content to wear whatever is hanging in his closet at the moment. As long as the clothes are clean (for my benefit) and comfortable (for his), he's happy.

So I was genuinely surprised by the interest he'd shown in a sweater. "You should have seen it," I heard him tell his teenage sister. "It was really nice."

She nodded her head politely as he spoke. And suddenly, I thought of all the sweaters on her shelf. Not sixty-five dollar sweaters, but sweaters nonetheless. Sweaters and sweatshirts, and skirts and dresses, and socks and shoes and a host of other items of apparel, purchased rather regularly because she shows enthusiasm.

Because she always seems to "need something" for the occasion. Because she "really, really loves" one item or another, because the purchases make her "so, so happy, Ma." And she says "thank you" with such feeling that I just cannot refuse.

As I listened to the teenage daughter and her pre-teen brother discussing the sweater, I suddenly realized that where clothing is concerned one has far more than the other.

And so it was that I decided to splurge. Right then and

there, I decided to spend the outrageous price of sixty-five dollars for a garment which he would outgrow in a year but which I knew would make him happy for the moment.

Two days later, armed with checkbook and pen, I fought my way through the holiday shoppers to locate the sweater he had loved. I removed it carefully from the rack, checked the size and color and draped it over my arm.

As I stood in line waiting to pay, I glanced once more at the price tag. And there, to my astonishment, I saw a thick red line running through the original figure. In its place was scribbled the new sale price of twenty-three dollars plus change—my reward for good intentions.

The Snow

From the window of the bedroom, I can see the clean white sheet of snow covering the ground. Not one person has left a footprint there. The color is perfect, pristine and pure in the afternoon sunlight. I pull aside the curtains and press my nose closer to the glass. "Dare I?" I wonder. "Might I?"

But I do not. Instead, I make a cup of coffee and reminisce about the good old days before the children had to go to school. When they were little, not so very long ago, I loved to take them out to play in the snow. I'd bundle them in hats and scarves and waterproof pants and knee-high boots.

I'd drag them around the yard on sleds. I'd build snowmen with them. I'd throw snowballs at them and make snow angels with them until their cheeks were fire-red. And then, I'd usher them inside for cups of cocoa at the kitchen table.

The best was when we played outside at night—riding sleds down slopes lit by a winter moon. I'd sit in the back holding one or the other of my children against my chest, whooshing past the evergreens.

But they are older now, in school all day. And I'm alone here at the window, feeling sad because they're growing up, which means I have to grow up too. They still like sledding, of course, ice-skating and building snowmen, but they like these things in a different way—in a way which doesn't require a mother on the scene.

It's not that they would mind me there. They think I'm funny when I want to play outside with them. They humor me by hurling snowballs at my back, by pulling ski caps over ears and asking for hot chocolate when they're tired of the game.

But it's not the same—not the way it was when I would have to show them how to stick a carrot in the snowman's nose. It's different now that they can ice-skate with more agility than I. It's not the way it was when they were small and I introduced them to the winter wonderland—gave them their first lick of an icicle, helped them build a snow fort in the yard.

I loved it when their little friends trooped after me to warm themselves around the fireplace in our house.

But everyone has gone to school today. And the snow is still untouched. I could, I know, go out there by myself to make an imprint on the unmarked slate. I could hurl snowballs at a tree or break off icicles from the roof.

However, I would soon be bored. And lonely. And so, I'll content myself with a solitary walk or a cup of cocoa at the kitchen table . . . until the kids get home.

CHOLENT

It was a dreary Friday morning in winter.

The phone rang.

I answered.

"How do you make *cholent?*" she wanted to know.

And the question brought tears to my eyes.

"*Mazel tov,*" I responded and proceeded to give her the recipe, both of us aware, of course, that the precise measurement of beans had little to do with the dish. It was what would lay beneath the food which counted.

You see, this, her first *cholent,* would symbolize her decision to embrace the *shomer Shabbos* world. With this pot of beans she would say to herself and *Klal Yisrael* that henceforth she would no longer light a fire on *Shabbos*—that she needed a recipe for a meal which would cook all night because she had taken this significant step.

And she wanted to let me know.

Just as I had wanted to let someone else know when I was ready for a pot of *cholent.* Back then, some four years ago, in that time before the classes and the courses, before the conversations, the study and the practice, back when I leaned heavily on someone else, I, too, called for recipes. And there was someone who answered. There was a woman who understood more than my surface questions, an individual who led me gently through the maze of rituals, who gave me confidence. There was one woman in particular who introduced me to *blechs* and *bentchers,* to the concept of *Shabbos.* And it was she who gave me my first taste of *cholent.*

So I cried when I received the call. I cried with joy at the evidence of continuity—at a heritage which dates back three thousand years. I smiled as I gave her my recipe and listened while she thanked me profusely, just as I had thanked someone else four years ago.

Then I heard her ask how she could repay me for the help she thought I'd given—just as I had wanted to repay another. And I answered with the answer that was given to me. I told her that her call was my reward. She said she did not understand.

"You will," I promised, "some day soon. When, on a dreary winter morning, your phone rings with someone wanting to know your recipe for *cholent*."

*T*ZEDDAKAH

Why was he there, shrouded in shadows on a winter evening? What kind of man was this, picking furiously through mounds of garbage overflowing from the huge metal dumpster in the corner of the parking lot?

And how did I, with my bag of newly purchased groceries, dare to drive away from him in the cold, dark night?

"Should we leave the food?" I asked my son as we approached the site. "Should we open the door and set the bag on the ground?"

But my son sensed the hesitancy in my voice and shook his head. "I don't think so, Ma," he said.

"I have a twenty dollar bill in my wallet," I said. "Should we hand him the money?" But I continued driving as I spoke, not really intending to stop. "I would have liked to," I told my son by way of explanation. "I really would have liked to help him. But I'm afraid. What if he has a gun? What if he is violent?"

What if he had not been hungry after all, but was instead

mentally incompetent, deranged? What if, despite a home and hearth, he had chosen to rifle through refuse like a cat? And what if all this were true, or none of it? I asked myself later.

Suppose I came upon this man with a full stomach and a twisted mind—a mind which had set him to scavenging just after dinner? Would that have made him any less in need of my concern?

But then again, what if his stomach was empty and he had no home to which he could return? Might not my twenty dollars have paid for a meal and kept him from having to sleep in the doorway of some suburban shop?

Had I imagined a battered suitcase there beside him? Was there a worn blanket inside which would serve as his shelter for the night?

Should I have gone directly to the police station to tell them of the man? Should I have said, "Go help him, please—take him in, take him to a shelter—give him a meal—do something for him"?

And what kind of lesson did my apathy impart to my son who had sat beside me in the car? What had I said about compassion and charity? How had I dared drive by?

How solicitous I am, how charitable when a helping hand means writing out a check or knocking on the neighbors' doors to collect for one charity or another. How giving I am when a telethon allows me to feel good about myself by phoning in my pledge. And how sympathetic I seem to be when tisk-tisking over the plight of the homeless in the big cities, as portrayed on the paper's front page.

But what of the true test—the man looking for something in the dumpster in the corner of the suburban shopping center two blocks from my house?

THE PARKING LOT

They look a little ridiculous standing in the parking lot, pecking at invisible bits of food on the macadam. Sometimes, I stand still to watch them as they make their way among the cars—seagulls on bird feet, walking in the shopping center. Aren't they silly, I think, to be bothering with asphalt and tar when there are beaches to the north and south of here? Don't they miss the ocean fish or the roar of the waves? Wouldn't they prefer a seafood dinner over our inanimate garbage? Or don't they remember their roots?

It makes me sad to watch them circling overhead, swooping down as I have seen them do a thousand times on sandy shores. It disturbs me that these elegant creatures settle for the refuse thrown behind pizza shops and delicatessens. Where is their pride? And their sense of direction?

Yesterday, I heard them flying overhead, uttering their distinct cry as they grazed the treetops in my back yard. Shading my eyes with one hand, I watched them soar gracefully against the backdrop of a winter sky. And I shook my head from side to side. They looked so out of place, competing with the crows.

I believe they belong on sand dunes or swirling around fishing vessels anchored at sea. They belong on weathered beach house fences and rooftops, on boats moored to docks for the winter.

It bothers me to see them here. It shakes my sense of order. And yet, the sound and sight of them does bring back happy memories—of childhood summers spent on clean white beaches, of winter excursions to Atlantic City when the boardwalk was the sole attraction of that place, of the ocean at peace and the ocean in turmoil—always with gulls in the sky.

Perhaps it is not the sea gulls, but change itself which ruffles me. I like predictability and routine. I prefer that things and people, seagulls too, remain in their appointed places—in their natural homes or natural habitats.

Maybe I feel safer when all is where I think it ought to be. I imagine hazards in the wake of change. I worry when things are not as they once were. And yet, despite these fears, I understand the value of a challenge, of moving out and on and up within the world. And so I suppose I should in some way admire these birds who've picked up stakes to try their luck at life in the parking lot.

WARM MILK

It was well past one a.m., less than five hours before we would have to wake up, and yet, we continued to sit. The wind rattled against the eaves of the house. The room felt chilly. But still, we stayed.

"Would warm milk help me fall asleep?" my daughter finally asked, swinging back and forth on the rocking chair. "I wonder if I'll remember the taste from when I was a little baby."

"Maybe," I answered, smiling broadly at the thought.

Long ago, nearly fifteen years ago when my daughter was a newborn, she and I spent many moments together while the rest of the world was sound asleep. At that time, it seemed as though my firstborn always would remain an infant, waking me with cries of hunger in the middle of the night.

Back then, I thought she would forever need me to

cuddle her in the dark while other people dreamed their nighttime dreams. When she was small, I truly believed that I always would be humming softly, carrying her from window to window to peer at the stars and the moon.

And then, one day or over the course of weeks or months, this infant stopped needing me at two a.m., stopped whimpering or howling to rouse me from my rest. Somehow, without my being quite prepared, my daughter learned to sleep until the morning.

I remember being jolted into full consciousness the first time I met daylight with unbroken sleep. I recall running headlong to her room to make sure she was fine, certain that somehow I had missed her cries at two a.m., worried that I had neglected her in her hour of need. But apparently, I had not.

As time went on, I found that she awakened less and less. Eventually, she learned to greet the dawn all by herself, viewing the world from the corner of her crib, talking gaily to her mobiles and stuffed animals.

Even then, though, when I was most grateful for the gift of unbroken sleep, even then, I sensed that I would one day miss the midnight rendezvous with my child.

I used to like the glow of the tiny night light in her room and the long shadows it cast on the wall beneath the window sill. I used to like the feel of her soft hair against my cheek. And sometimes—often, I think, I would sit with her long after she had had her fill of warm milk and fallen back to sleep. I sensed then the poignance in this mother love which blooms before the break of day.

And so, despite the lateness of the hour and the knowledge that both of us would awaken tired, when she said she couldn't fall asleep, I agreed to give my daughter a cup of warm milk, and I asked her to sit with me a while.

THE QUESTION

"Where do you come from?"

The question seemed strangely phrased. I turned it around in my head and decided he'd meant to say, "Where do you live?"

But why would he want to know, I wondered, squinting my eyes at the young gas station attendant who was filling my left front tire with air? In the second or two between this inquiry and my response, I found myself doubting his motives, but I decided, finally, that he was simply being conversational.

"Spring Valley," I answered.

He was not satisfied. He rose and looked me in the eye. "I mean," he said in a serious tone, "where do you *really* come from?"

"Spring Valley," I repeated firmly, annoyed by the insistence in his voice. "And where do you *really* come from?" I asked, thinking I was being clever in tossing the question back to him.

But he seemed pleased that I had asked. He paused a moment, nodded his head slightly and answered, "India." Then he smiled and walked away. And I drove off, feeling somewhat silly at having misinterpreted what he had said and vaguely flattered at the possibility that he had thought me foreign-born.

Had he perhaps mistaken me for an Indian or a Frenchwoman or an Israeli? Maybe he'd seen my dangling earrings and decided I hailed from some exotic shore. Then again, I thought he might pose this question to every customer who comes his way. He may keep a running log of countries to be tallied by the month, a kind of rough-hewn census on the gas station wall.

Whatever the case, his question has caused me to think. Since that brief encounter, I have found myself wondering rather frequently about the birthplace of some person or other standing behind me in a checkout line.

I've felt myself trying to pinpoint the origin of an accent overheard in a crowded restaurant. I have, through the words of the gas station attendant, become more curious.

And there is something to be said for curiosity. It's the first step to education, a tool of learning, a way of expanding our world. Knowing where we're *really* from demands our looking backward. It insists on history and honesty and introspection. It is not just where we live right now but where we've lived before which counts. It's where our fathers lived and their fathers. It's who we are and who we were and who we want to be.

Where we're really from is more than an address and therefore worthy of some thought. And while I didn't understand the attendant's question at the time, I hope it's not too late to say that I am from Romania and Russia and Poland and Hungary, from *shtetlach* and cities and farms and villages. I am from centuries of European history and centuries of history before that. I was born in the United States of America. I live in Spring Valley, New York. And I thank you for asking.

 ISH STORY

The following is a fish tale.

Although the ten-gallon tank has for years now sat atop the dresser in my son's room, I remain the official caretaker of the goldfish. I clean the tank, I turn the fluorescent fish light on and off, and I feed the fish. I am therefore the one responsible for the obesity of the two remaining goldfish living in the tank. And it was this task of feeding which caused me to enter the darkened room at ten o'clock on a recent Saturday night.

I approached the tank as I normally do, reaching for the small container of food and lifting the protective glass top in one swift motion. As I stared down into the tank, ready to flick sustenance into the water, I noticed that one of the fish had swum halfway into the hollow plastic log which rested on the bottom of the tank. Swimming through this log has never before been a feat worthy of note. For more than a decade, I've watched our various fish flaunt their prowess as navigators, gracefully entering one end of the imitation tree stump and reappearing moments later through an opening in the center of it.

Once or twice, I've found an ailing fish suspended in the water within the dark innards of the log, looking for all the world as though he'd gone there to die in peace and solitude.

And that was the thought which crossed my mind when first I saw the back half of the fish's body sticking out of the side opening of the phony log. With its filmy tail wagging furiously, I thought the fish was hurrying to enter the burial spot. And I stared for several moments before I understood the truth.

The fish was stuck—halfway in and halfway out of the plastic fallen oak. Instinctively, I grabbed the fish's bottom half and felt him wriggle frantically against my fingers. I tugged gently, but the movement sent him further into the log.

I called my husband, who came running to help. I lifted the log out of the water and tried to shake the fish free—until my husband reminded me that a fish can't breathe in air. My husband tried to push the fish all the way into the log. We contemplated breaking the log in half. All the while, the fish squirmed and wriggled and bashed its gossamer tail against our hands.

Finally, with one of us holding the log and the other using a cloth to grab the slippery fish tail, we freed the old fellow from his fate.

He looked rather dazed as he floated crookedly, a sharp white indentation circling his middle where once had been golden scales.

"Do you think he'll live?" we said to one another, watching worriedly as the fish wobbled unsteadily above the small blue stones.

I gave him two extra pinches of fish food and talked to him through the glass of the tank. Then I threw the plastic log in the garbage can.

As I write this, it is several days since the ordeal. The fish is eating well and swimming normally. Only a slight depression on his back and a ring of white around his belly attest to his brush with death. But I feel like a heroine.

THE BAR-MITZVAH TRIP

DEPARTURE. "Here's the salami," she said. "Thanks so much for taking it. When you get there, just make a left through the side door of the *yeshivah*. Ask one of the boys to find my son for you. Tell him we love him, please."

"No problem," I answered, and I meant it.

As far as I was concerned, the salami signified another

plateau. I had become a *shaliach* of sorts. No longer a first- or even second-time tourist, I would be visiting Israel the way one visits a family matriarch—with an armload of gifts. A computer monitor from a friend whose nephew lives in Tel Aviv, a half-dozen letters to be hand-delivered or placed in mailboxes upon arrival in Jerusalem, fifty-six dollars in *tzeddakah* money, a salami and the phone numbers of six *yeshivah* students and three seminary students whose parents had asked that we call "with regards from home."

I was delighted to accommodate, thrilled to embark on the momentous occasion of a *bar-mitzvah*, laden with messages of good will. "And be sure to ask my boy to help make the *minyan* at the *Kosel*. And maybe my daughter and some of her friends will join you for *kiddush*. And if you need any help contact my parents in Ramat Gan, my sister in Rechavia, my mother, my father, my *rebbe*, my rabbi, my student, my teacher. Call them or just show up at their door. They'll be more than happy to give you a meal, or a place to sleep or a tour of the city. After all, they're family, they're *mishpachah*."

BIRDS. Two, three, five birds flew above me against the clear blue sky and perched amidst the greenery sprouting from crevices between the stones. I smiled, pressing my ear to the *mechitzah*, peeking through the latticework, trying to catch a glimpse of him, my son, the *bar-mitzvah* boy, *laining Parshas Yisro* in its entirety at eight a.m. on *Shabbos*, at the *Kosel* in Yerushalayim.

I tried to keep my place in the *Chumash*, but I could not concentrate. I was too nervous, too excited, too enchanted by the scene and by our being here.

Where the boy was concerned there had never been a question. He'd seen no need for a staged affair in a synagogue or a fancy party afterwards. What he'd wanted instead was "the *Kosel*." And we had understood. We, his parents—his mother and father and stepfather—had listened to our son and we'd agreed.

Perhaps I should have cried, standing there making my way through the silent *Amidah*, fumbling with the Hebrew, reverting to the English. Maybe I should have felt some measure of guilt for having denied the grandparents the *nachas* of observing a grandchild become *bar-mitzvah*. But the tears did not come. What enveloped me instead was a sense of gratitude and joy.

"They know me, Mom," my son had said some months before. "They'll be happy for me. I'll be thinking about them, and they'll be thinking about me even if they can't be there. They're gonna want me to be in Israel. They're gonna tell us we should go."

And they did. Of all the various grandparents involved, my husband's father alone was able to make the trip. I could hear his thunderous voice as he *davened* aloud in the warm Jerusalem air. "But even though they aren't here, the other grandparents are just as glad for me," my son had told me when I'd fretted aloud at dawn. "They're proud of me, Mom. You heard what they said. 'Go. Go in good health and with our blessings and love.'"

I smiled, recalling the words.

TSFAS. We recognized the song and the singers instantly. This was undoubtedly the Tzlil v'Zemer Boys Choir. The high clear voices carried through the open door of the tiny restaurant.

"Shh," we whispered to one another, goosebumps rising on our arms. "Listen."

"That's you," my daughter said, pointing to her brother.

And so it was. Seven thousand miles from home, at the

crest of a steep and narrow hill, the words my son had sung some months before in a studio in New Jersey reverberated through this winding street in Tsfas. "*Ki necham Hashem Tzion, necham kol chorvoseha.*"

I thought I could distinguish the voice of my boy from amongst the voices of the other boys on the audio tape. "*Vayasem midbarah k'eden v'arvosah kigan Hashem.*" How many concerts had we attended, filled with pride at the sight of our son on stage? How many times had we driven him to and from practice? How moved and touched had we been with each rendering of the melody?

But never, never, had the verse had such meaning as it did this day, as we stood there listening to the choir on a narrow street in Tsfas.

THE MARKET. I took pictures of the olives and the avocados. With the crowds pressing in from all directions, I stood on tiptoe to capture close-ups of the oranges and the peppers, the eggs and the grapes, the cartons of fresh fish, the bottles of *schnapps*, the organized chaos, the carnival of fruit.

The candy. I captured it on film. The mountains of candy in celophane wrappers beside the bins of figs and dates. I caught in the photos the color of produce, the faces of shopkeepers, the lights overhead. The baskets of meions and the trays of nuts.

I stood before the stalls where men hawked their wares— freshly *shechted* chickens, freshly baked bread, bananas in bunches and cakes and wine. Natives and tourists, husbands and wives. Elderly women with nylon sacks.

And children and old men rushing through the aisles adding their voices to the music of the marketplace— Machaneh Yehudah on Thursday at dusk.

THE SOUND

More than once, I've wanted to tell her how lovely is the sound—how cheerful and sweet to hear it in the middle of the afternoon at the office.

More than once, I've wanted to let her know how often she makes me smile. But I've decided against complimenting her lest she become self-conscious and stop her little tunes. It is the quality of peace and joy in her voice and the fact that she does not know she is being overheard that make her melodies so pleasant.

If I were to tell her how much I like her music, I'm afraid the tunes would cease. And that would be too bad because there is something contagious about them. Unrehearsed and unaccompanied, they are not unlike laughter, bubbling up from a happy source, making the listener feel good, brightening the day.

And she is not the only one whose wordless songs have met my ears. I have a nephew who hums when he eats. A father who hums when he drives and a son who sings when he does his homework.

Throughout my life, I have been surrounded by business associates, relatives and friends who set mundane tasks to music. And I envy them all. Not merely because they can carry a tune, but for their attitude toward life. I admire their ability to rise above the task at hand, to put something pretty into the routine.

I believe that those who whistle while they work are setting priorities and making statements about the way they view the world. I believe that a song a day does at least as much good as an apple, particularly when the singer is unaware of the gift he is giving.

I still can recall the sound of my grandmother's voice as

she intoned the refrain of some half-remembered melody from her own childhood. As she sewed or cooked or sat with me, she would repeat the phrase again and again, thereby preserving the legacy of the gentle tune and passing it on to me.

And so it is that my grandmother, my father, my nephew and the young woman in the office have separately given rise to my belief that a change in mood can be purchased for a song.

REFLECTIONS

The Hebrew Day School—it's as much my school as it is my children's. It is the place which has given me a daughter who now attends Yeshiva High School and a son who learns *Gemara* every day. But more than that, it has given me the ability to appreciate what it is my son and daughter have achieved. And further, it has touched something within me.

From the time seven years ago when my children first entered this place, I would volunteer to serve hot lunch as often as I could—not so much because I wanted to give something to the school but rather because I wanted to take something from it. I never told this to anyone, but long before I understood the meaning of the *Birchas Hamazon*, I used to stand just outside the lunchroom doors to listen while the children *bentched*. And I would cry at the sound of their voices.

And whenever I could, without seeming overly anxious, I'd pick up the children from school on Friday afternoons so I could watch the *oneg*.

Without their knowing it, I used to practice all the songs the children learned in school. I'd sing them to myself before I learned to read the words.

And then, one day, I had the courage to ask my children to teach me how to read. Which they did, with patience and with pride. Each day, they'd help me stumble over letters until, at last, I could follow one line and then another. And every afternoon when they'd come home from school, I'd borrow my son's first grade book, and he would help me print the letters.

And then, they told me that they'd learned in school that we could build a *sukkah* in our own yard if we'd like, and they said, "Please," and my pulse quickened, because I think it meant as much to me as it did to them—and then their classes came to visit—came to visit our *sukkah*. And I served them fruit and juice and cookies in our *sukkah*—and I had to turn away because my eyes were filled with tears—again.

And I volunteered to serve lunch at every model *seder*, because I needed to see the children in their beautiful clothes, sitting beside Jewish children they'd invited to share the meal, sitting beside Jewish children who are deaf, Jewish children who are retarded, sitting beside strangers, reaching out to strangers with whom they shared something in common. And, in their reaching out, I learned to reach out, too.

And I chaperoned the class trip to the Kosher Food Fair in New York. And I chaperoned the class trip to the Brachos Bee. And my son was asked to join the Tzlil v'Zemer Boys Choir because the music teacher who taught here was the choir-master. And while my son sang his heart out, I sang silently, always grateful to this little school.

And our family visited Israel, where my children could understand the language and the road signs, could converse with the people, could shop in the supermarket, could talk to the children, could show me our history.

And on *Purim*, we received baskets of fruit and candy and the children called them *shalach manos*. And we made baskets of fruit and candy and we called them *shalach manos*. And we drove all over Monsey and Spring Valley delivering them.

And I dressed as a clown because it was *Purim*, and my son played the saxophone at the *Purim* party.

Oh yes, and then one of the teachers invited us to spend a *Shabbos* at her home—and she taught me how to make a pot of *cholent*, and our children played with her children and it was wintertime—*Chanukah*—and when we came home, my son and daughter said, "Let's keep *Shabbos*."

And we did. And we do. And it's beautiful. And it has to do with the day school which I love—very much.

THE DAY

It was the first warm day of the season. I hesitated on my way from one appointment to the next. Should I stop? Did I deserve a twenty-minute break? I bickered with myself even as I parked the car and headed for the store. I was in a hurry. As usual.

I rushed through the aisles with determination at my heels. I made my selection with record speed, and I found my way to the check-out counter quickly—quickly. But I had no cash.

"No cash," I must have said aloud because the cashier looked up at me from beneath her glasses. "Do you take checks?" I asked, quite certain I'd wasted my time.

But the woman smiled at me and answered yes with a disturbingly cheerful lilt to her voice. And I thought I saw a twinkle in her eyes.

"The date?" I inquired of her next. "Do you happen to know the date?" I must have appeared somewhat over-whelmed at this point, because she seemed to feel a need to commiserate.

"Don't worry," she assured me. "It happens to us all. Can't remember the date or the time, or even the season. Time flies, doesn't it?" she asked rhetorically. "Seems like only yesterday it was December and now it's spring." And here she paused to announce the date. "But it's a shame, really. Too bad. We don't take time to enjoy the days—just let 'em slip right by. Once was a time when only the older folks would lose track. But that's not so anymore. Now even the little children can't remember the month, let alone the week or the day. And you want to know why?"

I said I did.

"Because," she continued, "we're all too busy. Even the kids. Too many things to do. Too many lessons and classes and courses. Too much work and not enough rest. No time to play. No time to ride a bike on a nice warm day like this. No time to sit back and enjoy ourselves.

"And the mothers and fathers all running back and forth to work and meetings. Nobody just sitting and talking to neighbors anymore." She clucked her tongue against the roof of her mouth.

"People are getting heart attacks and ulcers from all this hurrying. And I'm just as bad as the next guy." And here she offered a list of activities planned for the ensuing weeks. "Whew," she said. "Time sure does fly."

Then she took my check, handed me the package and

said, "Have a very nice day." A slower day is what I think she'd meant to say—a day slow enough to allow me to observe the clouds, a day free of anxiety, a day tinged with boredom, a lazy day, a gone fishin' day, an old-fashioned summer's-on-its-way day. By "nice," she'd meant the kind of day which seems to have gotten lost—a day which I plan to find.

To See Shabbos

It depends on how you look at it. But first you have to look at it.

And that is the problem. If I could get them to see what I see, they would want it, too. But I think they do not want to want it.

And I understand that, too. Wanting to want *Shabbos* might appear to be an admission of some previous error in judgment. Wanting to want tranquility, family harmony, peace, joy, solitude—all that might be acceptable under the general title of ethics or humanism. But to call it *Shabbos*, to bring the Almighty into it—that would smack of constraints, and constraints are unthinkable unless they are self-imposed.

So I bite my tongue and do not say that with the lighting of candles the whole world stops, that the flowers look so pretty in the center of the *Shabbos* table, that the workweek is finished when *Shabbos* descends.

I want to tell them the food tastes better because it was cooked with a different purpose in mind, because it is not eaten in a hurry, because the meal includes laughter and songs and stories and conversation.

I want to say there is always dessert and coffee and the feeling of not wanting the meal to end. That after the table has been cleared there is still the long evening together—with no telephone calls, no intrusions—that in the morning we awaken to the sound of quiet, that even breakfast is different—there is cake and milk and the walk to *shul*, the *davening*, the walk home together. And there is yet another meal and another, with more songs and friends and conversation.

If they could only understand the concept of *Shabbos*, its ability to replenish, the fact that it is a gift.

But I know they think it is foolish, antiquated—that *Shabbos* is somehow synonymous with self-sacrifice. I know this because they have told me so. And I don't know how to change their minds.

NO DRIVING HOLIDAY

"Is this another no-driving holiday?" she asked. I could hear the resignation in her voice. She's gotten used to my not answering phones on certain days. Not stopping by to say hello. She's adjusted with some humor to my fanatic adherence to certain rules and regulations—though she readily admits, she "could not live" the way I do.

And yet, I think she would have liked the cheese cake and the blintzes. Not that it was either one of these which gave me so much joy. It was neither the eggplant parmesan nor the baked stuffed shells, nor the driving rain which beat against the window panes as my husband and son and several friends sat around the table studying through the night. Nor was it the hot chocolate served at two a.m. It was not the brilliant sunshine which flooded the streets as we walked to *shul* in the morning while others readied themselves to go to work. It was not the little *shul* itself, nor was it the people who filled the rows of seats on *Shavuos*. It was not the walk under darkened skies for late-night meals shared with like-minded friends, nor was it the holiday lunches eaten with company at their house or ours. It was not the group of us walking together each day, spanning the breadth of the smoothly paved roads. It was not the sound of our voices rising and lowering in unison as we *davened* or the jumble of our good wishes as we parted ways at various street corners throughout the neighborhood.

It was not one of these things in particular but each of these things especially and all of them combined which seemed to give a clarity to this holiday.

So the Torah is mine, I found myself thinking over the whipped cream pie and the cheese souffle. Mine to share with all these lovely people walking to and from *shul* with me, praying with me, eating meals with me. Mine to share with all the children—the little children, the teenage children gathered with siblings and parents and friends at kitchen tables and dining room tables and backyard picnic tables to reaffirm our connection to one another.

So the Torah belongs to me, I thought, and with it the celebrations. The wonderful, beautiful commemorations, the hours and days set apart from time, the spaces protected from the mundane, the shining, thrilling, mysterious, rich rituals which reoccur.

"A no-driving holiday?"

Yes.

UBURBIA

"We're moving to Brooklyn," he said. He was only half-kidding.

It was 7:02 a.m. The sky was a pinkish lavender behind my husband's head as he crouched in the driveway among the garbage cans, scooping the debris with his hands.

I smiled at him. Yesterday, he'd threatened to buy a condo in Manhattan, tomorrow it will be Queens.

"Nature," he wrinkled his nose. "The country," he smirked.

I laughed. It's a trade-off for peace and fresh air, I almost told him, but I thought better of it.

It hasn't been too peaceful here of late.

It began at five a.m. or so. I was awakened by the sound of scratching in the kitchen.

"Do you hear something?" I woke my husband. "Wake up. Listen, I hear something."

He grumbled sleepily but sat up in bed. "What is it?" he whispered, and I could sense him cringing in the dark.

"Go see," I said from under the safety of the blankets.

"I think it's a gorilla," he told me, as he crept bravely into the kitchen to turn on the light, but the noise stopped when he approached.

It was difficult to fall asleep again with the thought of a gorilla gnawing at the floorboards in another room, so we kind of drifted in and out of consciousness for an hour, until the alarm clock rang. And then he headed for the shower, and I proceeded to pack lunches for the kids—until my daughter saw the bees.

"Bees . . . bees, Mom," she shouted, pointing just above the kitchen window where a misplaced hive erupted in mid-winter in our house.

And suddenly, as we stood there frozen to the floor, a hundred bees—maybe a million bees—swarmed in all directions, stinging and buzzing as they flew.

My husband ran into the kitchen and grabbed what he thought was bug spray from beneath the sink.

"This'll get 'em," he said, squirting with all his might as the rest of us huddled in the doorway. But the bees did not die instantly, and the spray had a funny smell.

"Like oven cleaner," said my daughter, pointing to the can. "You sprayed them with oven cleaner." So we sprayed again with the proper stuff. But the combined odors were so strong that we had to step outside, which is when we found the garbage strewn across the yard.

"And this critter . . . this thing . . . this, this . . ."

"Opossum," I told my husband. "A cute little opossum sound asleep at the bottom of our garbage can."

My husband said Brooklyn was a good idea.

17 KIDDUSH CUP

I am a person with simple tastes—a holdover from the Sixties. I pride myself on my not owning a set of crystal, fine china or a diamond ring. The absence of costly material objects in my home gives me a sense of righteousness. "Earth, sky, trees, people—these are the things that count," I say to myself. And I believe what I say.

So why, then, do I love the *kiddush* cup—the large one with the carved flowers and leaves—the one with the matching circular silver tray?

It's not the only *kiddush* cup we own. We have a number

of others, the plain little one we purchased for our son when he was six years old, the one with the single ring of letters carved at the base, the oddly shaped one which my husband received when he turned thirteen. All these *kiddush* cups we own and use. And yet, my favorite is the grandest one—the tallest, the biggest, the brightest, least delicate, most elaborate *kiddush* cup of all.

I love removing it from the box in which it remains packed throughout the week. I love polishing it with a soft, damp cloth. I love buffing it until it sparkles in the light. I love the color of the wine swirling near its brim.

I love this *kiddush* cup precisely because it is so far from the mundane—so different from the simple things that signify our daily lives. I enjoy this *kiddush* cup because it decorates the table with its shape and size and glow. This *kiddush* cup is not an object for everyday use. This *kiddush* cup was made for *Shabbos*. This was made to hold a special liquid for a regal meal on a sacred day.

I love this *kiddush* cup for what it represents, and I like the fact that I love the *kiddush* cup.

STUMPED

Stumped.

By slightly more than six percent.

You'd have thought one of us could figure it out.

But there was "no way," according to the young man in the brown leather jacket. He leaned on the glass countertop examining the merchandise. "Ask somebody else," he suggested.

So we did. We asked his blonde-haired friend who offered us a pleasant and thoroughly blank smile. "Not me," she said and shook her head from side to side, eyelashes closing over hazel eyes.

The woman wheeling her grandchild in a stroller laughed out loud when we approached her. "Math?" she asked. "You're kidding."

We were not. In fact, the cashier was nearing tears as we sought to help her solve the problem. But none of us could remember what to do, and the cash register would not work.

It was a midweek evening less than thirty minutes short of closing hour. My daughter and I had been on our way out of the mall, when we'd noticed the pretty candles for sale at one of those temporary booths situated between the potted plants and the escalator.

"Should we buy a couple?" my daughter had asked.

And I'd said, "Sure, how long could it take?"

But we hadn't known about the broken cash register or that no one near the booth had a calculator on hand.

"And I don't remember how to do percentages," the cashier admitted apologetically. "Can you help?"

But alas, I could not. Nor could my daughter (who, as a high school sophomore, has had more recent dealings with arithmetic than have I). Nor could the man and woman in line behind me, nor could the grandmother wheeling her grandchild, nor could anyone else we approached with a pen and paper.

Eventually, the cashier of a neighboring shop graciously tallied the figures on his cash register, thereby enabling us to pay and leave—but not without some second thoughts—about aptitude, education, memory and an increasing reliance on calculators, cash registers and the like.

DAUGHTERS

Her blue eyes darted about the room as she fidgeted with the small white hat atop her head. "I feel so stupid," she whispered, leaning towards me, squirming on a metal folding chair. She thumbed through the *Yom Kippur machzor.* "Look," she shook her head in dismay. "I don't even know where we are."

"Neither do I," I whispered back, tapping my daughter on the shoulder. "Find me the place, please," I said for the tenth time that morning. "I'm lost again."

Dutifully, my daughter turned the pages until she found the spot. Then, pointing to the Hebrew word, she handed the book back to me. I, in turn, found the place for the woman with the bright blue eyes. She mouthed "thank you" over the din of discordant chanting. "I always feel ridiculous when I come here," she told me. "I never know what's happening."

"Neither do I." I smiled back at her. "I'm trying to learn."

"Shh," someone hissed from the other side of the *mechitzah*. We were silent for several minutes before she bent closer to speak. I cupped my hand to my ear.

"Aren't you embarrassed when you don't know what to do?" she asked.

"No," I answered quickly. "I'm proud."

She raised her eyebrows in surprise.

"Watch," I told the blue-eyed woman as I nudged my daughter again. "Lost," I said. My daughter quickly found the place. A slow smile formed on the blue-eyed woman's lips. She turned her gaze to her own young daughter who, having arrived in *shul* somewhat earlier, had taken a seat near the front of the room. The child appeared to be following the service with apparent ease, as well she might.

"Because she has had a *yeshivah* education," I whispered softly, leaning towards the woman as I spoke. "Your daughter and my daughter and all of the daughters of all of the women on this side of the *mechitzah* have had as good a Jewish education . . . and in our cases a better Jewish education than have their mothers. Isn't that wonderful?" I said. "Isn't that reason to be proud?"

The blue-eyed woman adjusted her hat and squared her shoulders. Through the duration of the Day of Atonement, she and I occasionally asked our respective daughters for assistance in finding a page. Our daughters were capable and happy to oblige.

NSECTS

I rushed through the job, ripping individual leaves from the head of lettuce, passing them perfunctorily under the faucet, placing them on a towel to dry. What a pain, I thought to myself. What's the point? Even before I became observant I washed the lettuce. Even non-Jews wash the lettuce. But this business of thorough checking is a bit much. I scanned the leaves quickly for lurking insects. Since the moment I became observant, I have not found one bug on one vegetable, I muttered. It's all so unnecessary . . . so picayune . . . so ridiculous. I hurriedly bunched the leaves together, holding them firmly with one hand, placing them on a flat plate, moving a sharp knife swiftly across them to slice thin strips for salad. What's the point of all this minutiae? I worked with a vengeance. Clean is clean. Who needs to scrutinize lettuce leaves? I watched my fingers pull the knife through the center of the bunch. Bits of fresh green fell to one side, then the other. I observed the process with little interest until I saw—the moth—the large gray moth all but hidden in a fold of one lettuce leaf. The knife fell from my hand as I stared at the creature staring back at me. How had I missed him, I wondered, feeling vaguely annoyed that the moth had disproved my "clean is clean" theory. Still, I reasoned, it's the only time it's ever happened to me. The insect in the lettuce was a strange coincidence all right, but it represented nothing more than a well timed fluke. I shrugged my shoulders and, mildly amused by the pointedness of this chance happenstance, I rewashed the lettuce.

That chore completed, I moved on to green peppers and onions, wondering vaguely as I chopped, at the probability of events coinciding with thoughts. On occasion, I decided—rarely, I thought. I proceeded hastily to remove the plastic covering from the cauliflower. And there it was. Like a beacon or a stop sign, a lighthouse or the moon, there atop the fresh white head of cauliflower sat a fat brown slug. Nearly an inch in length, the fellow clung tenaciously to his resting place. I stared at him . . . speechless, feeling all the while as though someone, something was standing just behind me, just beside me, just above me, watching, gently prodding, possibly smiling, alleviating doubts.

THE CONVERSATION

"I hear you became religious," he said to me.

"Relatively speaking," I answered, wondering why he'd brought it up.

He paused for a few minutes before continuing. "You know, I was *frum* for a while."

"*Frum?*" I must have looked surprised. He wore no *kippah*, and I knew the food on the plate before him was not kosher.

"I had to give it up," he said.

And thus began our conversation. He and I have known each other by sight and name for nearly a decade. We'd met again on this particular day as guests of a newly-married non-Jewish mutual friend. My husband and I had stopped in to wish our best to the young couple.

"How *frum?*" I couldn't help asking.

He rolled his eyes heavenward. "Too *frum*," he said and proceeded to explain. An Israeli by birth, he'd arrived in this country before his twelfth birthday. Reared by an observant but religiously uneducated mother, he "gave it up" when he left home. "I never went to a *yeshivah*," he said. "I just did things or didn't do things, by rote, as a child. It never had much meaning." But then, it seems as he neared forty, he suddenly felt a need to know.

"So you took a few classes?" I asked.

He laughed, restating my words. "A few classes? No, not a few classes. I learned night and day. For two years, I did nothing but study, 'round the clock, with some of the most fascinating *rebbeim*. I read and thought and argued and shouted and tried to understand."

"And?" I asked.

"And I changed the way I ate."

"Yes," I said.

"And the way I dressed. And the way I spoke. And the way I thought. I changed my life. I changed my personality. I gave up everything—everything I had ever known—to enter this world of religious observance."

"What happened?"

"I couldn't handle it," his eyes took on a distant glaze. "I felt as though I was losing my mind. I began to judge people. If I met a Jew who wasn't doing what I thought he should be doing, what I'd learned he should be doing, I discounted him. I cast him off. I made fun of him. I became so holy, I was holier than thou . . ."

"And?"

"And then I couldn't sleep. All day long I'd run from this *rebbe* to that *rebbe* asking questions, trying to comprehend the answers. Trying to absorb the finer points before I understood the basics. I wanted to swallow it whole. I wanted so badly to conquer it that I filled my brain to the point of overload. Like a computer with unlimited memory," he said. "But . . ."

"But what?"

"But I'm not a computer. And I couldn't take it all in. I wanted things in black and white. The gray areas drove me to distraction. One scholar would seem to say one thing and the next would say another. I couldn't tell which or what was right. And then someone would come along to tell me that both answers were correct.

"I was frightened. Overwhelmed. How could I possibly grasp such a thing? There were people who'd devoted their lives to Torah and still had found questions, and I wanted it all in a couple of years. I was afraid of everything. Afraid to speak lest I say the wrong thing. Afraid to eat lest the *kashrus* not be this or that. I was afraid to marry, afraid not to marry, petrified of every step I tried to take." His mouth curved downward, mocking a smile. "Until one day I simply said that's enough . . . no more."

"And that's the end?" I asked, casting sidelong glances at my husband. "You mean, after all that study you're going to throw it away? You're sure you're never coming back to it?"

He took a long sip of his drink and sighed. "I am tired," he explained. "I went too far too fast. I tried to do too much at once, and no one told me when or how to stop . . ." He paused here, twirling the straw in the glass, perhaps to gather his thoughts. "Maybe some day I'll find the proper path, the place I belong. There has to be some middle road between nothing and everything, a spot that's comfortable for me."

"I'm sure there is," I told him, empathizing with his need to find definitive answers, to fit observance into a specific slot. I've come close to panic several times along the way.

"I miss some of it," he said.

We stood in silence for several minutes before bidding one another good-bye. "And good luck," he said to me. "Be careful. Don't rush things. Don't try to take it on all at once. Be cautious. Choose your teachers wisely. Don't ask the same questions to everyone you meet. Trust your husband. Trust yourself. I hope you find your way . . ."

GRADUATION

What a wonderful school, I thought to myself, perspiration dripping from my brow. What a fitting statement to personify the concept of Torah education despite all odds. I squinted in the darkness before snapping one picture, then another. A baby cried, eclipsing the speaker's words. Undaunted, the young man standing tall behind the podium continued his speech. Through the wall of windows opposite the stage, I watched the sun sink slowly out of sight. The room was swathed in a murky dusk. Someone in the audience produced a weak flashlight. The event proceeded according to plan.

This eighth grade graduation took place on the appointed date, despite a late afternoon's raging storm which had downed trees and power lines and left the school with nary a light. The young graduates stood before us, starched and sparkling, defying the ninety-seven degree temperature and the absence of air conditioning or a fan. With neither microphone nor spotlight, the event proceeded just as the school has persevered against probability—with overwhelming deficits, a lack of space and budget cuts. Eighth grade graduation occurred because the graduates, my son among them, understand the importance of moving forward no matter what the obstacles.

At the close of an era, these youngsters looked inward at themselves. They examined where they'd been and where they were headed. They listened carefully as their principal recounted the triumphs of their childhood years and projected a future filled with responsibility and joy.

How much has happened since my child, at six, first took his place among the students of this lovely little school. On that September day eight years ago, they placed a *kippah* on his head and handed him a pair of *tzitzis*. "Look what they gave me, Mom," he said back then. "Look at what I've got."

The words rang true as I sat in the fading light, listening to the graduates discuss issues and events: Soviet immigration to the United States and Israel, Ethiopian emigration, the future of American Jewry, the end of the Cold War, the value of a Torah education.

How strong and sure these children shone, how like the school itself, I thought. The graduates, the future of our people. Lights in the darkness, preparing to lead the way.

A PORTRAIT

I think everyone should write. I think everyone of every age should, if necessary, disregard punctuation, spelling and sentence structure for the sake of an idea.

I believe that everyone should scribble hidden feelings on little scraps of paper to be stored away for rainy days. And I think everyone will be happier for having followed my advice.

I say this now after having spent three hours sorting out two file drawers filled with "stuff" I've written over the years. In the end, of course, I discarded not one word but instead relived a lifetime of feelings in the time it took to clean the cabinet.

But what if I hadn't saved my thoughts? Would I remember who I was? Probably. Yet this is so much better, so much more interesting and so much fun. These scraps I speak of are not the published columns that appear in print each week but rather pre-columns or post-columns—fragments of joy and pain that wound up as letters never mailed, as lectures never delivered, as short stories, long stories, poems, lists of worries, thank-you notes, messages scrawled on napkins and paper towels, pieces of me as I once was.

And interspersed among these missives were the letters from other people, notes and cards—excerpts of others' lives as they related to mine.

As I sat poring over the reams of yellowed typing paper, I realized that the words drew pictures that photographs could not. The letters spelled ideas I'd never known I had.

In the back of dog-eared folders, I found furious rantings banged out on the typewriter in the middle of angry nights, a long time ago when I was a mother alone, frightened and battling the world. I found humor in my state of mind and determination in my run-on sentences.

Through the cryptic notes and lengthy essays, I saw myself from the inside out and now again from the outside looking in. I was mesmerized by the words, precisely because no one else had ever seen them or heard them or felt them. They were a secret portrait of me. And I believe a thousand words are better any day.

EPILOGUE • A PARABLE

"Are we there yet? Are we? Are we there yet?" Chanted in unison from the back seat of the car before you've made the first left turn out of the driveway. "How long is it gonna take, Ma? Is it gonna take long?"

And you tell them to quiet down.

"Play with your toys. Here," you say, reaching into the bag beside you on the seat, "have a cookie."

And the car swerves a little as you strain to deliver the treat to the waiting hands and mouths. But the quiet lasts only as long as it takes for them to chew and swallow.

And the refrain begins again. "Are we almost there? Why's it taking so long, Ma? It's taking too long . . ."

And so you console them with a song or a story which you dispense while watching for signposts and landmarks along the way.

"Were we supposed to turn off here?" you ask yourself aloud.

And the children whimper knowingly. "Are we lost

again, Mommy? Are we ever gonna find the place?"

But your voice is reassuring. "Of course we are," you tell them. "I'll just pull over and ask someone directions. Then, we'll be on our way."

And you give them each a stick of licorice and a boxed juice drink from your endless supply of snacks.

"They're probably worried about us, Mom," the children tell you when you're on the road. "Shouldn't we call to let them know we'll be a little late?"

You check the time. "No," you answer resolutely. "No, we'll make it. Don't worry," you say. "I know where I'm going now."

GLOSSARY

Amidah: central part of the prayers

Ashkenaz: Accidental Jewry

asimone: Israeli telephone token

bar-mitzvah: *halachic* adulthood

bashert: preordained

bentcher: booklet containing Grace after Meals

besser: better

bimah: pulpit

Birchas Hamazon: Grace after Meals

blech: metallic covering for stove

bris milah: civenant of circumcision

chalav: milk

challah: *Shabbos* loaves

Chanukah: Festival of Lights

chassidic: relating to *chassidus*

chazanus: cantorial music

cholent: special *Shabbos* stew

Chumash: Book of the Pentateuch

daven: pray

Eibershter: the Almighty

eiruv: demarcation of private domain

ess mein kind: eat, my child

frum: observant [Yiddish]

Gemara: part of the Talmud

glatt kosher: strictly kosher

hakafos: circumnavigations

hamantashen: *Purim* pastry

Havdalah: concluding ritual of *Shabbos*

kapote: frock

kashrus: state of being kosher

Kiddush: sanctification of *Shabbos* or Festivals

kittel: traditional white garment

Klal Yisrael: the Jewish people

klezmer: musicians
klutz: dunce
Kol Nidrei: opening *Yom Kippur* prayer
Kosel: the Western Wall
kugel: *Shabbos* dish [Yiddish]
laining: reading of the Torah [Yiddish]
latkes: *Chanukah* pancakes
lehitraot: good-bye
leichter: candelabra
machzor: prayer book for high holy days and festivals
mah nishtanah halailah hazeh: why is this night different
matzah: unleavened bread
mazel tov: congratulations
Meah Shearim: old section of Jerusalem
mechitzah: partition
megillah: scroll
mein zonenyu: my son
menorah: candelabra
mezuzah: scroll affixed to doorpost
mikveh: ritual bath
minyan: quorum of ten
mishloach manos: sending of gifts (on *Purim*)
Mishnah: part of the Talmud
mishpachah: family
misnagdim: opponents of *chassidus*

mitzvah: Torah commandment
nachas: satisfaction
neshamah: soul
niggun: tune
oneg: pleasure
Parshah: portion of the Torah
Pesach: Passover, early spring festival
peyos: earlocks
Purim: Festival of Lots
rebbe: Torah teacher
Rosh Hashanah: New Year
s'chach: *sukkah* roofing
schnapps: whiskey [Yiddish]
seder: Passover feast
sefarim: books
seudah: feast
sephard: Oriental Jew
Shabbos: the Sabbath
shaliach: measenger
Shass: the entire Talmud
Shavuos: Pentecost, late spring festival
shechted: peformed ritual slaughter
sheitel: wig
sheva berachos: the seven nuptial blessings
shomer Shabbos: *Shabbos* observant
shtetl: Eastern European village
shtreimel: *chassidic* headdress

shuk: marketplace
shul: synagogue [Yiddish]
Simchas Torah: Festival of the Torah
simchos: rejoicings
sukkah: *Sukkas* booth
Sukkos: Festival of Tabernacles, autumn festival
Taanis Esther: the Fast of Esther
tallis: prayer shawl
tefillin: phylacteries
tichel: kerchief [Yiddish]
tish: table; *chassidic* gathering
Tishah b'Av: the Ninth day of *Av*; a fast day
tzeddakah: charrity
tzitzis: fringes
yarmulka: skullcap
yeshivah: Torah school
Yiddishkeit: Jewishness
Yom Tov: festival
Yom Kippur: Day of Atonement
zieskeit: sweetie